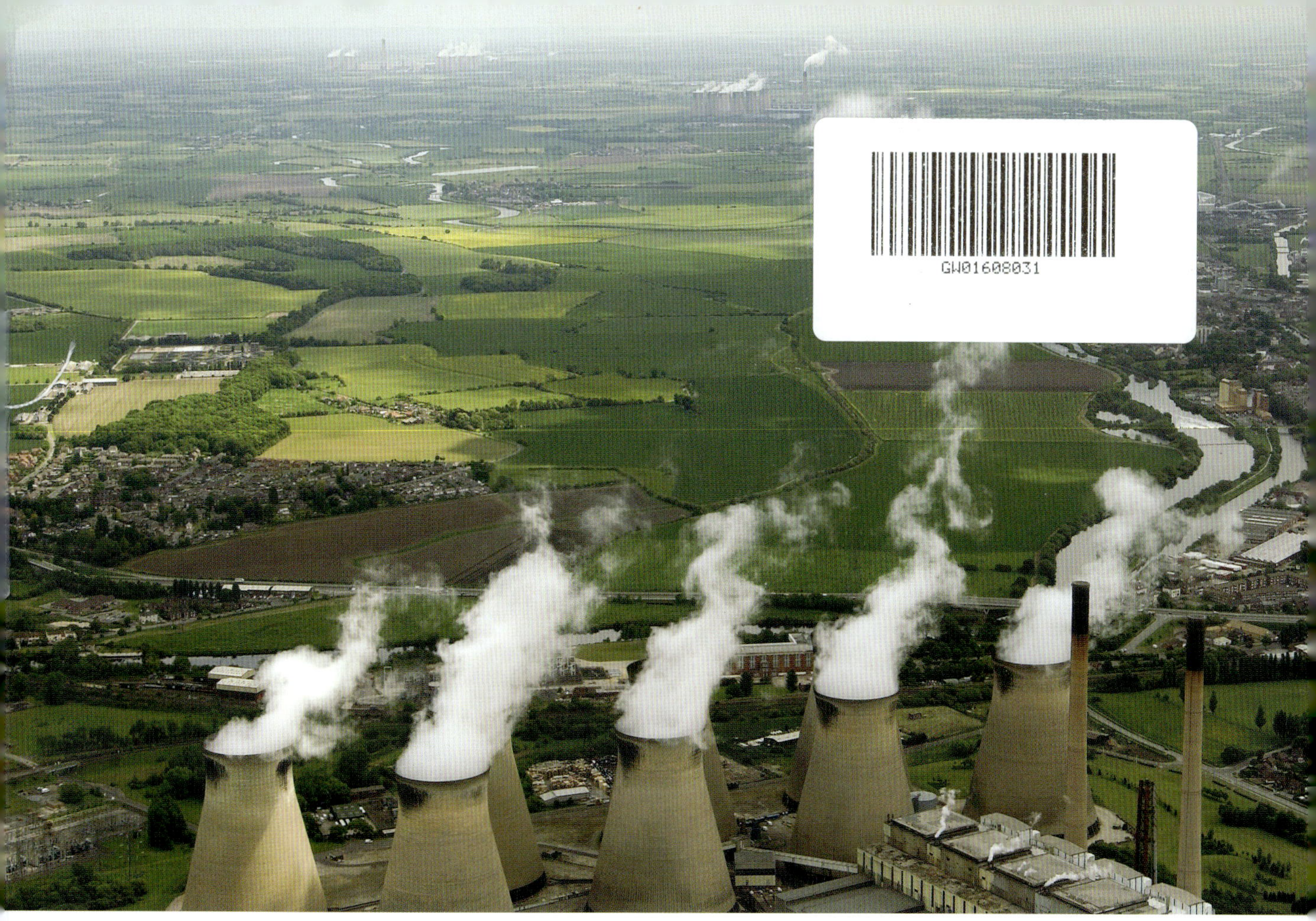

WEST YORKSHIRE
FROM ABOVE

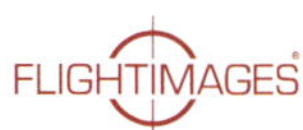

Photographs: IAN HAY, FLIGHT IMAGES
Text: MELVYN JONES

MYRIAD BOOKS

Leeds

Leeds, as *Loidis*, was first mentioned by the Venerable Bede in the early 8th century. It was given borough status by the lord of the manor, Maurice Paynel, in 1207. It thrived as a market town for hundreds of years, the original cloth market being held on Leeds Bridge. Daniel Defoe, in the 1720s, described it as "wealthy and populous" and said that its cloth market was "not to be equalled in the world". It was the development of water and rail transport that transformed Leeds into an industrial giant. In 1699 an Act was passed to create the Aire and Calder Navigation and in 1816 the Leeds and Liverpool Canal was completed. The first railway was the Leeds to Selby line which was opened in 1834 (linking the town to Hull), and in 1842 the Midland railway to London was opened, closely followed by the Leeds and Bradford railway and the Manchester and Leeds railway. Leeds became not only an important woollen cloth manufacturing centre but also a centre for the production of earthenware and a wide variety of engineering products including textile machinery. Today it is well-served by motorways (M1, M62 and A1M) and Leeds Bradford Airport. It is the commercial and financial metropolis of Yorkshire.

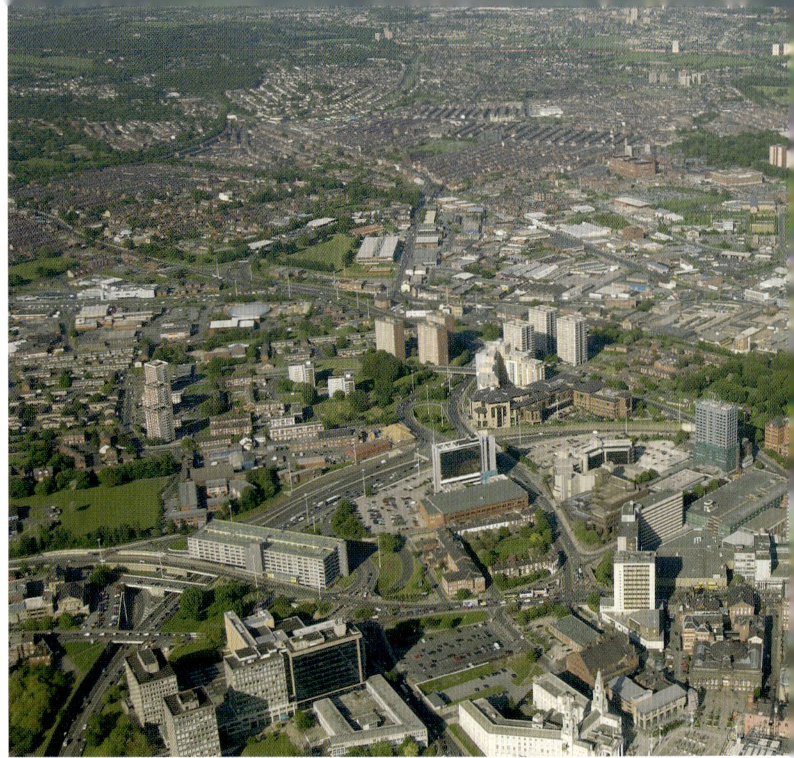

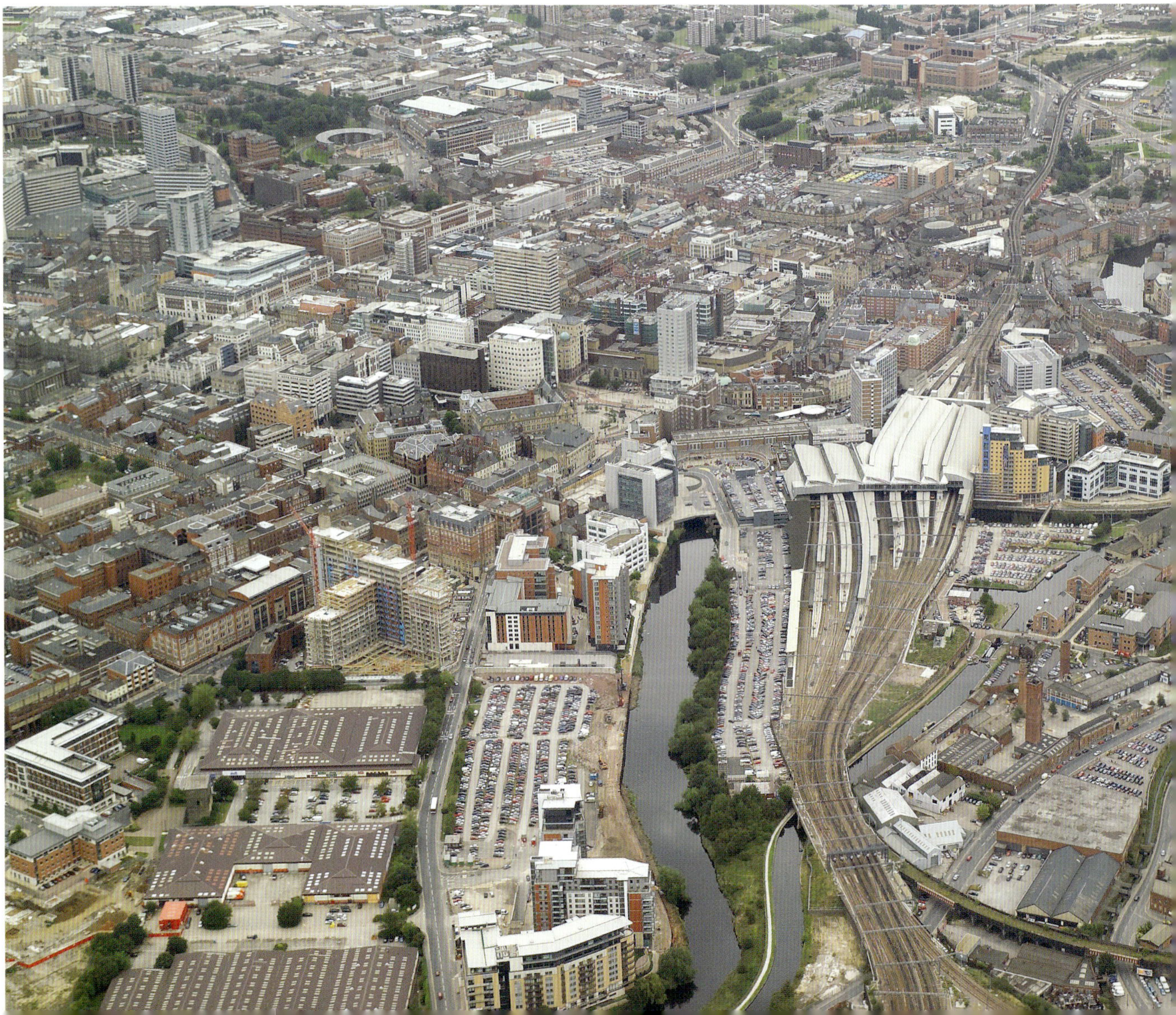

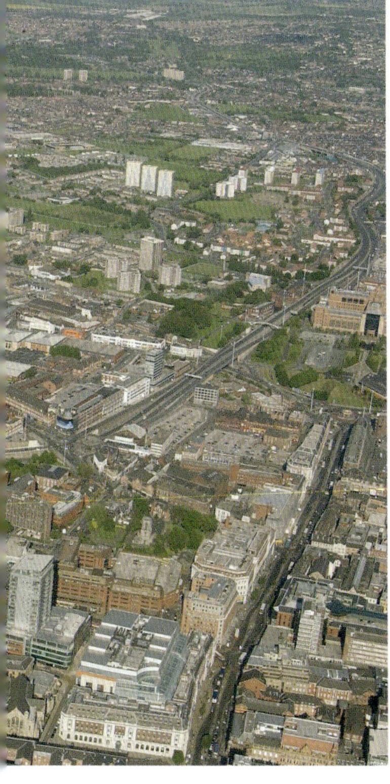

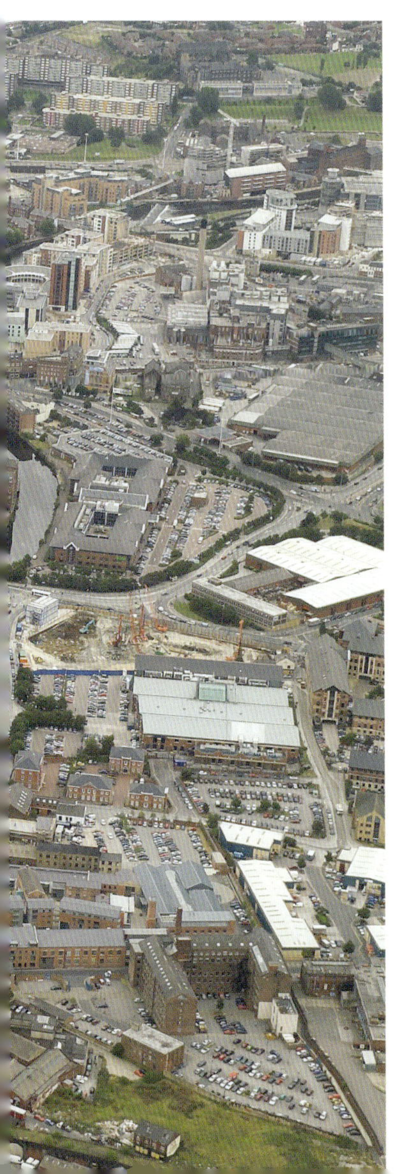

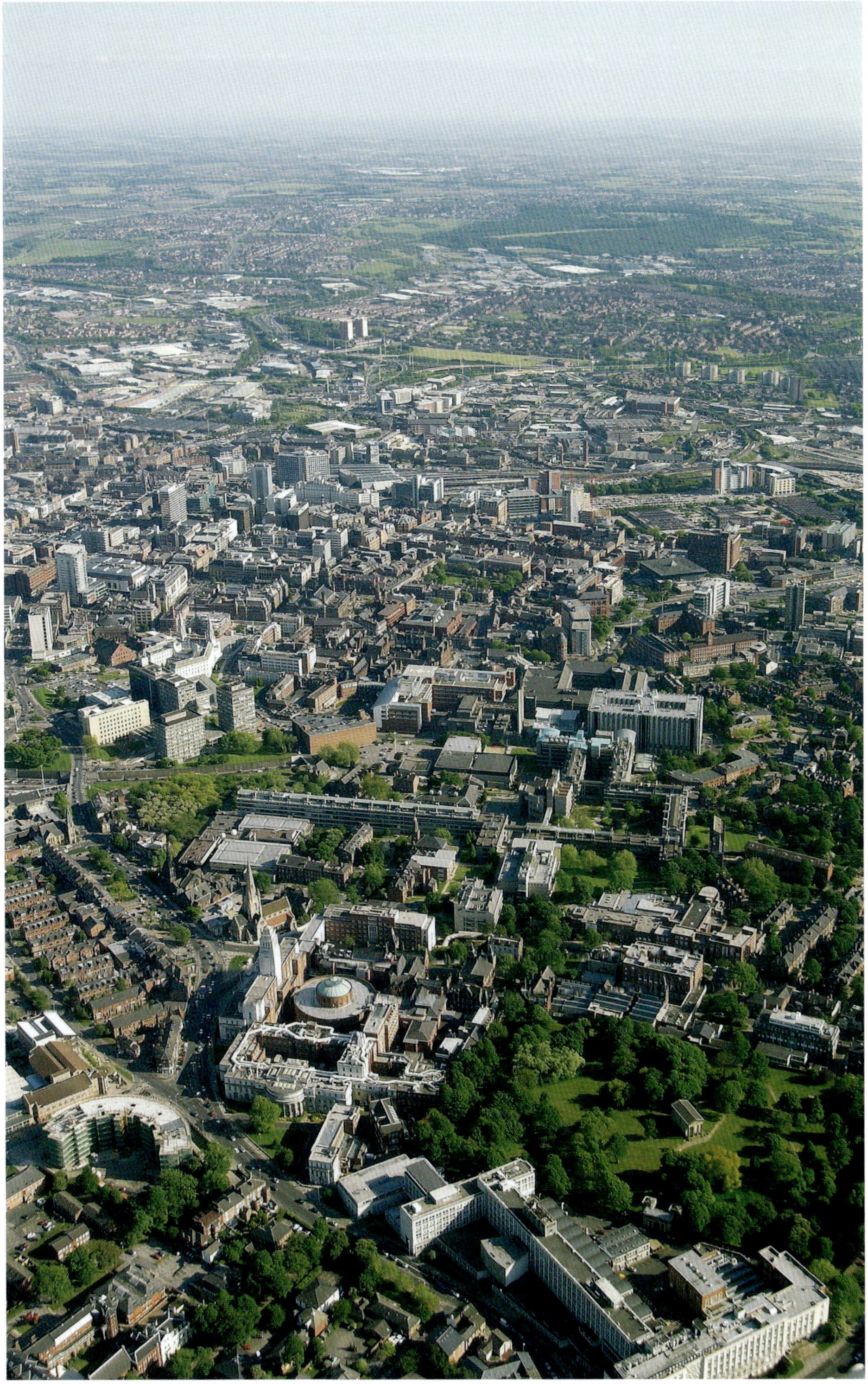

THREE VIEWS OF LEEDS

The photograph on the left shows the city from the west. In the foreground are the river Aire (on the left) and the Leeds and Liverpool Canal and Canal Wharf (on the right) separated by the railway lines running into Leeds City railway station. Leeds City Station came into being as late as 1938, as an amalgamation of the pre-existing New Station and Wellington Station. The new Queens Hotel which fronts the station on City Square was re-built at the same time to replace a Victorian hotel of the same name. The station was virtually re-built in 1960. The photograph above left is also a view from the west along The Headrow (bottom right) with the twin towers of the Civic Hall in the centre foreground looking towards Sheepscar, Chapeltown, Harehills and beyond. The photograph above is from the north looking over the campus of the University of Leeds with the prominent tower of the Parkinson Building, built in 1926. This university (there is another, Leeds Metropolitan University) was originally the Yorkshire College of Science, then the Victoria University in 1887 and the University of Leeds in 1904. Beyond the university is the city centre and beyond that the City Station and the suburbs of Hunslet and Beeston to the south of the river Aire.

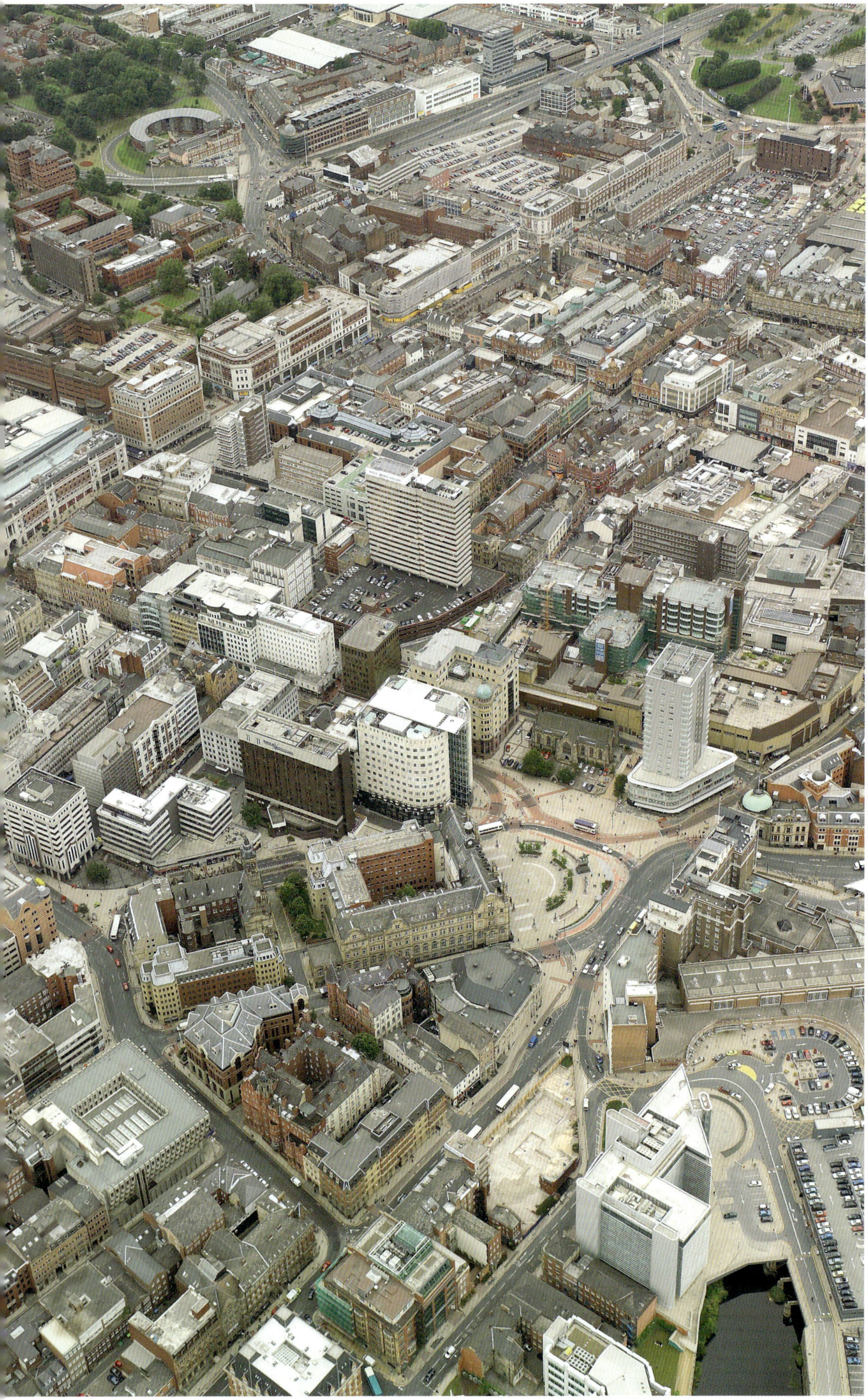

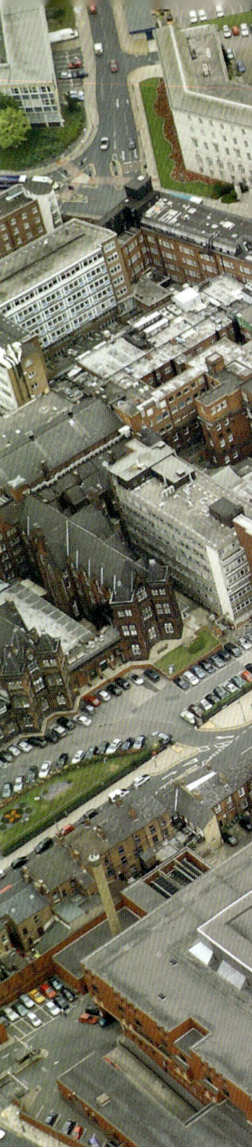

LEEDS CITY CENTRE

As the three photographs on these two pages show, Leeds has a "big city" townscape. On the left the view is over City Square outside the City Station looking eastwards with the river Aire in the foreground. The large square building with its central turret overlooking the western edge of the square is the General Post Office building built in 1896. The grid-iron street layout to the east of the square has The Headrow at the top left running away towards the roundabout on the A61 with the main junction formed where the The Headrow is crossed by Briggate. Beyond Briggate at the junction of Vicar Lane and Kirkgate stands the Baroque exterior of the City Markets (Kirkgate Market). In the streets between City Square and Vicar Lane are the famous shopping arcades of central Leeds.

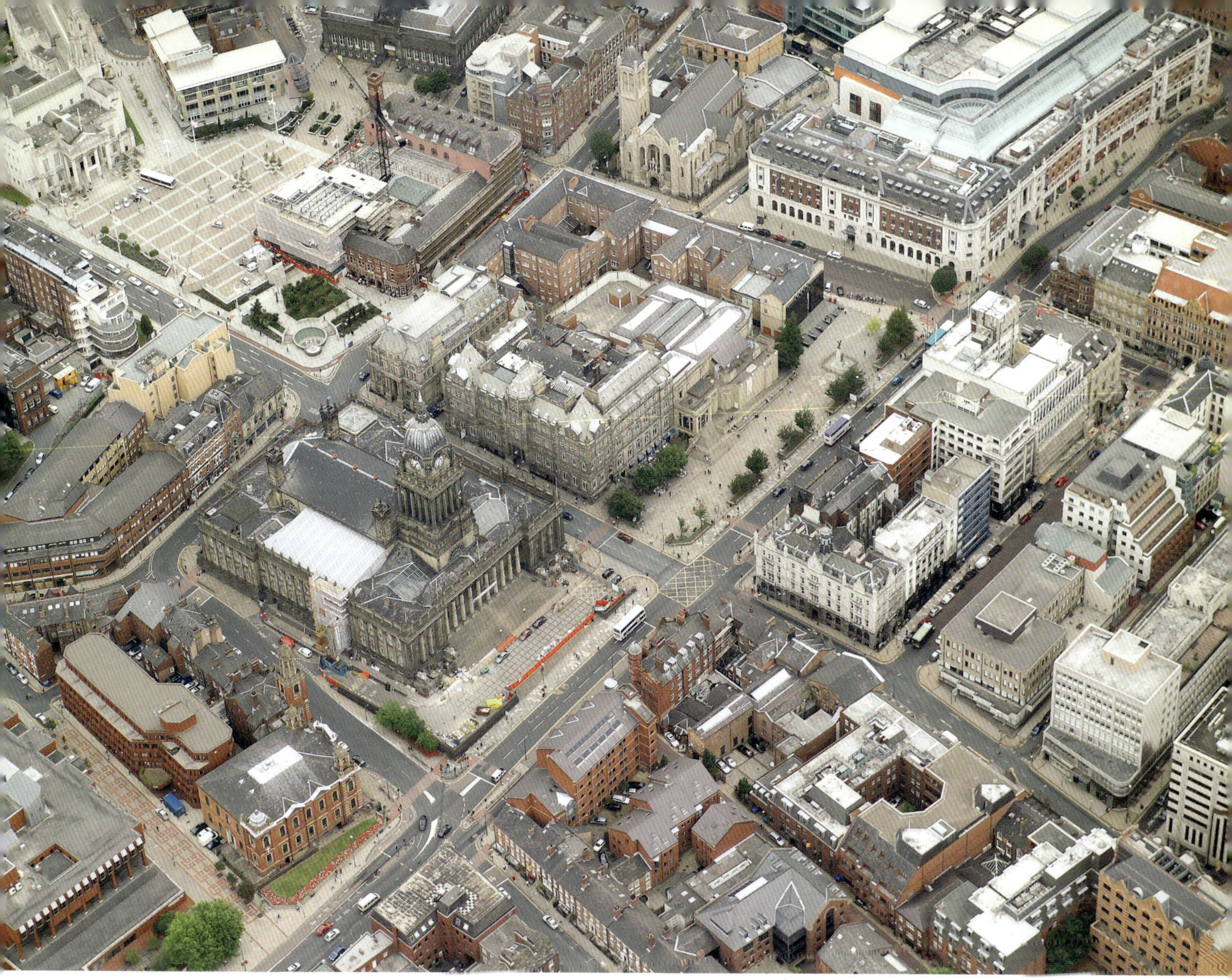

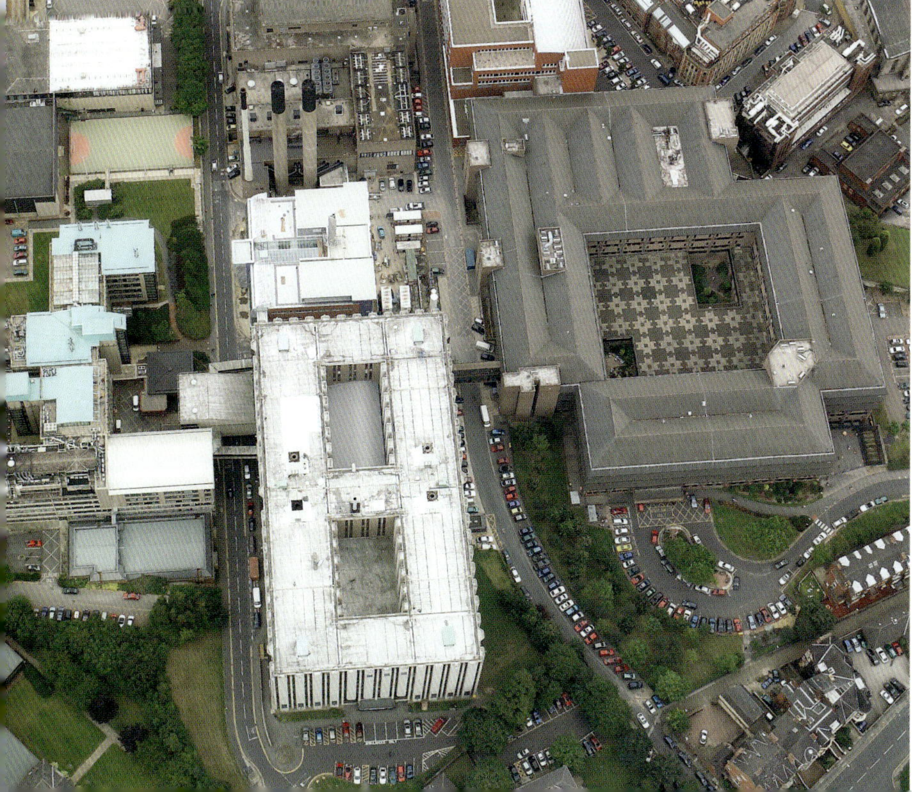

THE HEADROW *(above)*

The Headrow, which runs from the bottom-left to top-right across the photograph was the main east-west route through early Leeds. It was widened by Leeds town planners between 1928-32 creating the wide modern street. It is the civic and commercial heart of the city. Dominating the centre of the photograph is Leeds Town Hall, constructed between 1853-58 and designed by Cuthbert Brodrick, the Hull architect. It is a solid and confident flagship of a proud Victorian city on the move. The building is topped by a magnificent domed clock tower rising to 225ft (68m). Beside the town hall, across Calverley Street also facing The Headrow, are the Municipal Buildings designed in 1876 by George Carson, now housing the city's Museum and Central Library. Beyond the Municipal Buildings still on the north side of the Headrow is the former Leeds Permanent Building Society building (Permanent House), now "The Light" and containing shops, bars and a hotel. Behind The Light, on Cookridge Street, is the Roman Catholic Cathedral dating from 1902-04. At the top of the photograph beyond Centenary Square is the Civic Hall with its twin towers dating from 1933. Finally, of great architectural and social interest, are the town houses in Park Square East, across The Headrow opposite the western side of the Town Hall. Begun in 1778 and completed in 1794, Park Square is the only Georgian residential square in Leeds and was once the home of gentlemen, lawyers, merchants and surgeons.

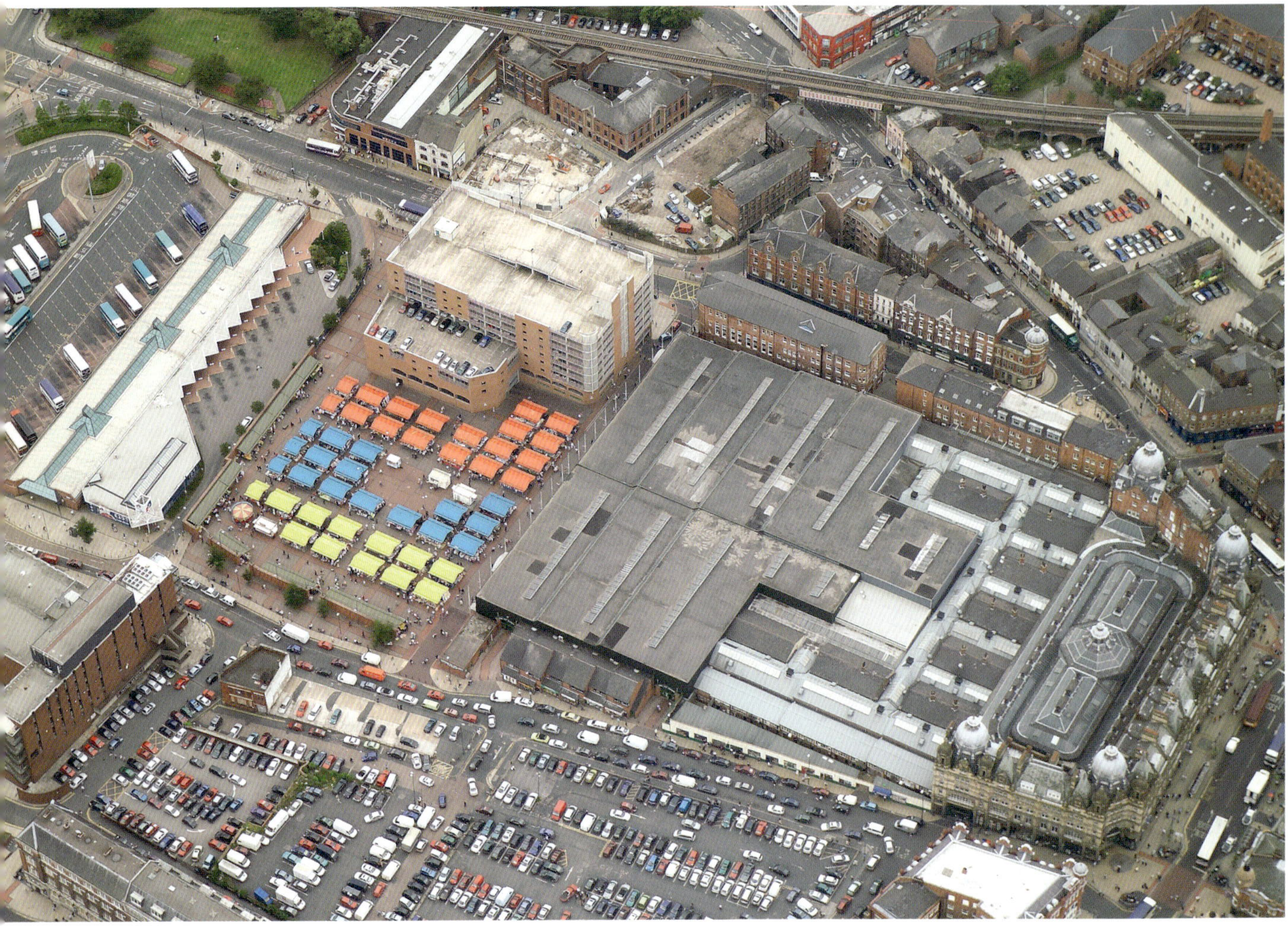

KIRKGATE MARKET

(above)

The original market hall was built in 1857 in the Crystal Palace style on land previously occupied by the open Free Market at the junction of Kirkgate and Vicar Lane. This was replaced by a new market hall in 1904 by architects John and Joseph Leeming. A disastrous fire in 1975 destroyed two-thirds of the interior and another fire in 1992 set back restoration work that had begun in 1991. Now the exterior stonework has been repaired, the domes rebuilt and shop units and stalls replaced or repaired in their original style. Other surrounding Victorian market buildings have been restored and the open market has been provided with new stalls and a central market square created.

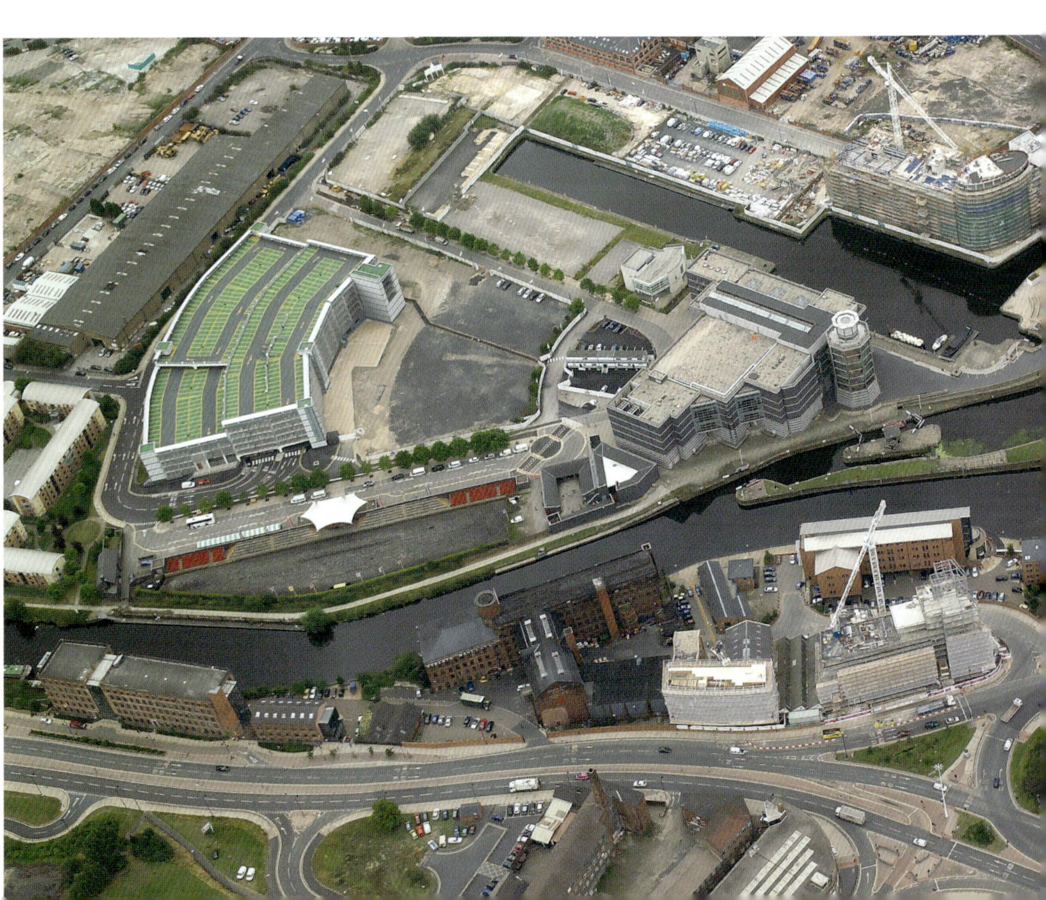

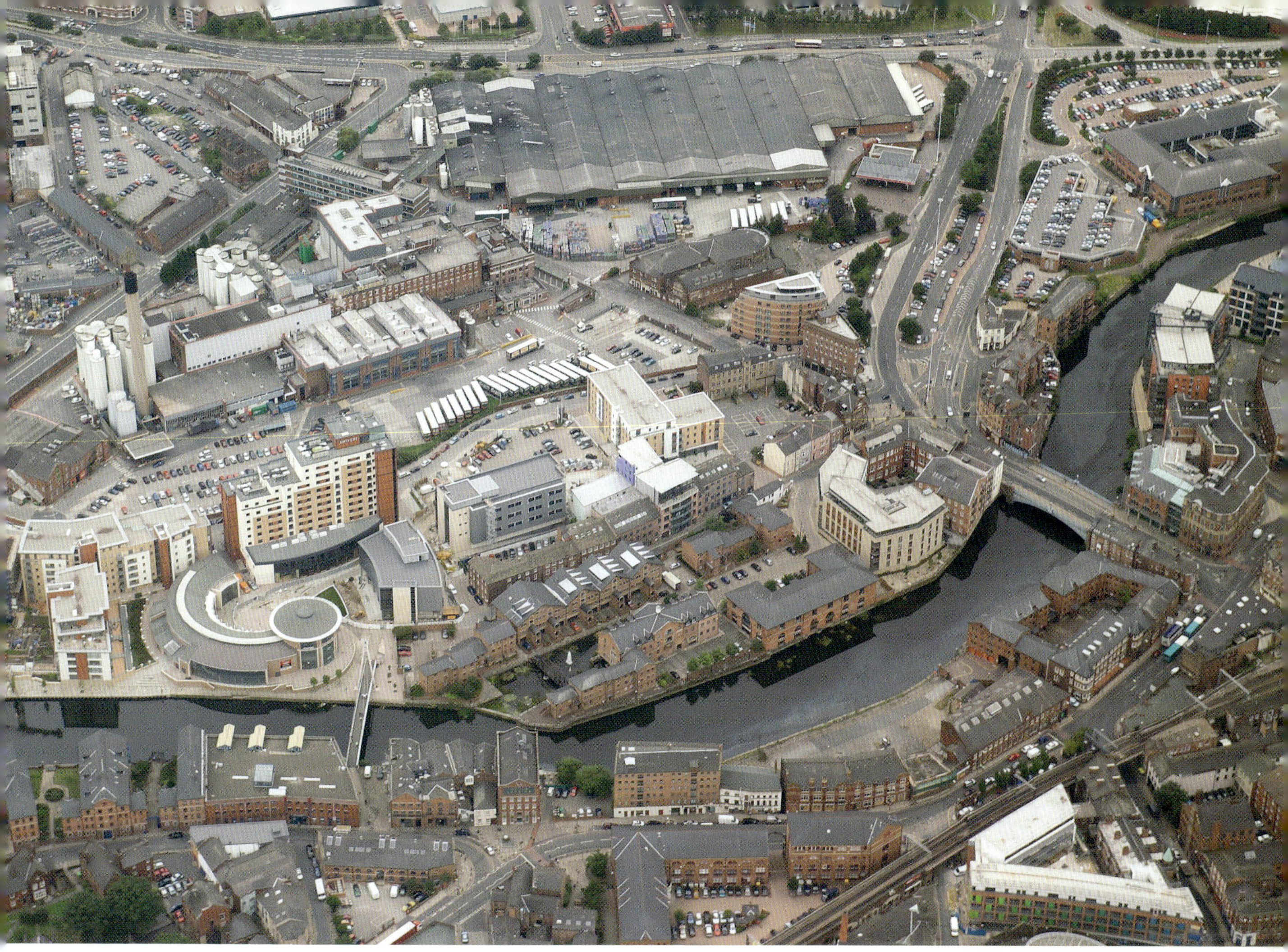

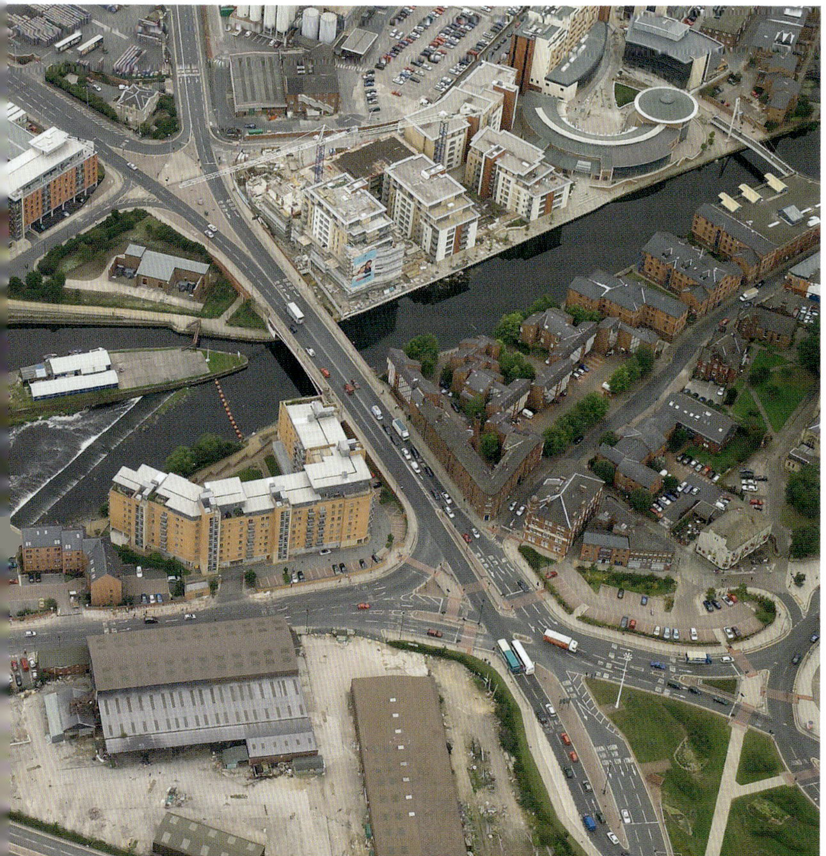

LEEDS WATERFRONT *(left & above)*

This was Leeds dockland area at the termini of the Aire and Calder Navigation and the Leeds and Liverpool Canal. By the 1960s this area was rundown and partially derelict. It has now been transformed, primarily through the enterprise of the Leeds Development Corporation working with both the City Council and the private sector. Existing warehouses have been converted into apartments and offices and new riverside apartments and office buildings have been constructed.

The photograph above shows the waterfront from the north with Leeds Bridge leading to Briggate (towards the bottom of the photograph) and the new development at Brewery Wharf on the south side of the river Aire (bottom left) with its high-quality office space, hotel, cafes, bars, restaurants and 360 apartments.

In the photograph to the immediate left a crane still towers over new building beside Clarence Dock on the river Aire in this revived area of waterfront to the south-east of the old city centre. The new building is a £200m mixed-use development which includes apartments, offices, shops and leisure outlets sited around the dock area. Pride of place, however, goes to the Royal Armouries Museum which relocated from London to Leeds and opened in 1996 between the dock and the river. This national museum of arms and armour has 5,000 objects on permanent display with five themed galleries on War, Tournament, Self Defence, Hunting and Arms and Armour of the Orient.

HOLBECK & HUNSLET *(right)*

This long view over southern Leeds from the north-west covers Holbeck (right foreground) and Hunslet in the background. Both Holbeck and Hunslet today are industrial as well as residential suburbs with a mixture of old industrial buildings, modern industrial estates and terraces, villas and high rise blocks. Holbeck was where the famous engineer Matthew Murray (1765-1826) set up his foundry at Mill Green in 1795 and his new works, the New Foundry, at Water Lane in 1802. Murray made his first steam engine in 1799, was the first to make machine tools and in 1812 made the first commercially successful steam locomotive for the Middleton Colliery a few miles to the south. This locomotive did the work previously undertaken by 50 horses and 200 men. A painting of one of Murray's locomotives at Middleton Colliery is famously featured in George Walker's *Costumes of Yorkshire* in 1814. Murray lived at Holbeck Lodge or "Steam Hall", probably the first domestic dwelling in the world heated by steam! Holbeck was transformed in the 19th century from a pleasant village and surrounded by meadowland watered by the Hol Beck into an industrial suburb of Leeds based on its rapidly growing engineering works. The need for sound housing for its working population gave rise to the foundation of a succession of "Holbeck Societies", deliberately short-lived but very successful building societies, the first one founded in 1845. These early societies led to the foundation in 1875 of the Leeds and Holbeck Permanent Building Society, the word "Permanent" being removed from the name in 1929. The Society is still going strong today. Hunslet is the location of the famous Garden Gate Inn, a complete Edwardian public house surviving in the middle of a modern council estate with its original tilework, mosaics, intricate glasswork and joinery.

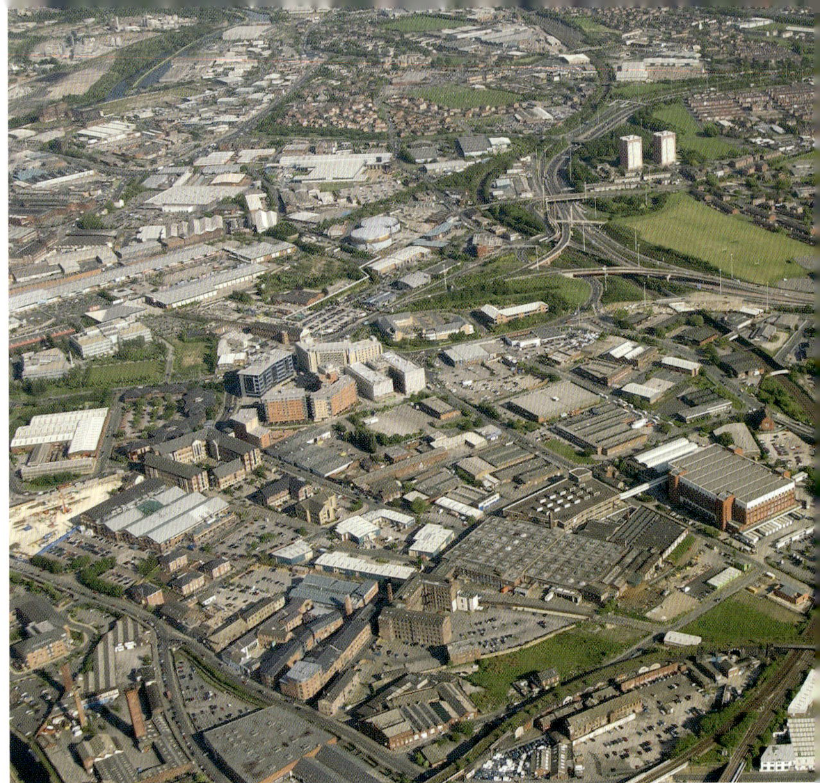

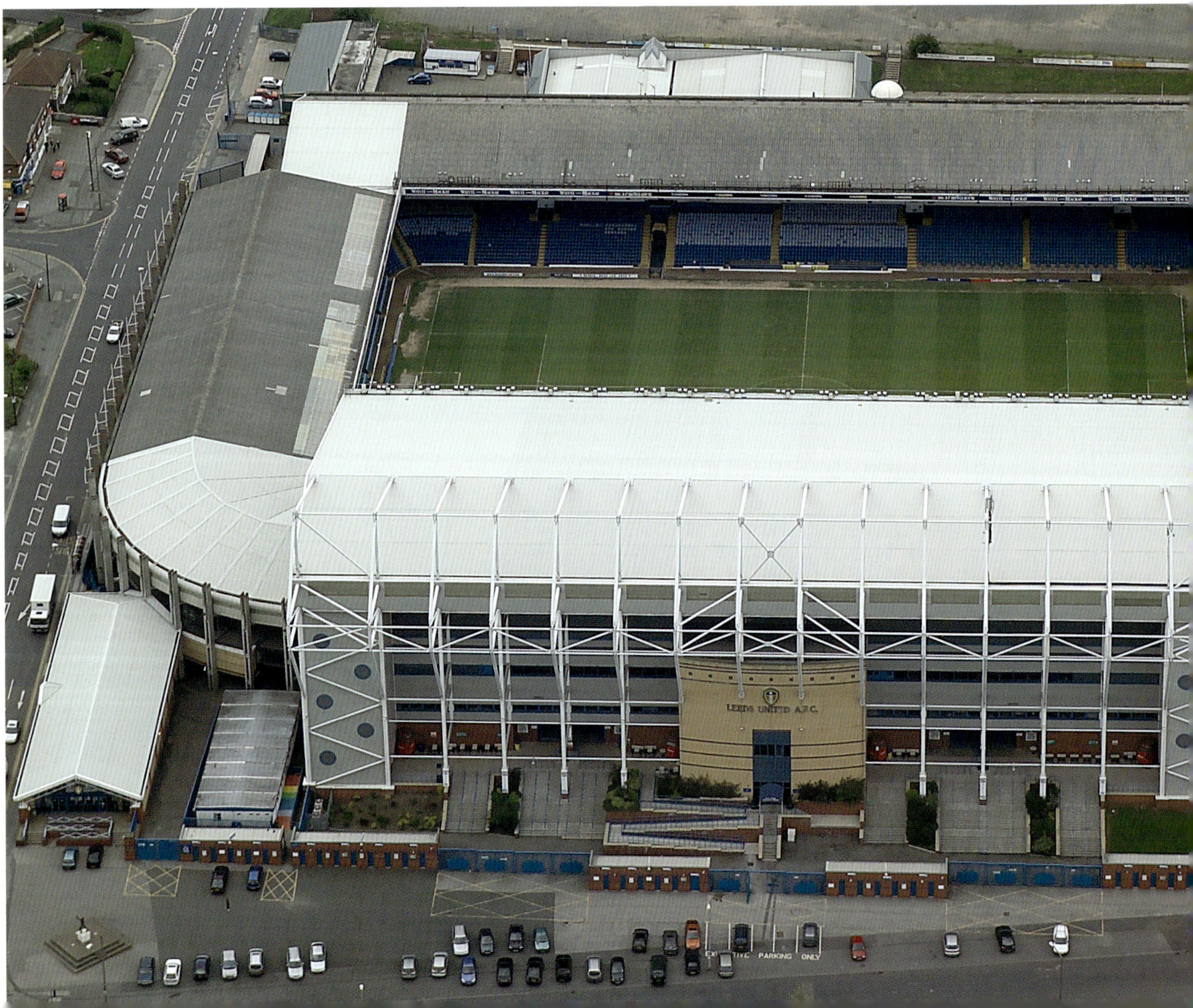

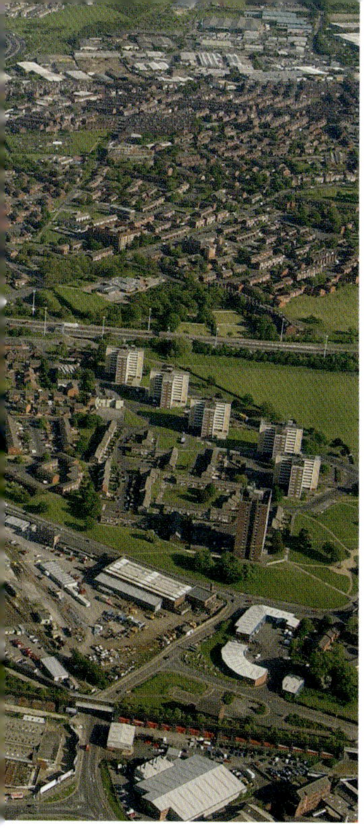

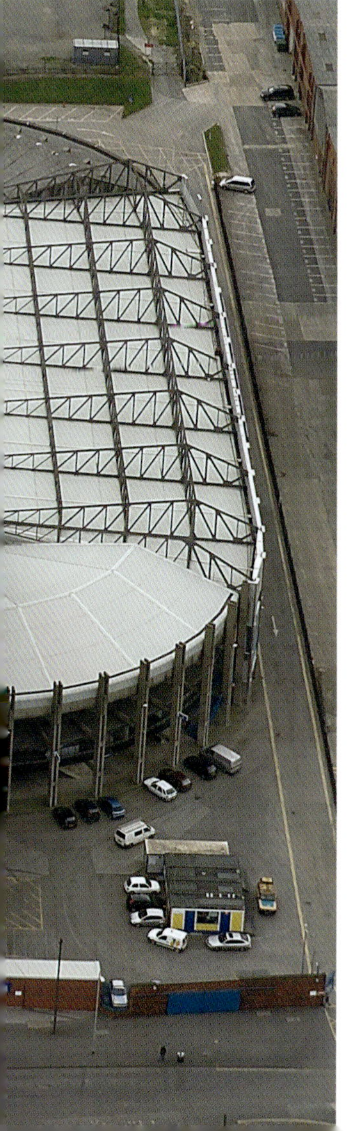

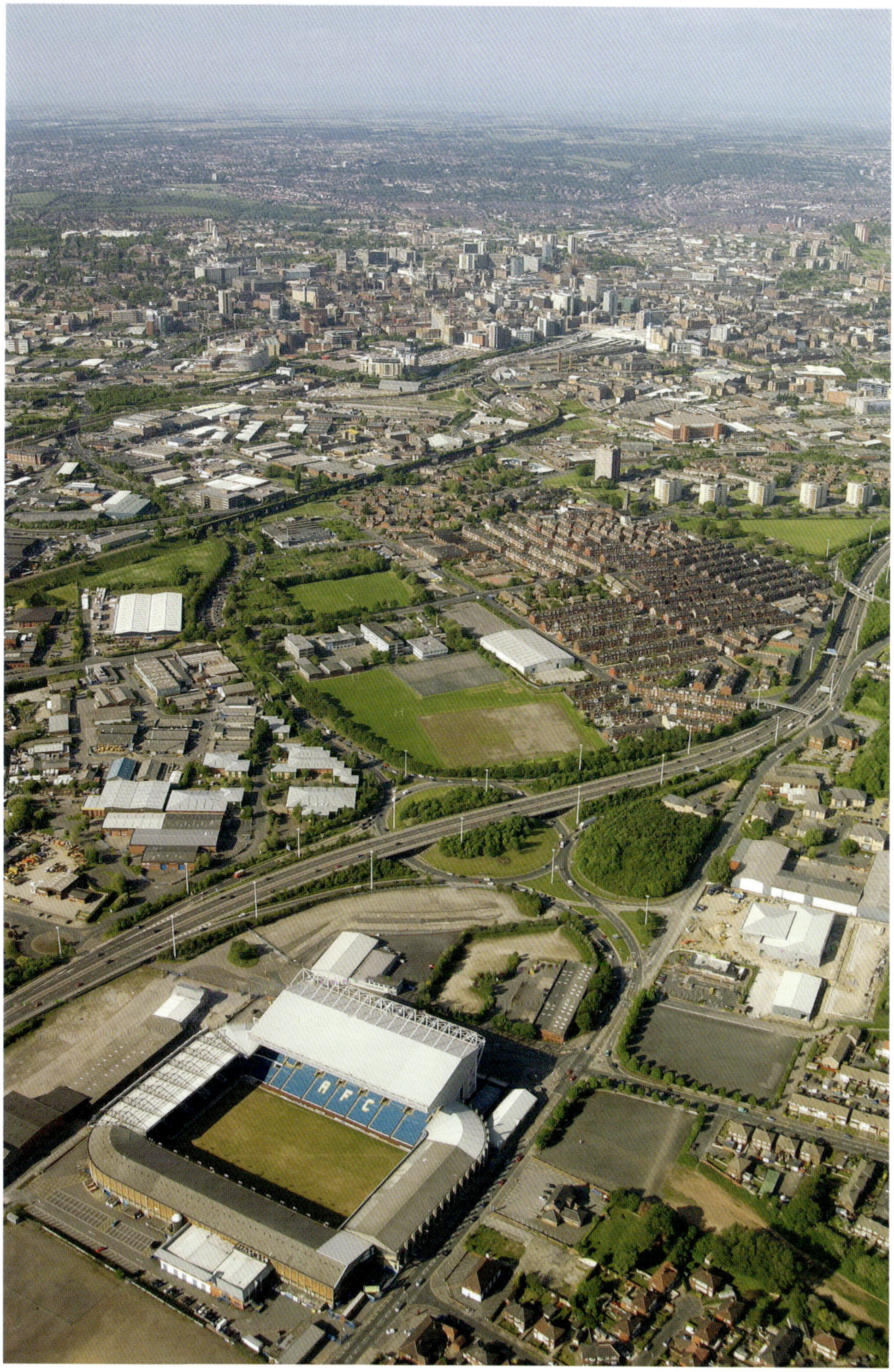

ELLAND ROAD *(above & left)*

Elland Road became the home of Leeds United Football Club following the ejection from the Football League of their predecessors, Leeds City, for making illegal payments to players. Leeds United were elected to the Football League in 1920. The development of the ground has gone through a number of important stages. The first stand, the West Stand, was built in the days of the Leeds City club in 1905 and this was followed in the 1920s by the so-called Scratching Shed and Spion Kop.

A new Kop (now the Don Revie Stand) was constructed in 1958 and in 1974 the Scratching Shed was replaced by the South Stand. The latest addition was the cantilever stand, the biggest in the world. The record attendance at the ground was 57,892 in a cup tie against Sunderland in March 1967. The modern ground capacity is just over 40,000. Leeds United won the First Division Championship in 1968, 1974 and 1993 and the FA Cup in 1972. The greatest period in the club's history came in the Don Revie era of the 1960s and early 1970s. During the period when Revie was manager (1961-74) the club won the First Division Championship twice, the FA Cup once, the League Cup once and the European Fairs Cup twice. The array of outstanding players at the club during that period was almost endless, including Billy Bremner, Jack Charlton, Johnny Giles, Eddie Gray, Peter Lorimer, Alan Clarke and Norman Hunter.

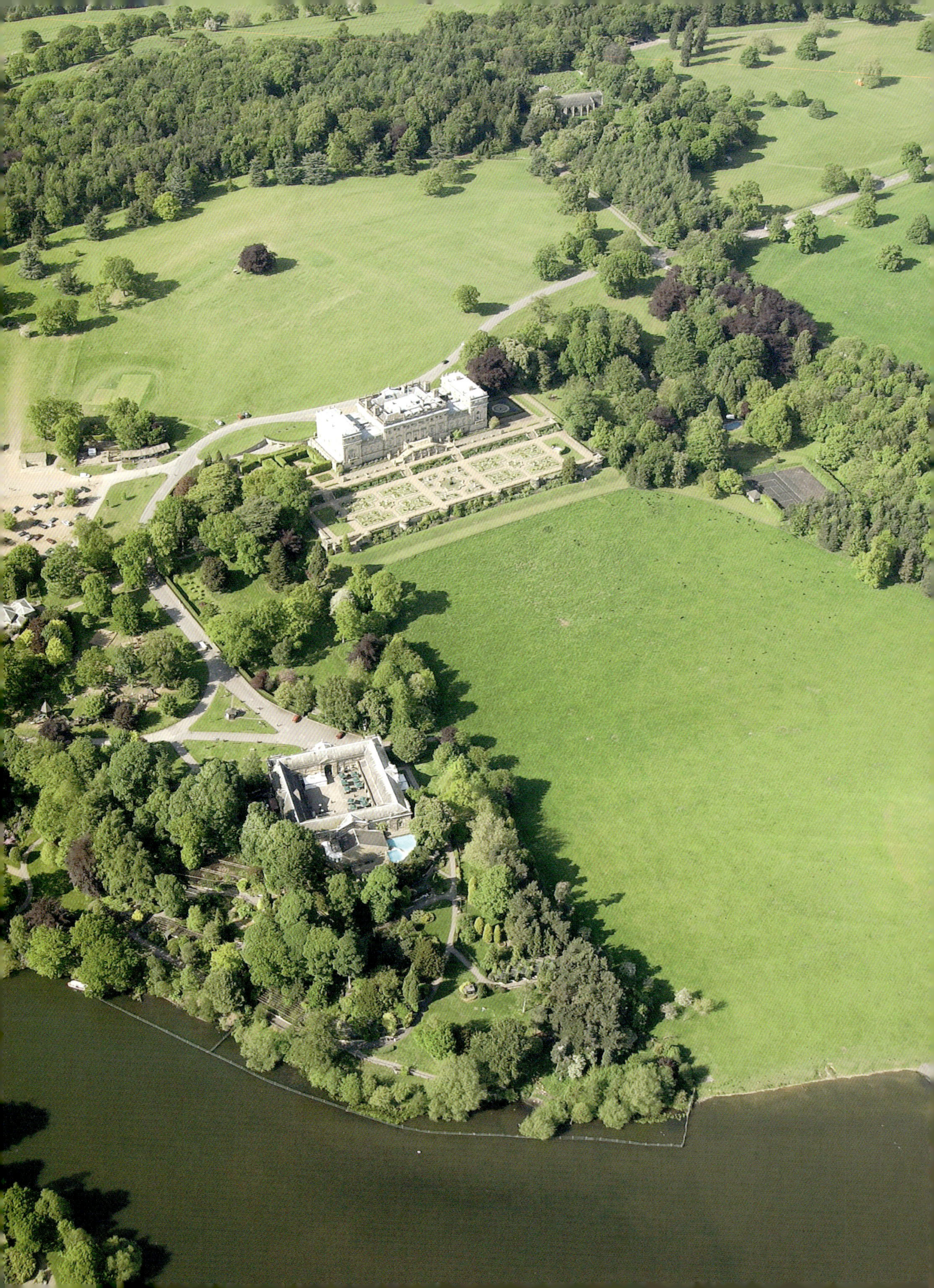

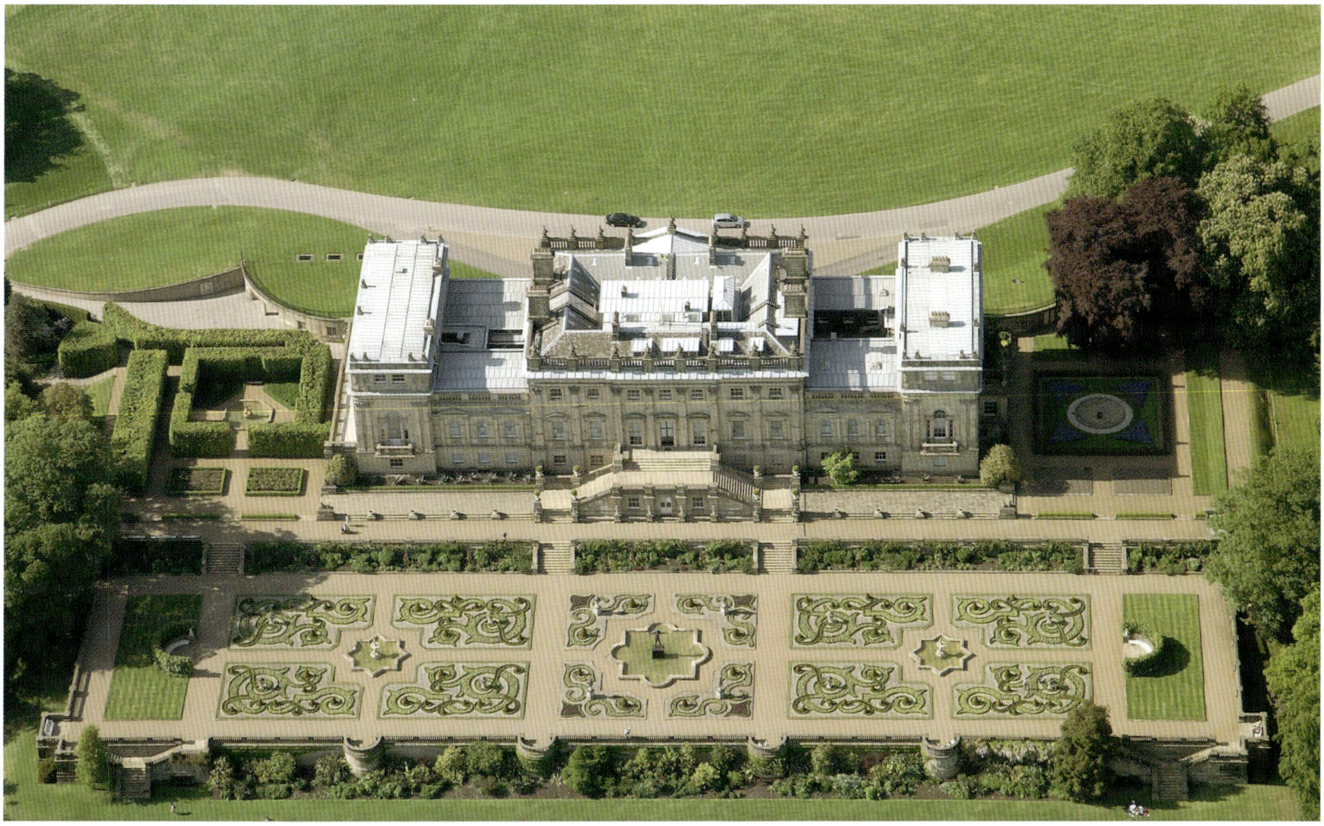

HAREWOOD HOUSE

This magnificent country house, the home of Earl and Countess Lascelles, was built by the York architect, John Carr, between 1759 and 1772 on the instructions of Edwin Lascelles whose father had made his fortune in the ribbon trade, from his position as collector of customs in Barbados and his directorship of the East India Company. The interiors were the work of Robert Adam and much of the furniture is documented work by Thomas Chippendale. In the 1840s the south facade of the house was remodelled by Sir Charles Barry, the architect of the Houses of Parliament. Immediately beyond the house to the south is an elaborate Italianate parterre with intricately-shaped flower beds, fountains and herbaceous borders. The grounds of the house, which include a serpentine lake, were laid out by Capability Brown.

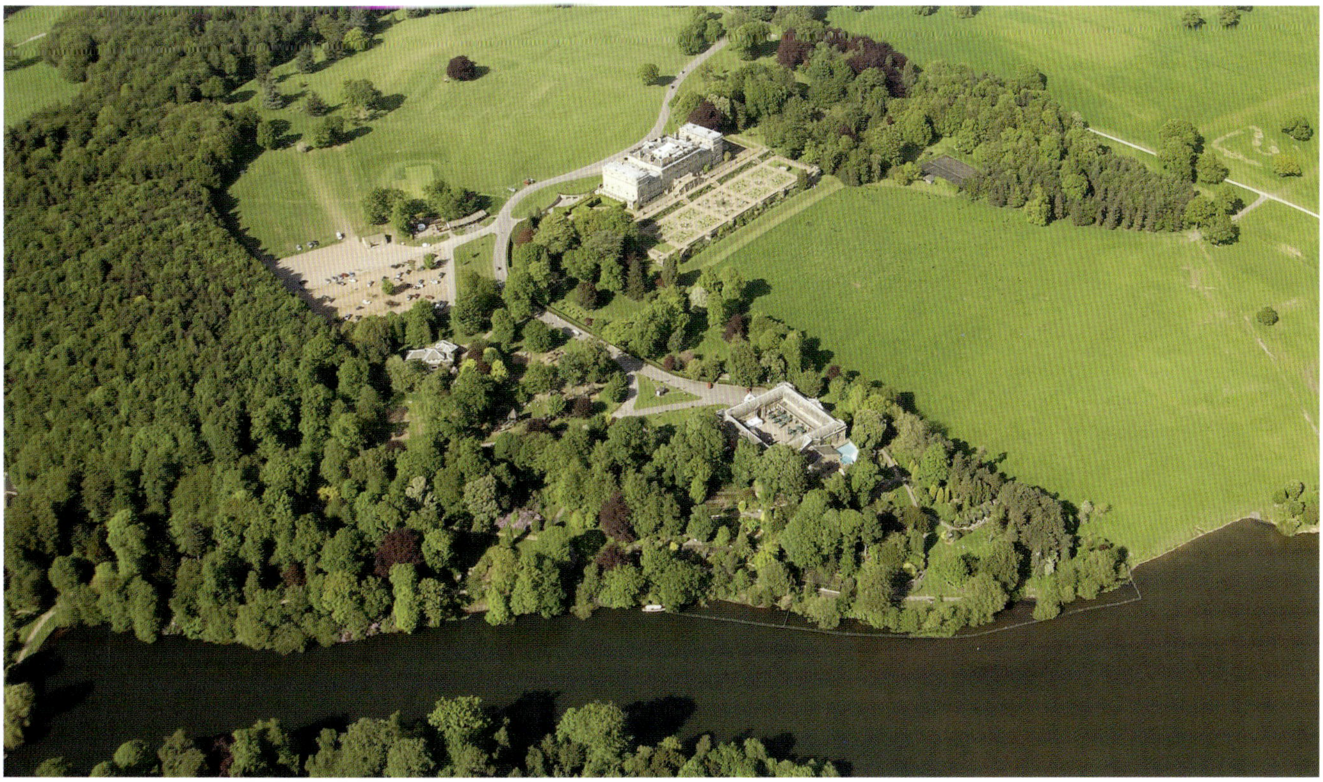

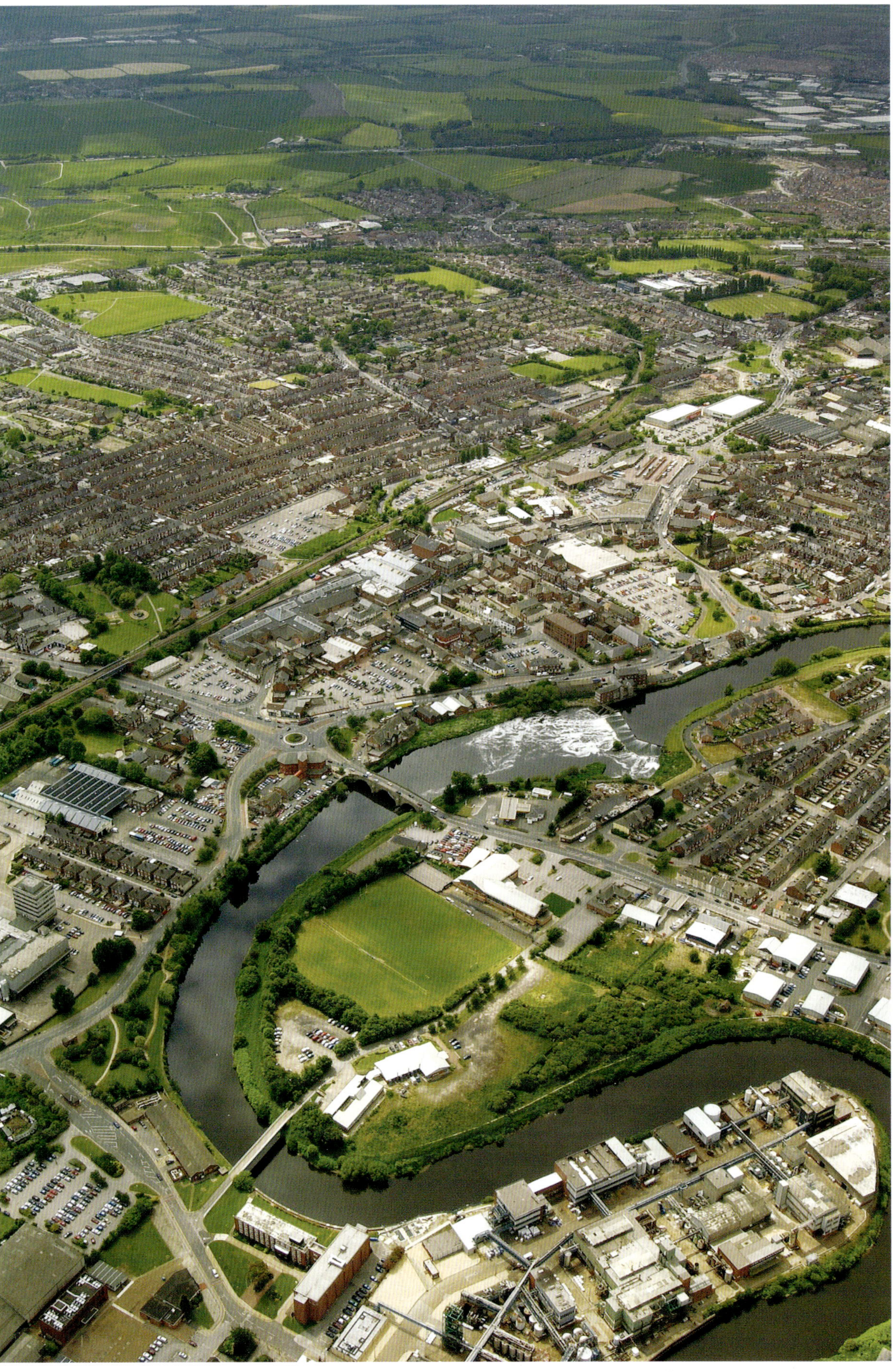

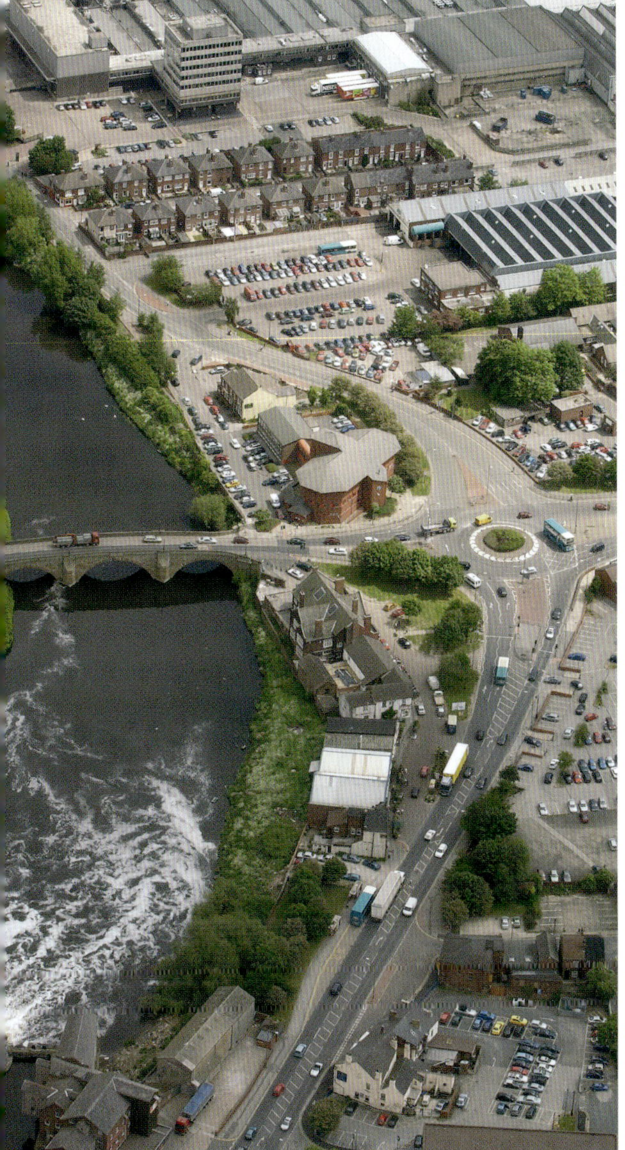

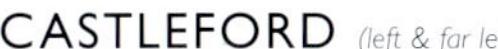

CASTLEFORD *(left & far left)*

The name Castleford is a corruption of Castreford, "the ford by the Roman fort". It was here, where the Roman military road Ermine Street crossed the river Aire, that the Roman station called *Legeolium* was located. The ford has now gone and the main river crossing is by means of a three-arch bridge built in the early 19th century. Castleford's growth was based on manufacturing and coalmining. The photograph on the far left is from the north-west over the town towards the M62 motorway which runs from left to right beyond the southern edge of the town. The site of Hickson's chemical works, the last chemical company in Castleford, can be seen in the foreground of the photograph on the far left.

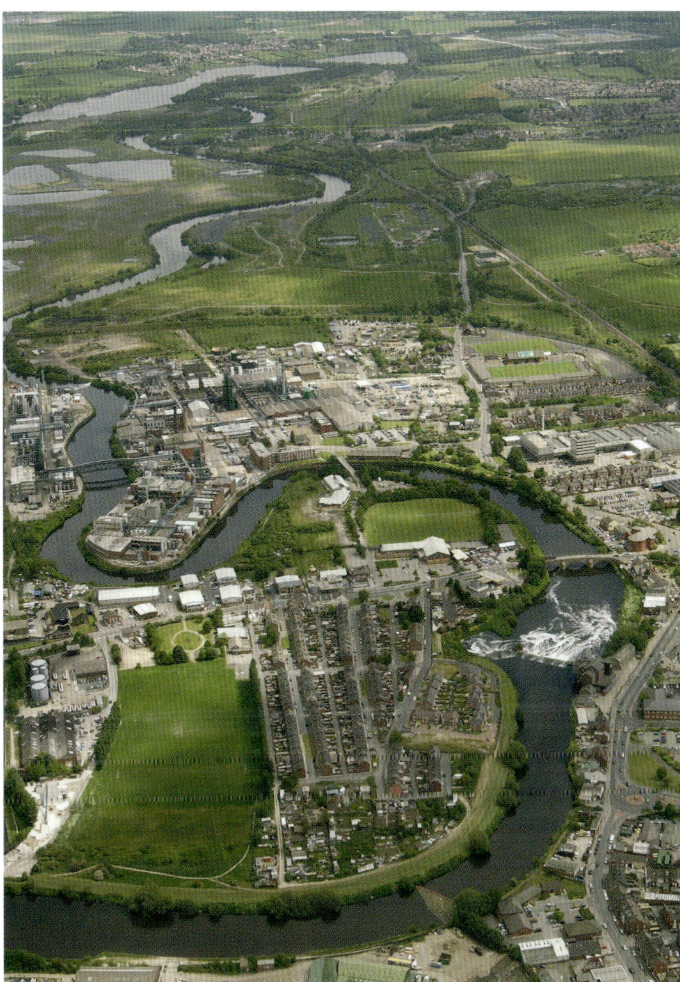

CASTLEFORD FROM THE WEST LOOKING TOWARDS FAIRBURN INGS *(above)*

This view of the town shows in the right middle ground Castleford Tigers rugby league club's ground, "the Jungle", on Wheldon Road and in the background Fairburn Ings RSPB nature reserve. This reserve is the ideal place to watch wetland birds. In summer redshank, snipe and lapwings breed and in winter there are thousands of ducks and geese. Many wading birds also visit the reserve on their autumn and spring migrations.

JUNCTION 32 OUTLET SHOPPING VILLAGE

(left)

This retail park (formerly Freeport Castleford) is a modern addition to Castleford's townscape. Located in Glasshoughton between junction 32 of the M62 motorway and the centre of the town, it is a designer outlet village with more than 65 shops selling a wide range of merchandise, designer fashion, children's wear, books and music. There is also a large DIY warehouse, a hotel and parking for 1,000 cars. Next door, with its sloping roofline, is Castleford Xscape where under one roof can be found real snow slopes, ice climbing walls, bowling alleys, a multi-screen cinema and cafes and restaurants. At night it becomes a "dine and dance destination".

KNOTTINGLEY & FERRYBRIDGE *(below)*

This view sweeps westwards across Knottingley, on slightly raised ground beside the river Aire, to Ferrybridge and its eight power station cooling towers. Electricity production began at Ferrybridge in 1927 when it became one of a large number of small power stations located near to the mainly urban markets they served. Massive expansion to make Ferrybridge Britain's largest coal-fired power station took place in the 1960s. The waters of the nearby river Aire have from the beginning been used not only to transport coal to the station but also to supply the steam-powered turbines.

PONTEFRACT CASTLE *(right)*

This is all that remains of what must have been one of Yorkshire's most impressive medieval stone keep castles. What can be seen here are the remains of the inner bailey with its surviving wall, and the remains of a postern gate and a chapel. Originally built as a timber motte and bailey castle in the late 11th century by its Norman lord Ilbert de Lacy, it was "slighted" (levelled with the ground) in 1649 following the end of the Civil War. The space was reputedly used for a time as a field for growing liquorice for making the famous Pontefract cakes. It is now a recreation ground.

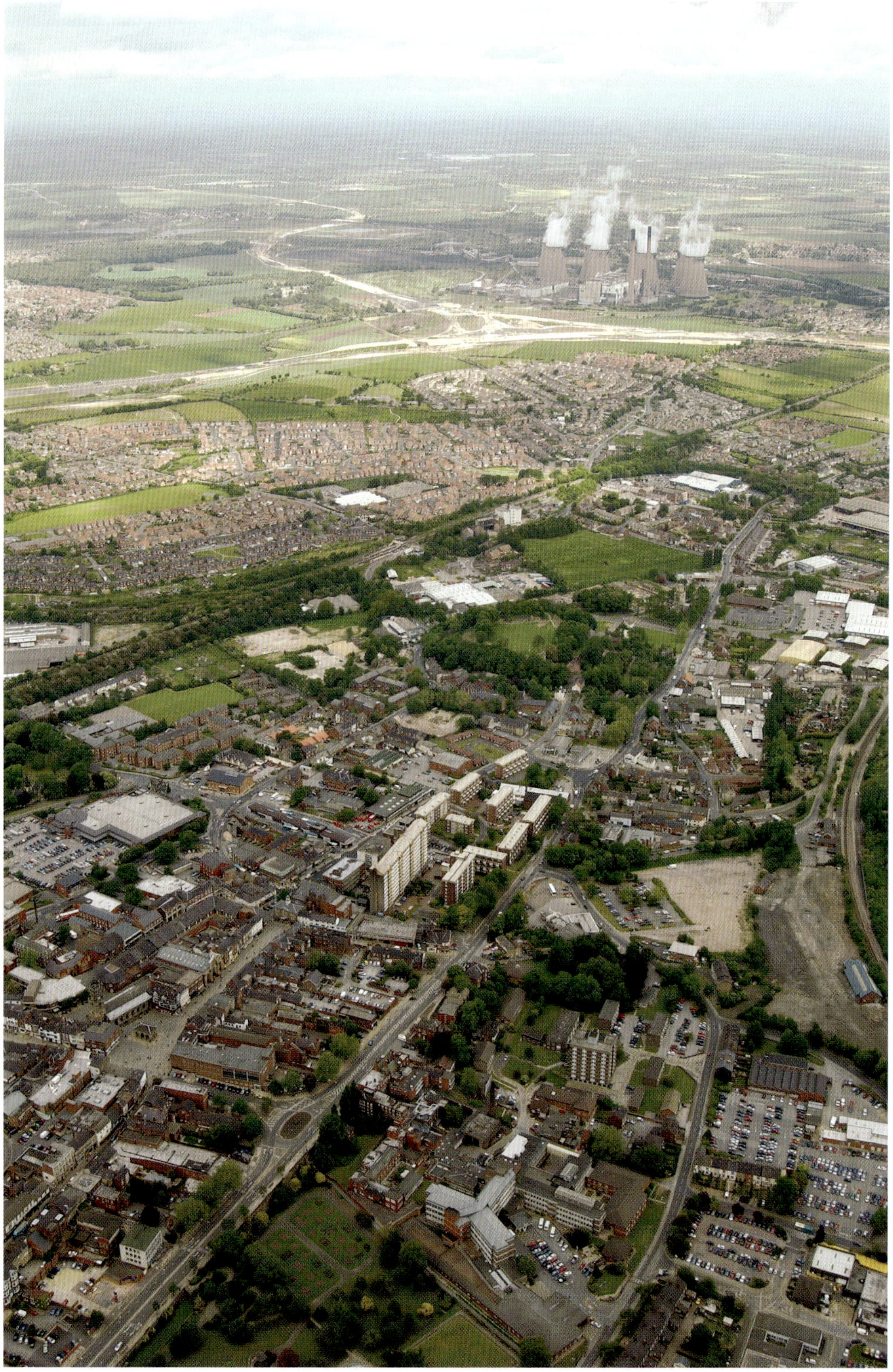

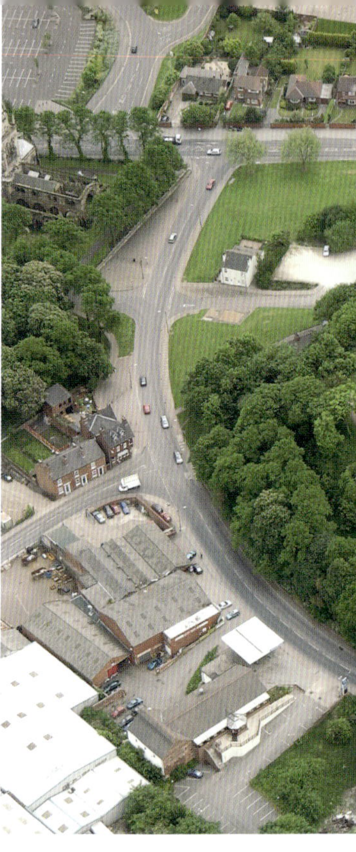

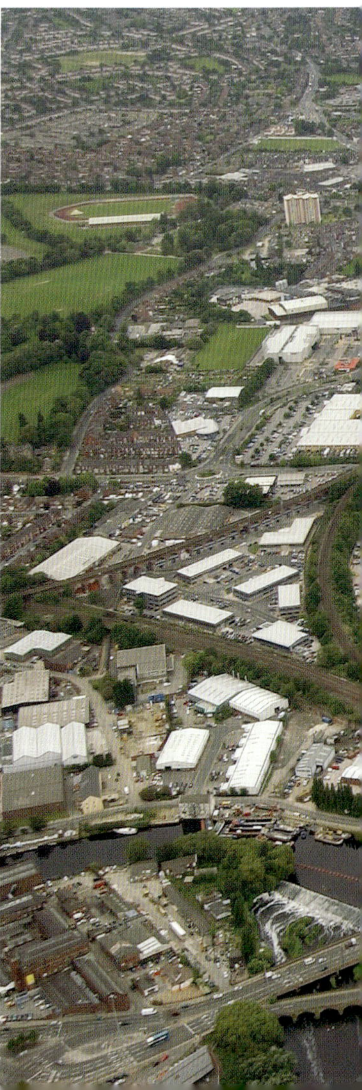

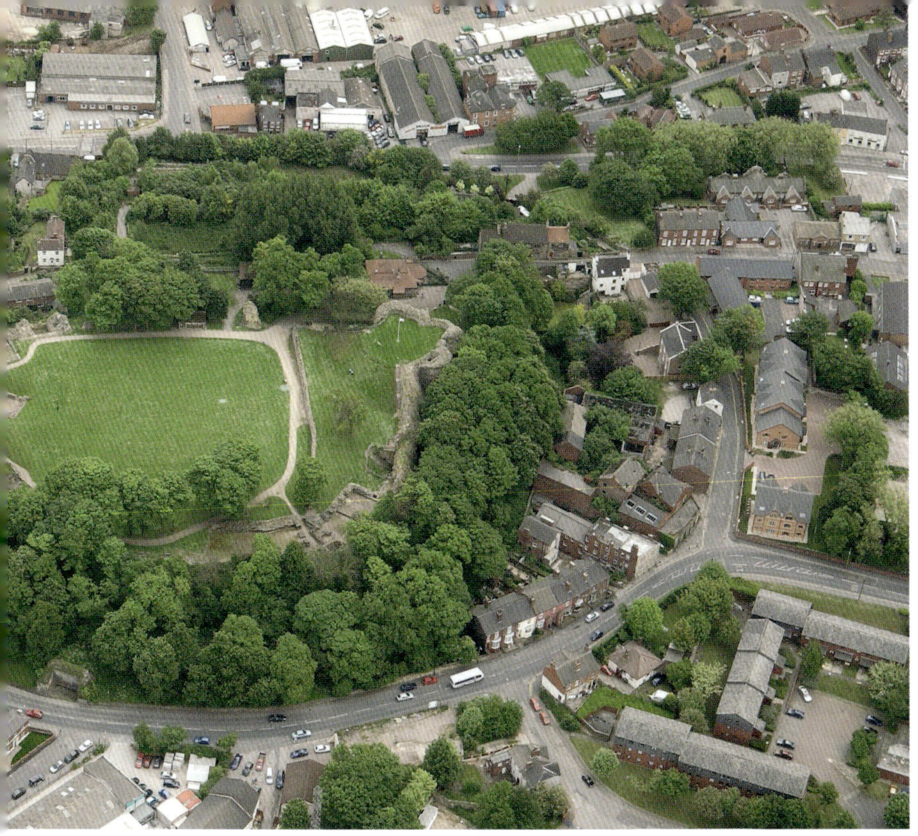

WAKEFIELD *(below)*

This panoramic view of Wakefield looks in a north-westerly direction over the urban area towards Wrenthorpe. In the medieval and early modern period Wakefield was an important market town and was the centre of the Yorkshire clothing trade before the rise of Leeds and Bradford. In the 1720s Daniel Defoe described Wakefield as large, handsome and rich. Until 1974, and local government reorganisation, the town was the administrative capital for the West Riding County Council. Its early importance is reflected in two important medieval buildings that survive. In the foreground can be seen the medieval chapel built about 1350 on the bridge over the river Calder, one of only four surviving bridge chapels in the whole country. The other fine medieval building is the Perpendicular-style cathedral, until 1888 the parish church of All Saints, standing on Kirkgate (Church Street) in the centre of the town. Sir Nikolaus Pevsner commented that Wakefield had what few towns in England could boast – a skyline. The highest feature in Wakefield's skyline is the cathedral spire, 247ft (75m) high. Two other important features of Wakefield's skyline stand in Wood Street, the tower of the Town Hall rising to 190ft (58m) and the domed tower of the former West Riding County Hall rising to 130ft (40m).

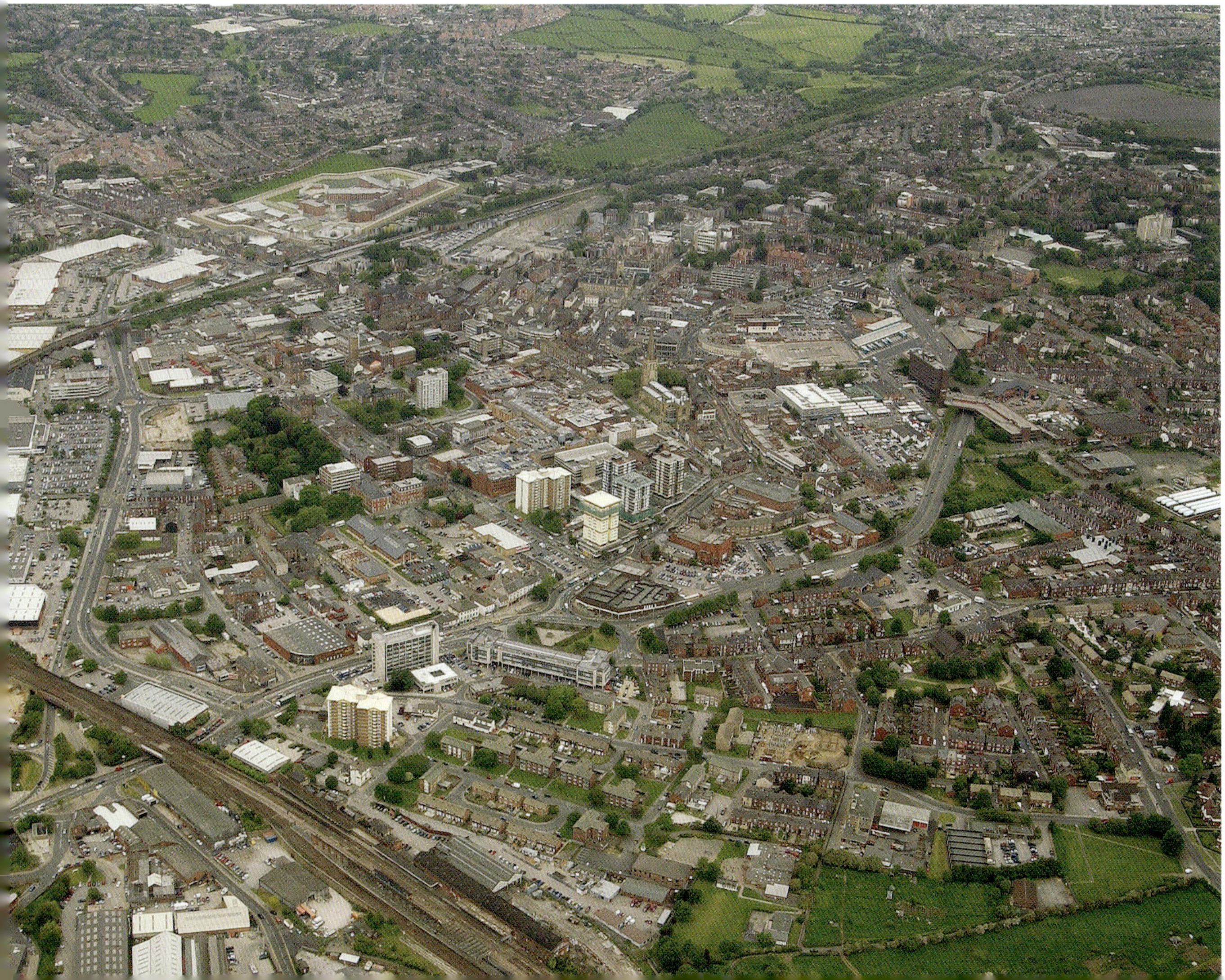

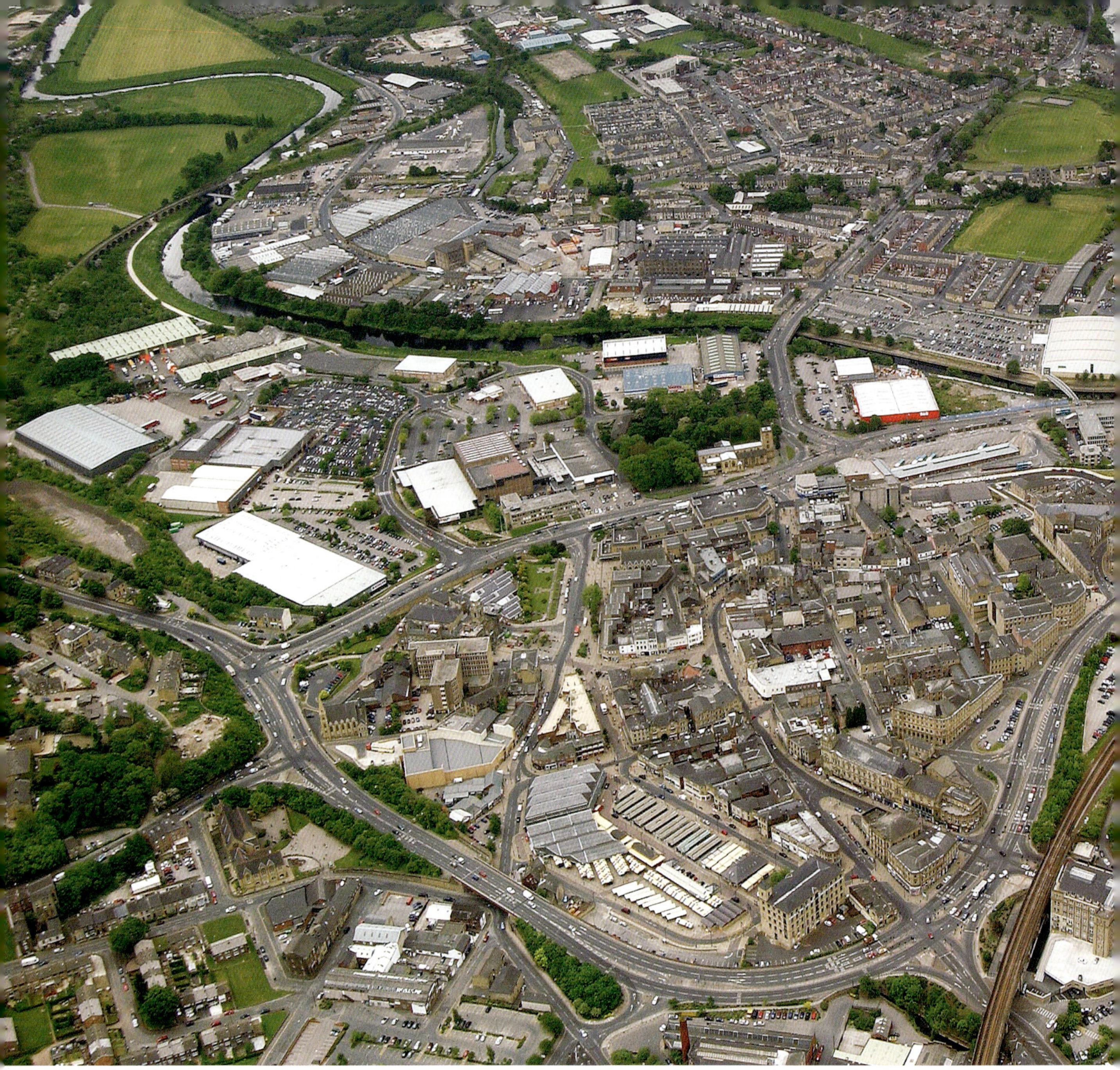

DEWSBURY *(above)*

This panoramic view of Dewsbury shows the town from the north with the town centre lying outside a great meander on the river Calder. The river is bridged in three places, with the principal road (Wilson Street leading to Saville Road, the B6409) linking the town centre with extensive industrial, warehousing and residential development in Saville Town which occupies the level ground within the meander itself. In the foreground most of Dewsbury's town centre is hemmed in by the modern road system of Dewsbury Ring Road and the railway line between Leeds and Huddersfield. The town street names such as Market Street and Old Westgate betray its medieval origins while Nelson Street and Wellington Street reflect its 19th-century expansion. Some of the most striking buildings in and around the town centre are 19th-century multi-storey textile mills and wool warehouses that stand out in stark contrast with the modern flat-roofed one-storey warehouses, workshops and stores. Also well in evidence are the stalls of Dewsbury's outdoor market.

LEEDS-BRADFORD AIRPORT *(right)*

Originally known as Yeadon Aerodrome, Leeds-Bradford International Airport is on the former Yeadon Moor, six miles north-east of Bradford and six miles north-west of Leeds. The first club flight from the aerodrome took place in 1931 and scheduled flights began four years later in 1935 to Blackpool and the Isle of Man, Newcastle and Edinburgh. RAF 609 squadron was formed at Yeadon in 1936 and civil flights stopped in 1939 with the outbreak of the Second World War but resumed again in 1947. During the war military aircraft at the nearby Avro works received their first test flights at Yeadon. By 1955 international flights to Ostend and Dusseldorf had been added to the domestic destinations. Scheduled flights to London began in 1960 and in 1978 the first flight for holidaymakers to Spain took place. The terminal building was destroyed by fire in 1965 but was rebuilt and re-opened in 1968 and significant extensions and improvements have been made since then. Two million passengers flew from the airport in 2003.

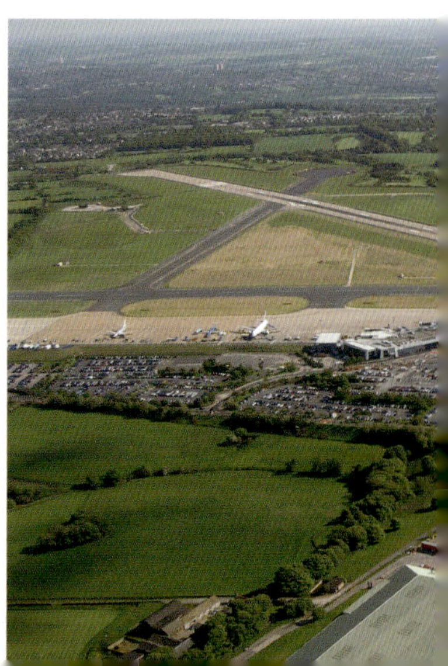

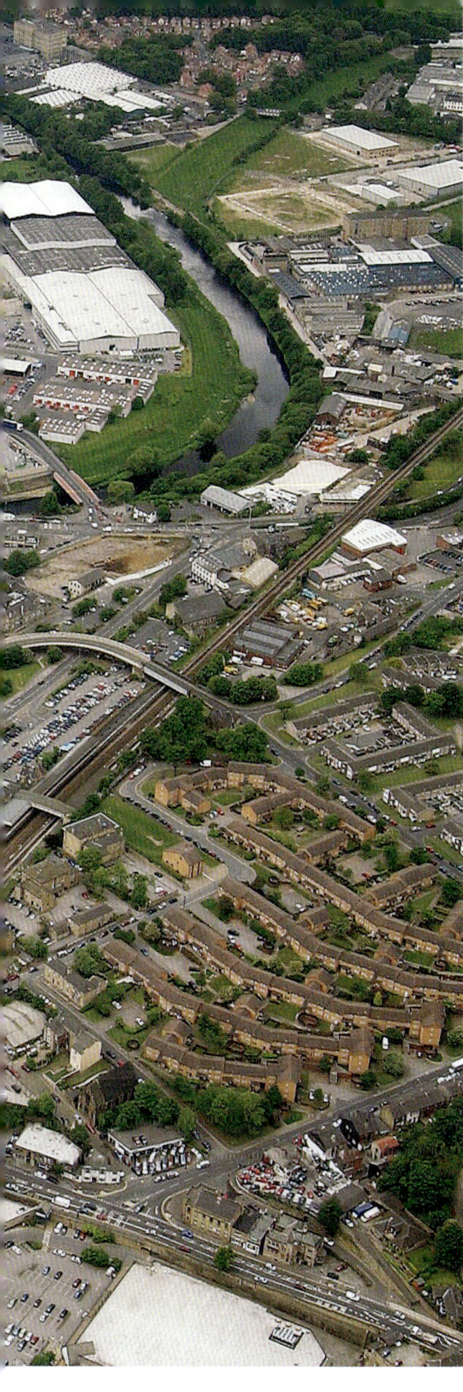

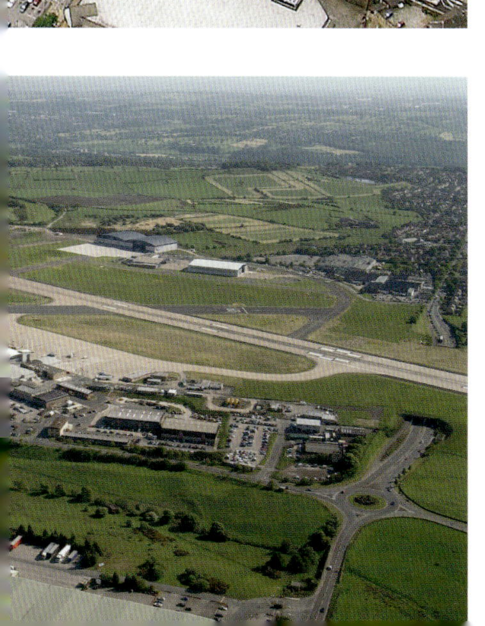

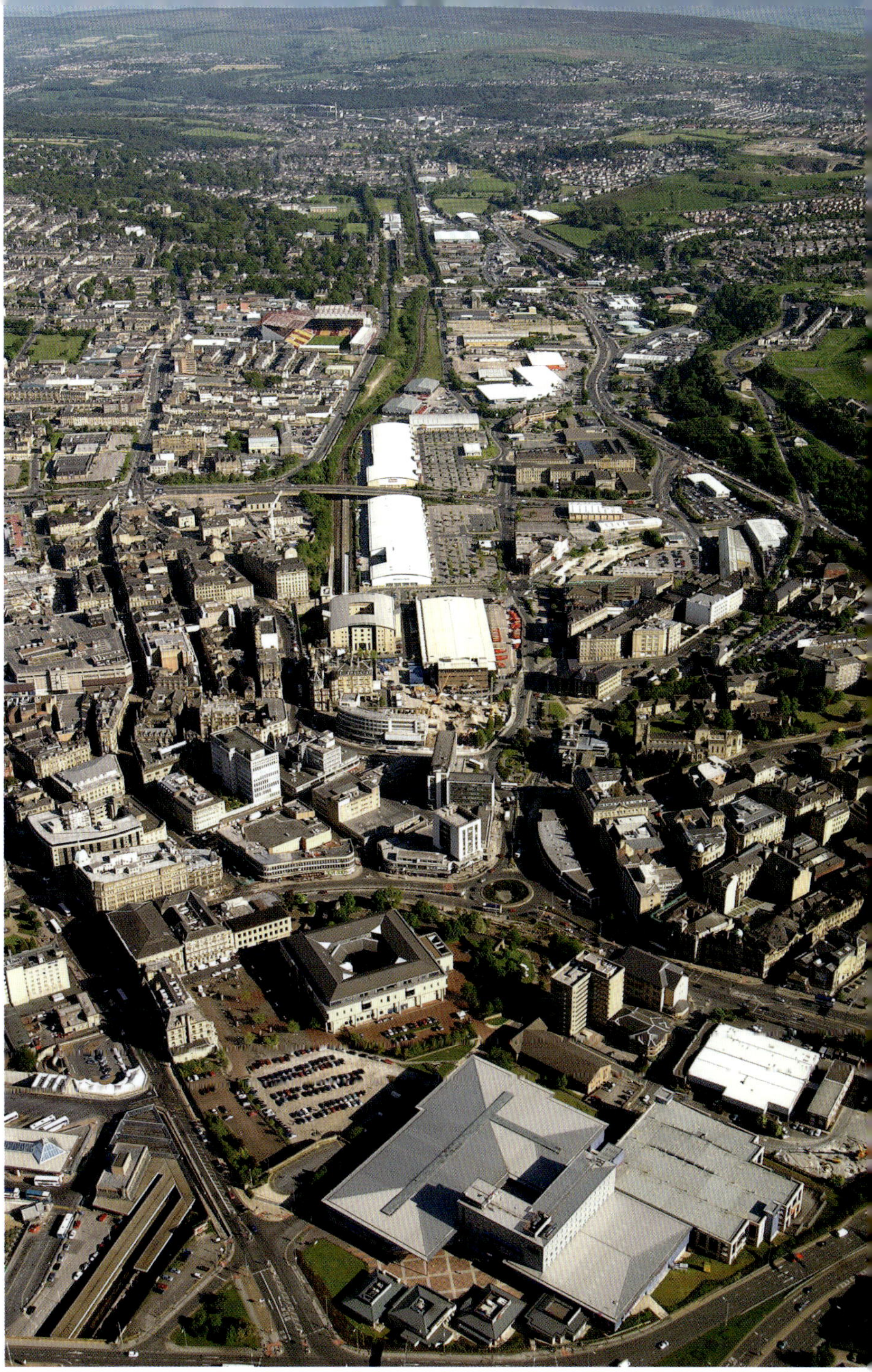

BRADFORD *(above)*

The cloth trade had made Bradford a wealthy town by the late Middle Ages and this prosperity continued through the Tudor and Stuart periods. But its great period of expansion came in the 19th century when the population grew from about 13,000 in 1801 to 280,000 a century later. The Bradford branch of the Leeds and Liverpool Canal opened in 1774, the railway that came in 1846, and local collieries that produced the fuel for the textile mills were key factors in this period of sustained industrial expansion. Popularly known as "Worstedopolis", Bradford was the world centre in the Victorian period for the production of worsted, made from long wools.

This view of Bradford today is from the south-east looking over the city centre with the railway terminating at Forster Square Railway Station just to the south of the flyover carrying the A6181 (Hamm Strasse) beside the Forster Square Retail Park. Along the line of the railway can be seen Valley Parade football stadium and beyond that the outer suburbs of the city and on to Shipley and Baildon with Rombalds Moor rising in the background.

Now fighting not to be dwarfed by modern development, Bradford Cathedral stands on a slight rise on the eastern (right) side of Forster Square. This was St Peter's parish church until raised to cathedral status in 1919. Made of millstone grit it has a fine Perpendicular western tower constructed between 1493 and 1508. In the immediate foreground can be seen The Leisure Exchange, 205,000sq ft (19,000sq m) of space, the tenth largest leisure scheme in the UK.

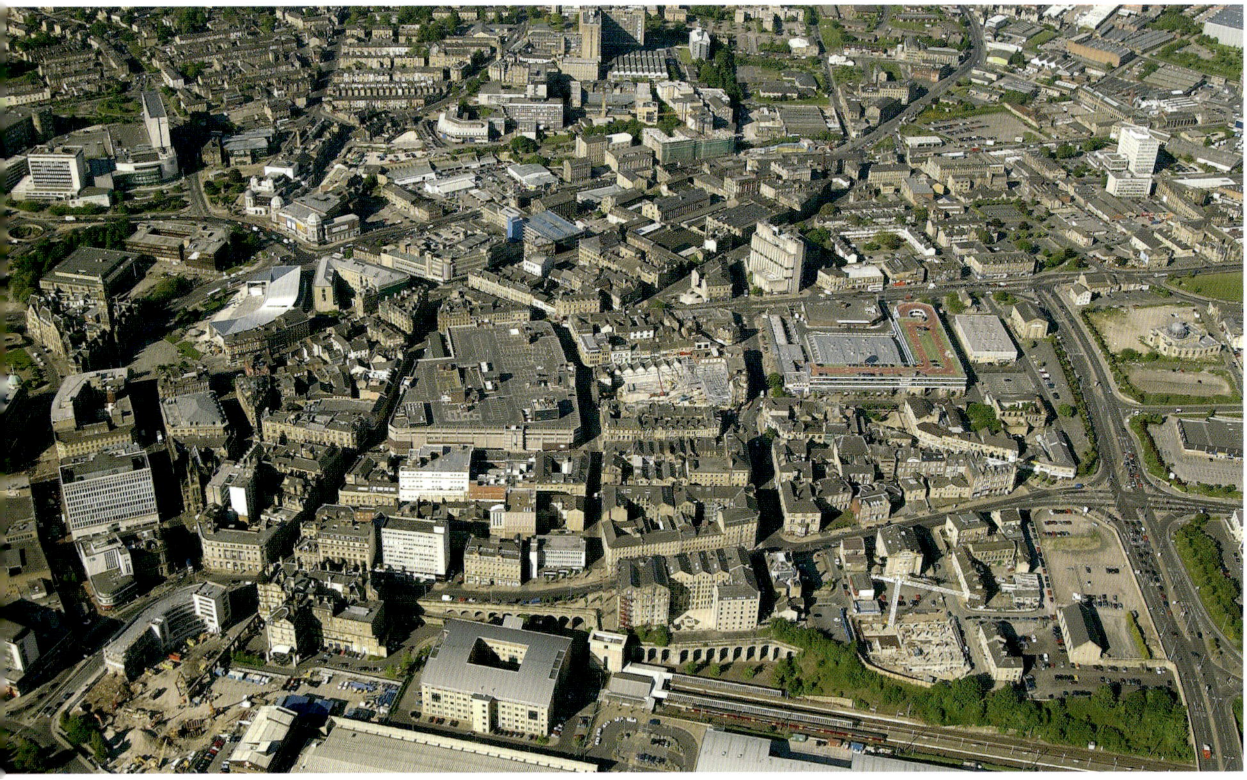

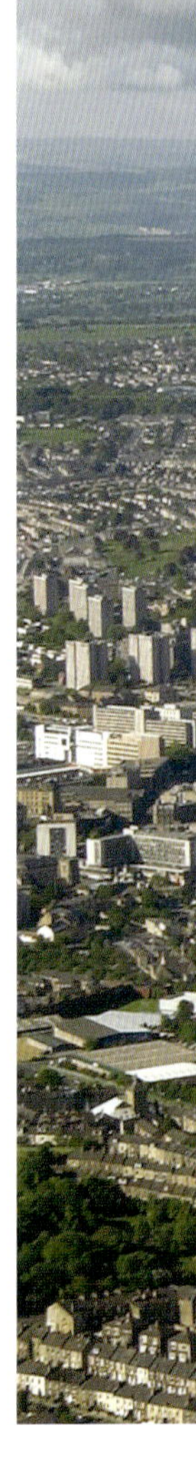

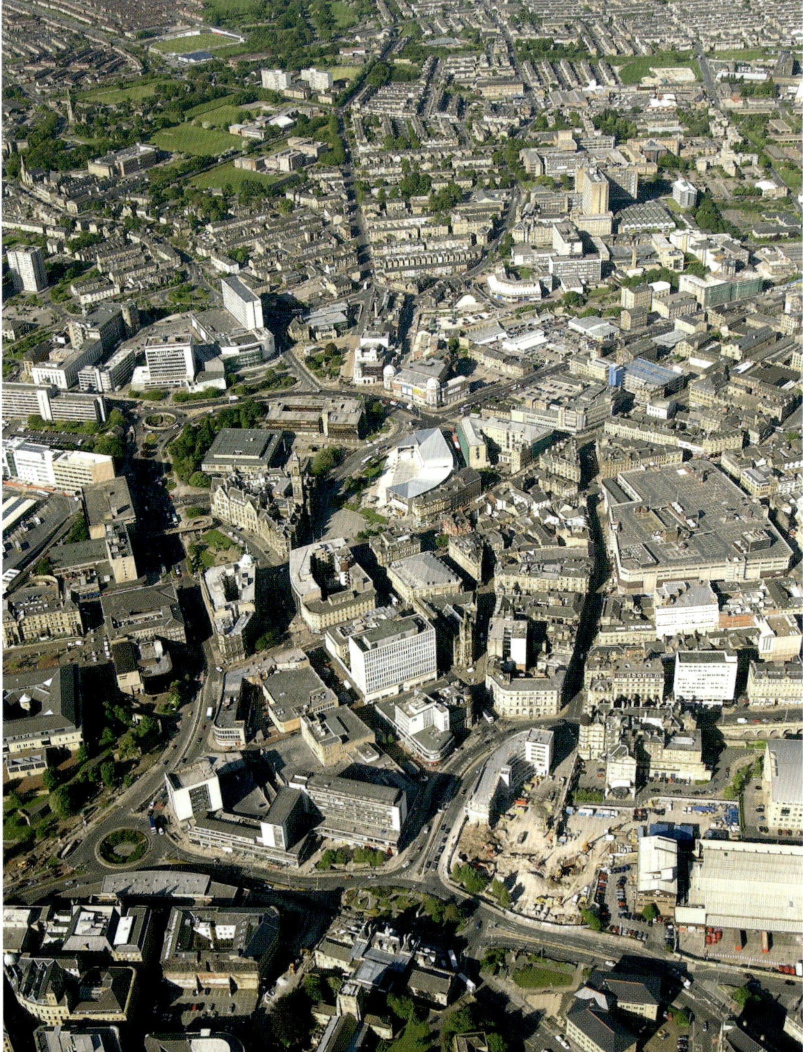

THREE VIEWS OF CENTRAL BRADFORD

(above, left and above right)

All three photographs show various parts of central Bradford from the east. In the foreground of the photograph above can be seen the railway terminus at Forster Square. Running away on the right-hand side of the photograph is the A6181 (Hamm Strasse) with the junction with Manningham Lane, Manor Row and Cheapside and further away the junction with Westgate/Godwin Street, all clearly visible. Between the railway and Westgate/Godwin Street can be seen the roofs of Rawson Market, John Street Market, and the Arndale Centre and Kirkgate Market.

The photograph above right shows the same part of Bradford in the left middle ground but also taking in a wider view of the suburbs to the north and west of the city centre (including Thornton where the Brontë family lived before moving to Haworth) and beyond to the peripheral villages of Denholme and Oxenhope on the edge of the Pennine moors.

The photograph on the left shows a view of central Bradford looking along Hall Ings and Kirkgate to Godwin Street and beyond along Thornton Road. In the immediate foreground is a small part of that district of Bradford called "Little Germany" where 19th-century German wool merchants built their spectacular warehouses in Greek revival, Italianate and Gothic styles (seen more clearly in the photograph on the previous page). Also visible are the law courts and the roof of the Arndale Centre and Kirkgate Market.

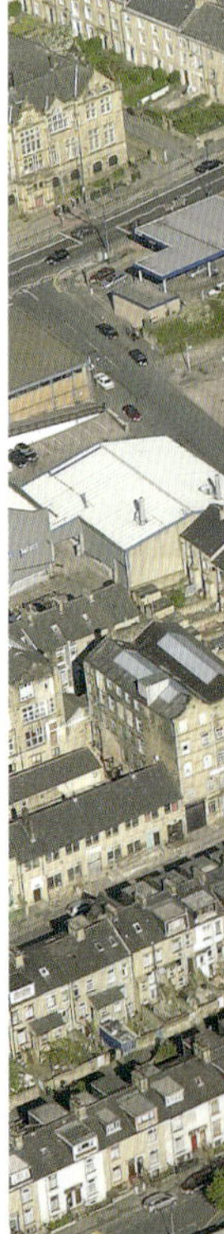

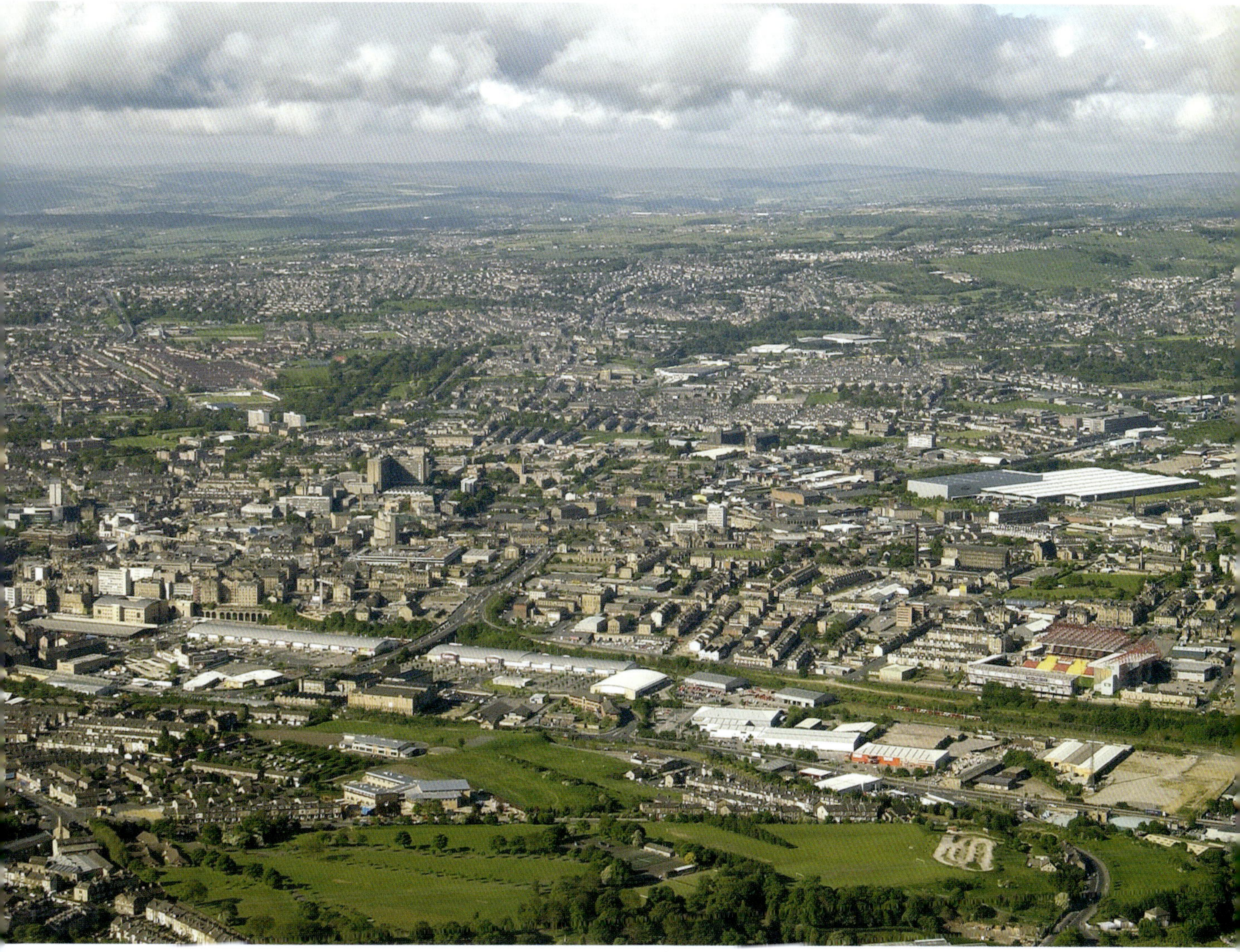

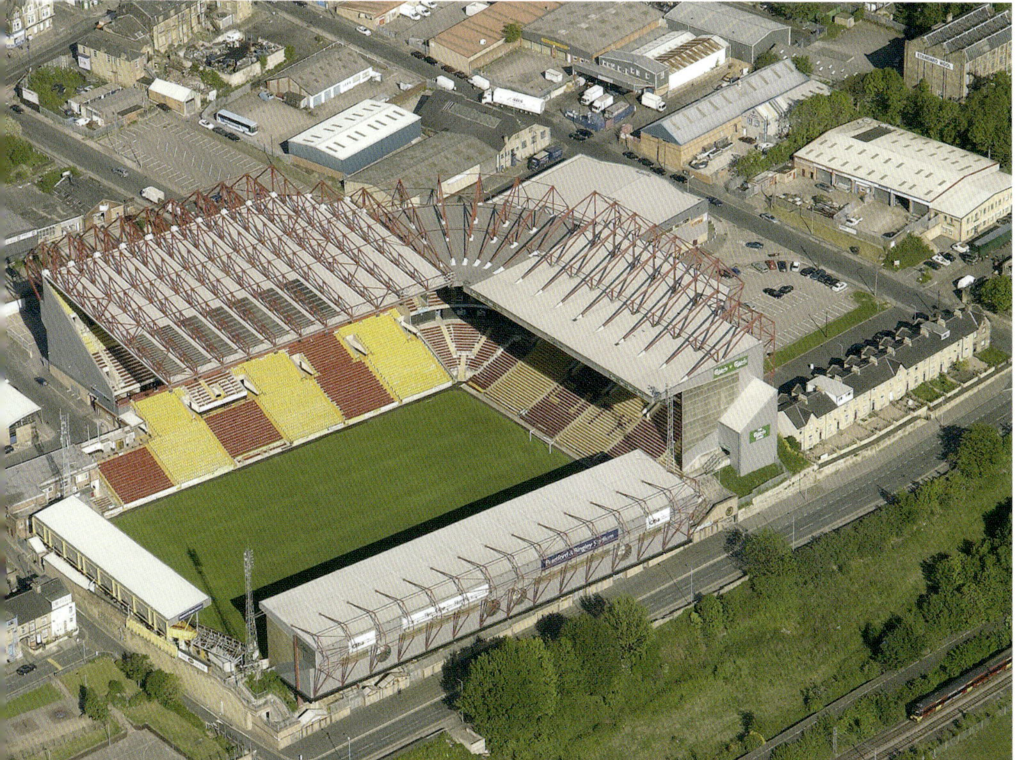

VALLEY PARADE *(left)*

Valley Parade is the home of Bradford City football club founded in 1903. The team colours, reflected in the colours of the stand seating, are claret and amber. They were FA Cup winners in 1911, the first holders of the present trophy which coincidentally was made in Bradford. The record attendance at the ground was 39,146 at a cup tie against Burnley in March 1911. The modern ground capacity is 25,136. Disaster struck the club, the ground and the city on 11 May 1985 when a fire, thought to have been started by an accidentally discarded lighted match or cigarette end in a polystyrene cup in the old Main Stand, caused the death of 56 spectators and injured another 265. The subsequent enquiry led by Mr Justice Popplewell resulted in new legislation about safety regulations at the country's sports grounds. For a whole season the club played its home fixtures at neighbouring grounds before the new stadium was re-opened in May 1986 when the club team played (and beat) an England XI.

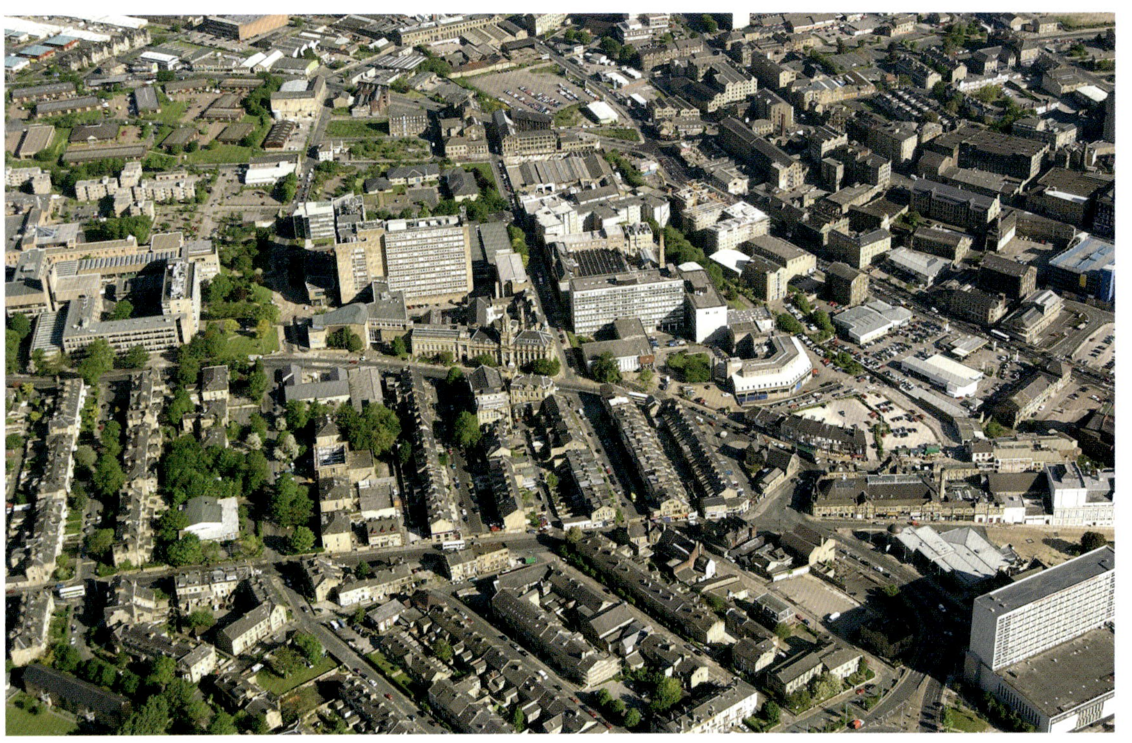

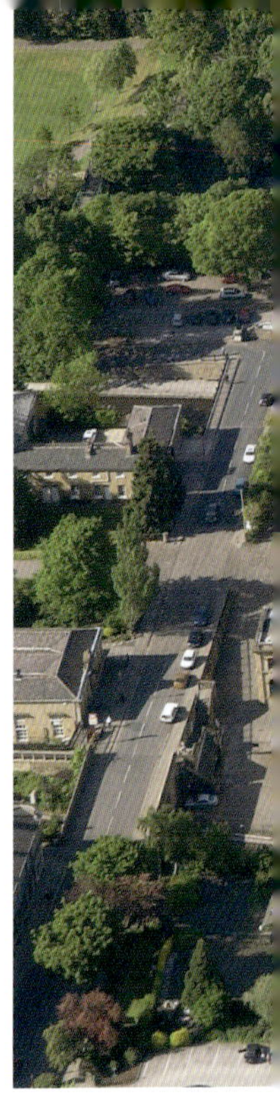

UNIVERSITY OF BRADFORD *(above)*

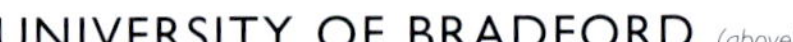

Bradford Institute of Technology received its Royal Charter to become the University of Bradford in 1966 and its first Chancellor was Prime Minister Harold Wilson. The university library is the JB Priestley Library, named after the Bradford-born novelist, dramatist and essayist. The university campus occupies a compact site just to the west of the city centre bounded by Listerhills Road in the north, Smith Street and Carlton Street in the east, Great Horton Road in the south and Shearbridge Road in the west. Millions of pounds continue to be invested on the campus to create a "21st Century Learning Village". Today Bradford is ranked number one among universities in the north of England for graduate employment.

MANNINGHAM MILLS *(below)*

Originally built in 1838, Manningham Mills (also known as Lister's Mill) were re-built in 1871-73 by local architects Andrews & Pepper for Samuel Cunliffe Lister following a fire. They became the largest silk-spinning and weaving mills in the country. The façade of the mills along Heaton Road is 350 yards (320m) long and the campanile chimney, which is based on one in the Piazza San Marco in Venice, is 249ft (76m) high and dominates the skyline. The imposing entrance has above it the Latin inscription *Fidem Parit Integritas* (Integrity produces confidence). A 19-week strike at the mill in 1890-91 played a major role in the formation of the Independent Labour Party. After years of dereliction the mills are being renovated and converted into stylish apartments.

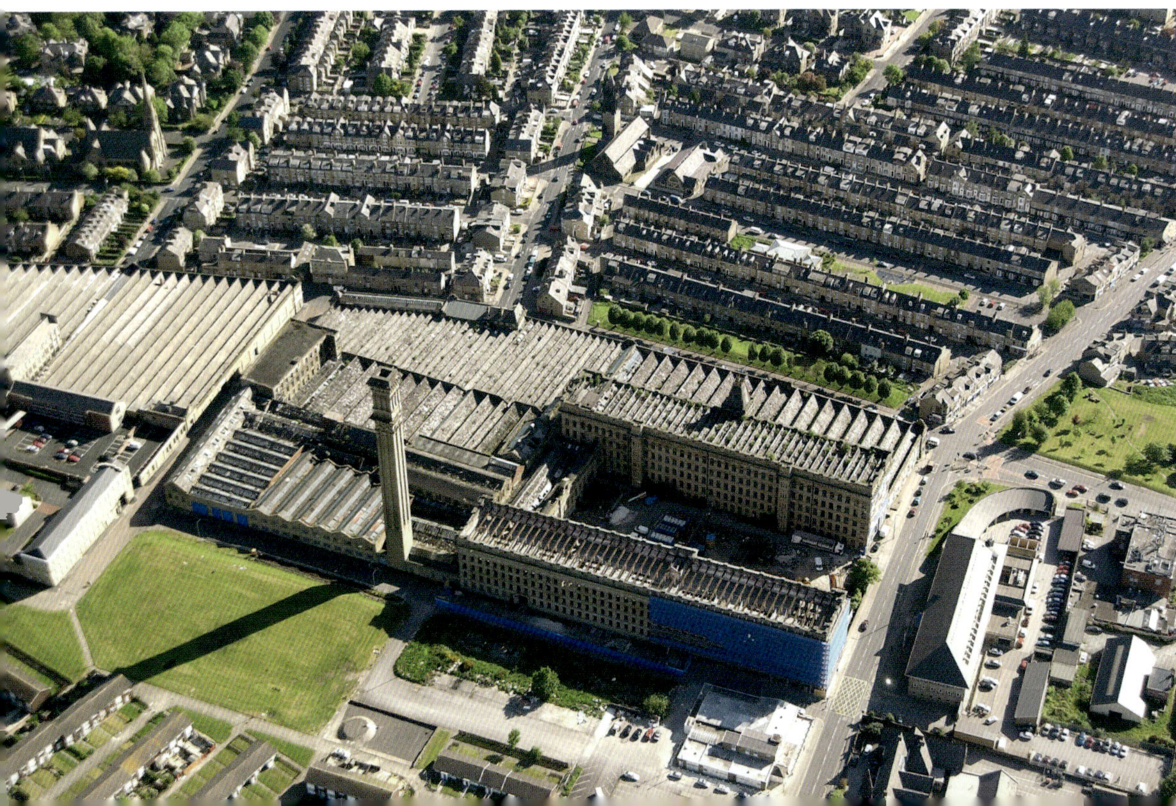

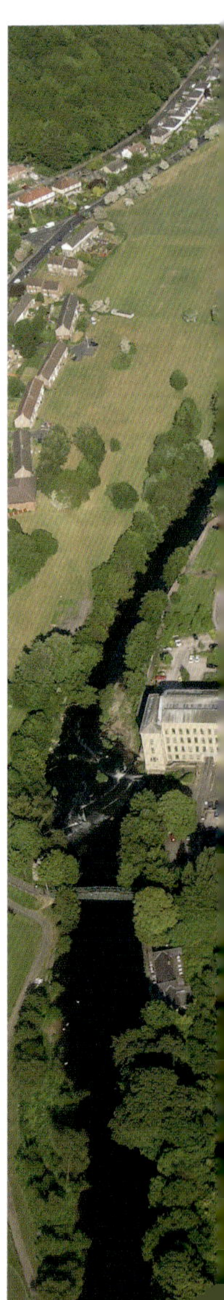

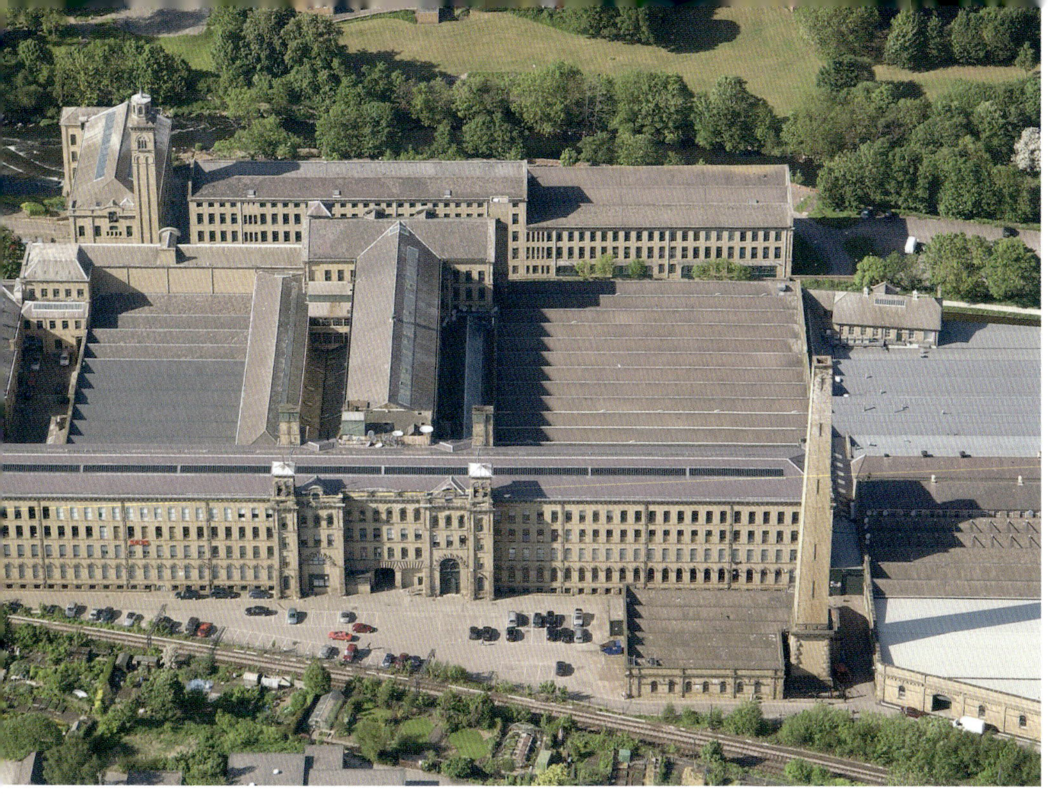

SALT'S MILL & SALTAIRE

(left, and below left & right)

Wealthy alpaca and mohair woollen cloth manufacturer, Sir Titus Salt, moved his mill and his workforce from Bradford to a more rural and healthy location to the north-west of the town in the Aire valley in the 1850s. He called his new industrial village Saltaire and the first large T-shaped six-storey mill to the south of the Leeds & Liverpool Canal was completed in 1853. Another mill, the New Mill, was completed in 1868, separated from the first mill by the canal. Both are in the Italianate style and have very tall campanile chimneys. Beside his mills Salt arranged for housing, places of worship and a school but there were no public houses. Altogether he built 895 houses laid out on a grid-iron street pattern some of which can be seen in the bottom left photograph. His architects also designed and built a beautiful congregational church which can be seen in both photographs below. Saltaire has been declared a World Heritage Site.

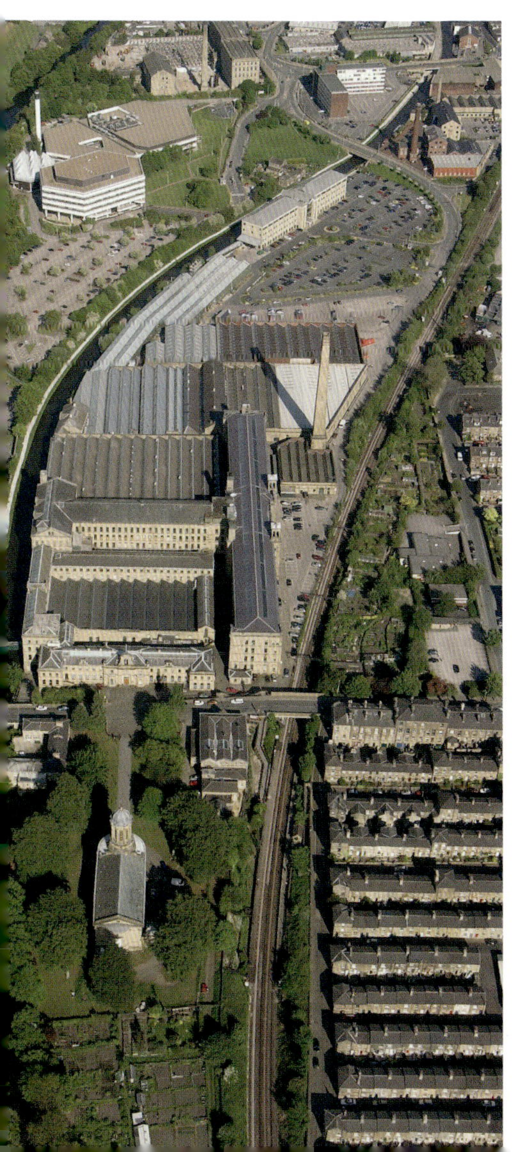

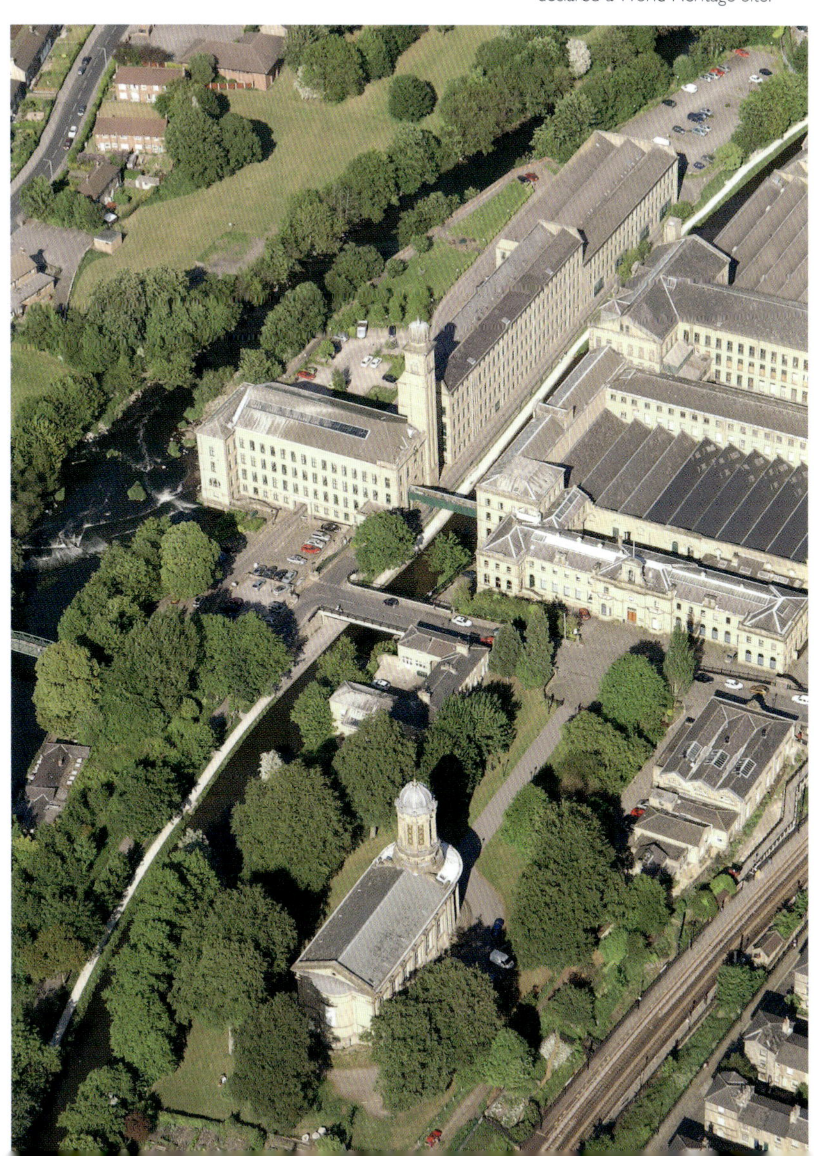

HAWORTH *(below & right)*

The photograph below shows Haworth from the north and the one on the right shows the village from the east. The steep main street of the village is still cobbled and contains antique shops, antiquarian bookshops and an old-fashioned apothecary shop. There is a network of footpaths from the village into the surrounding countryside. Visitors still flock to the Parsonage Museum, once the home of the Brontë family, where the three famous sisters, Emily, Charlotte and Anne wrote their well-loved novels: most famously Emily's *Wuthering Heights*, Charlotte's *Jane Eyre* and Anne's *The Tenant of Wildfell Hall*. The Brontë daughters were the children of the Revd Patrick Brontë who took his family to Haworth from Thornton near Bradford in 1820. Their mother died of cancer in 1821 and they were brought up by their aunt and mostly educated at home.
The most romantic approach to Haworth is by steam train on the Keighley & Worth Valley Railway (which can be seen in both photographs), lovingly portrayed in the 1970 film *The Railway Children*. This railway line was opened in 1867 by local mill-owners, but was closed by British Railways in 1962. It re-opened in 1968 and has been operated ever since by volunteers from the Keighley & Worth Valley Preservation Society.

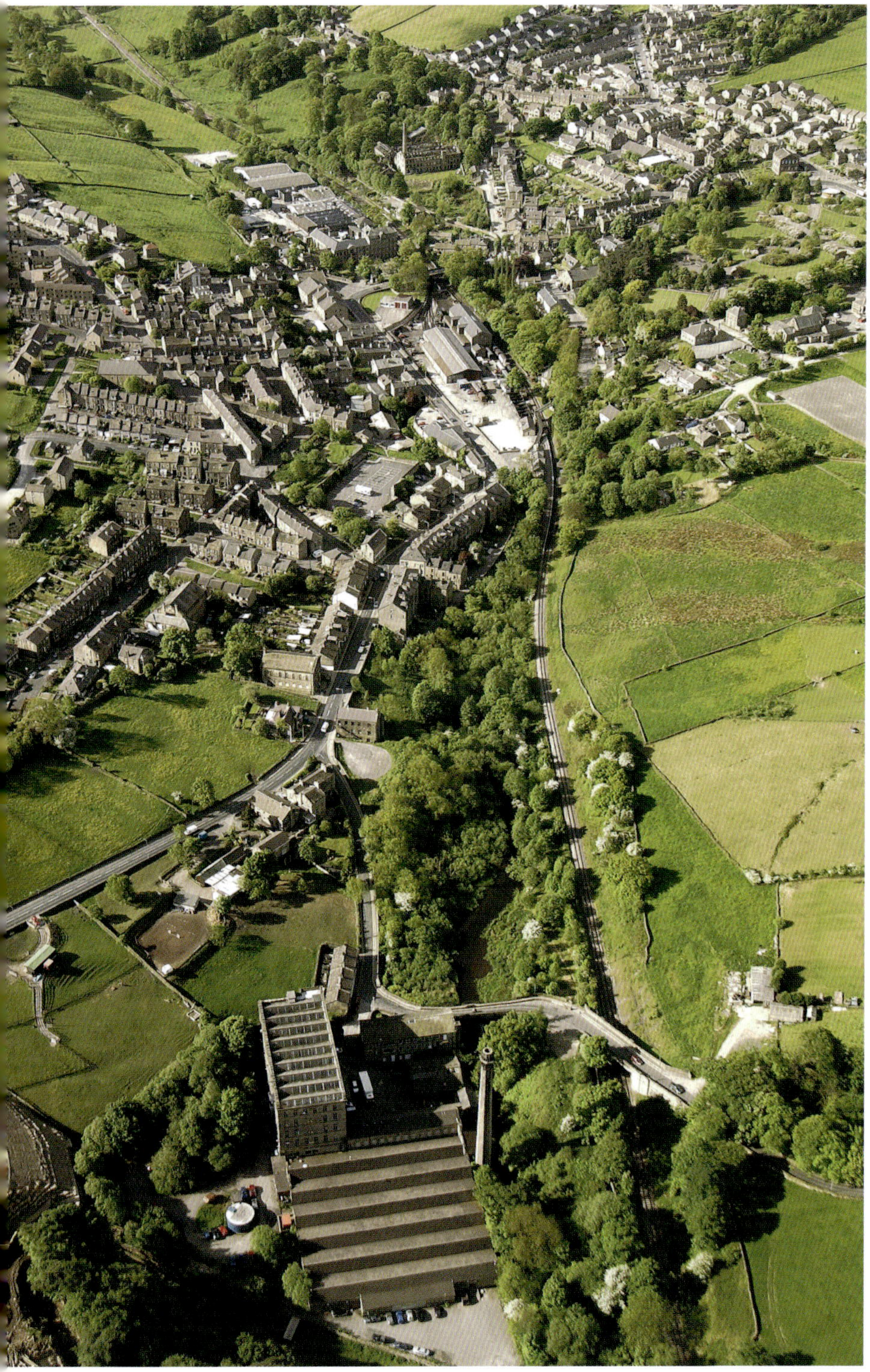

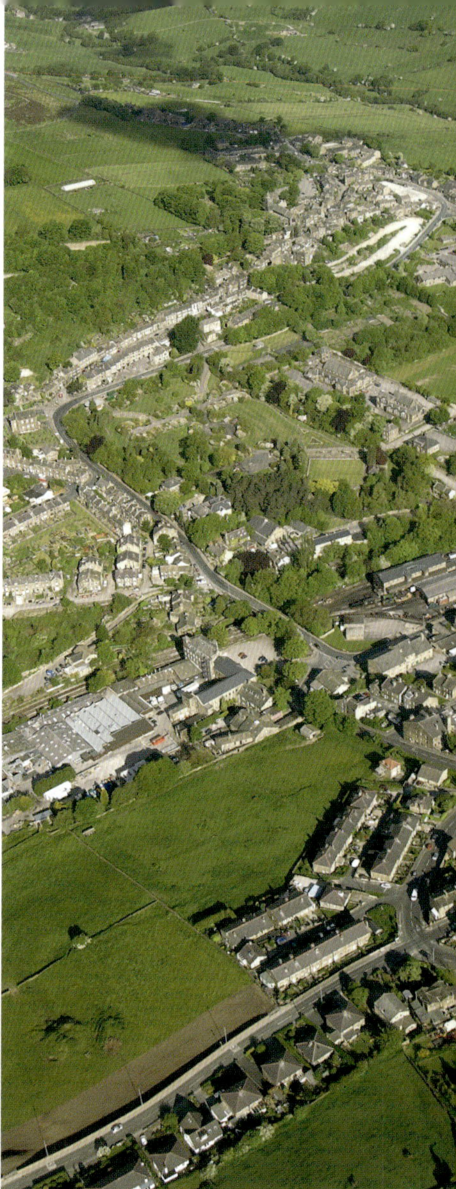

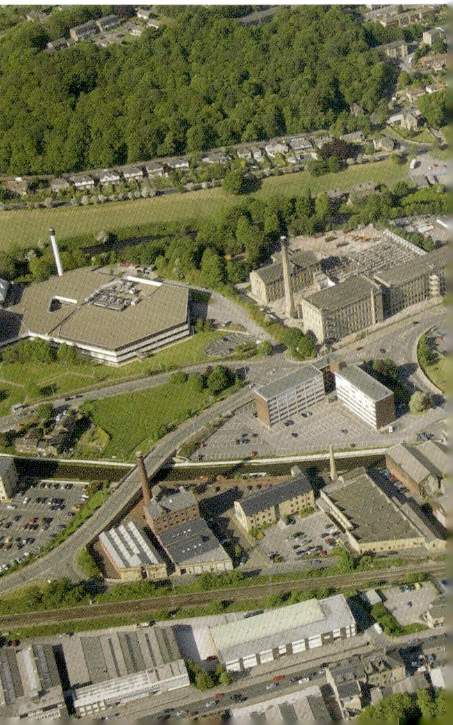

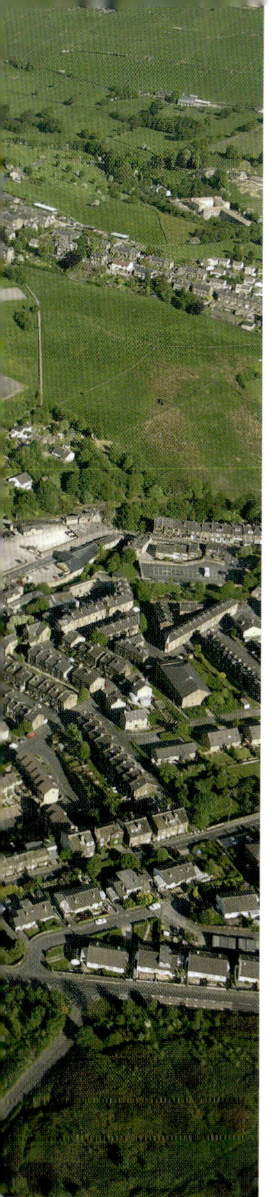

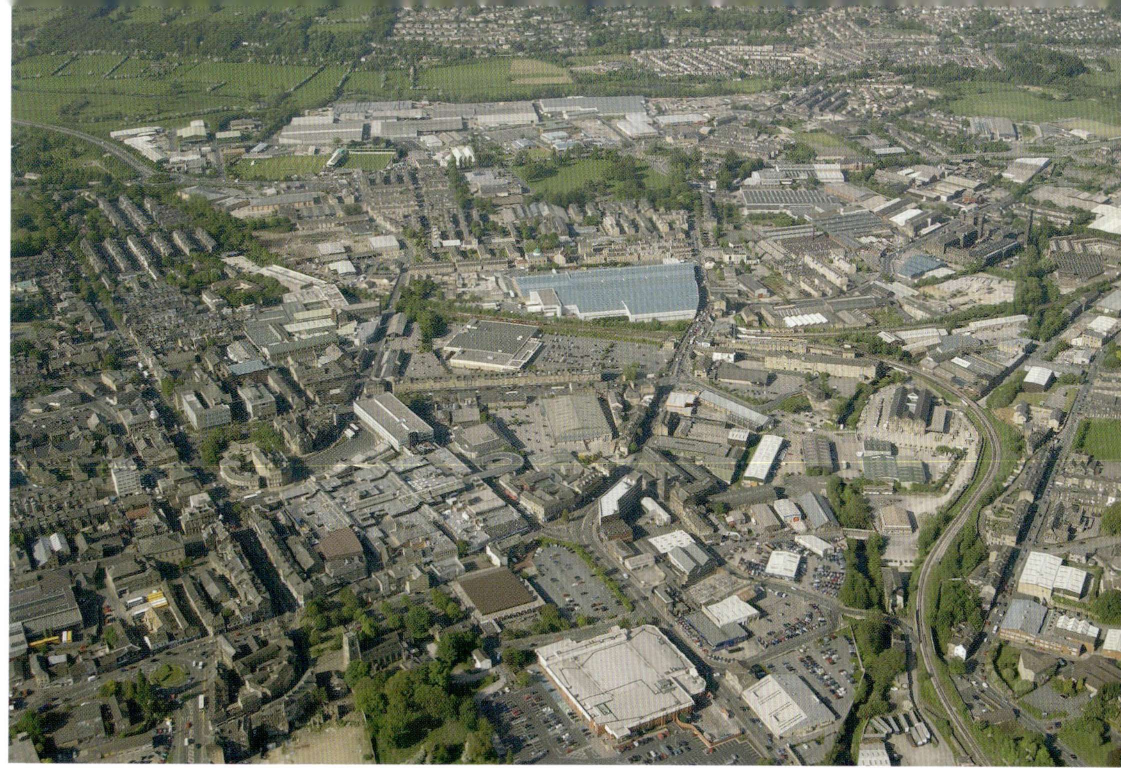

KEIGHLEY *(above)*

Keighley (pronounced Keith-ley, of course) grew up on the banks of the river Worth to the south of its confluence with the river Aire. It is best-known today for its railway station, the terminus for the steam trains that run on the Keighley & Worth Valley Railway which can be seen on the right. The view shows the industrial parts of the town beside the river Worth looking towards Eastwood and Aireworth with the town centre on the left. The blue roof is a large distribution centre.

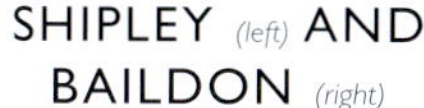

SHIPLEY *(left)* AND BAILDON *(right)*

Both of these small industrial towns in Airedale to the north of Bradford expanded initially because of their position beside the Leeds & Liverpool Canal. The photograph on the right is a view along the Aire valley north-eastwards from Shipley with much modern industrial development on the flat land beside the river, canal and railway in Baildon. The photograph on the left shows the northern part of Shipley just to the east of Saltaire beside the river Aire, the canal and the railway. Standing side by side between the river and canal are the Victoria Mills, currently being converted into luxury apartments, and the modern hexagonal-shaped Inland Revenue Accounts Office. Another interesting mill with its tall chimney stack, occupied by Aldon Brearley Print, stands between the bridge over the canal and the railway line towards the left-hand edge of the photograph.

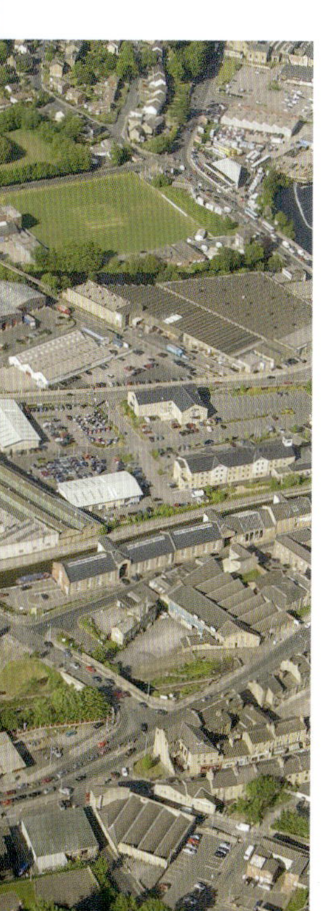

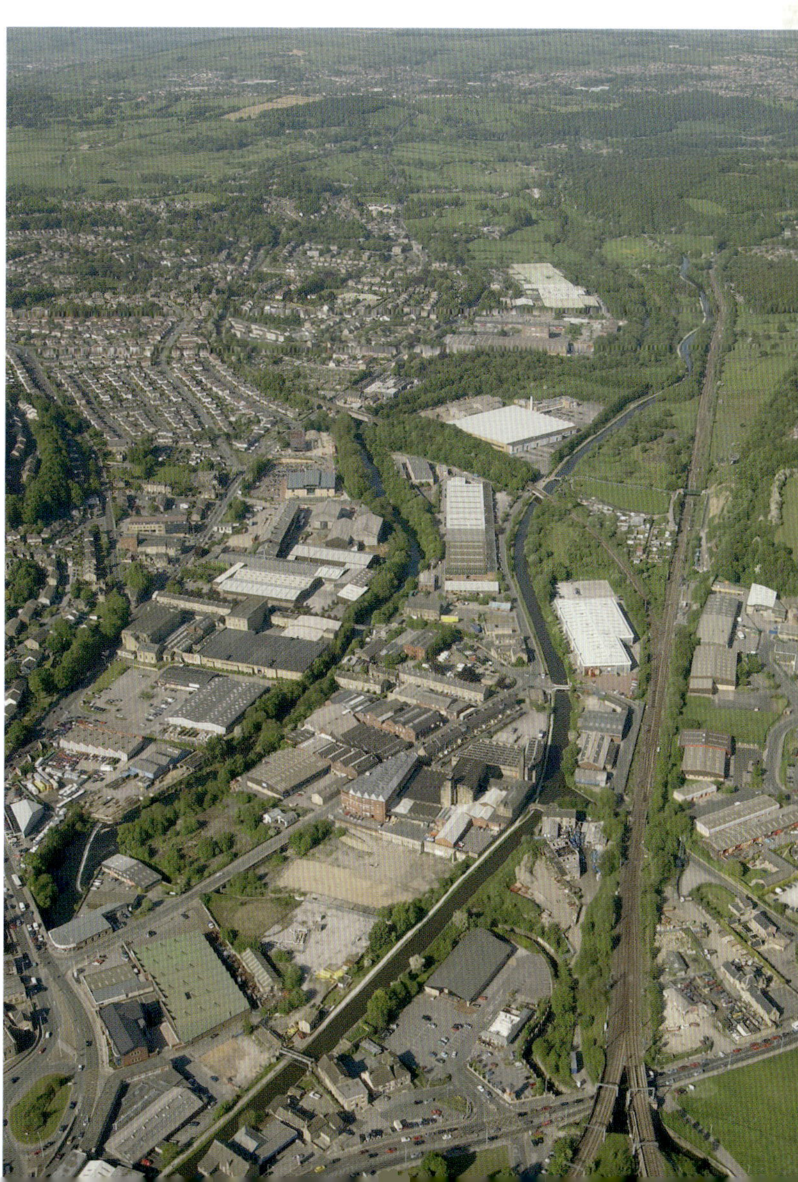

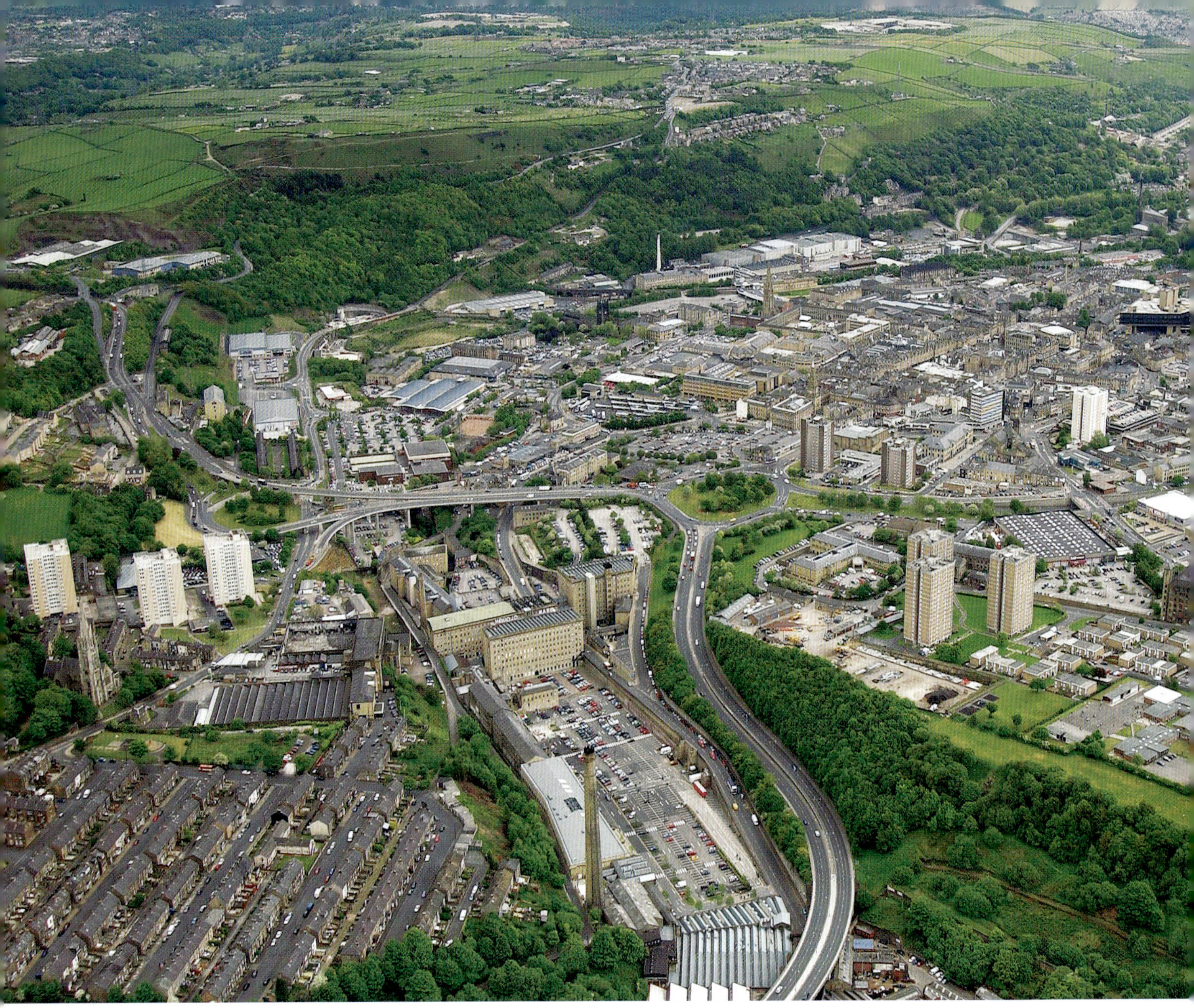

HALIFAX *(above and far right)*

Halifax originally grew up beside the river Hebble, a tributary of the river Calder, but with industrial development the town expanded in the direction of the Calder valley and the canal, and later the railway that linked it with Manchester and the port of Liverpool to the west and to the port of Hull to the east. The town has the distinction of having one of the earliest records of the wool textile industry in West Yorkshire: a carving of a pair of cloth shears in the porch of the parish church is thought to mark the burial place of a mid-12th century clothworker. The view above takes the eye along the Ovenden Road, past Dean Clough and over the town centre with the head office of Halifax plc (formerly the Halifax Building Society) and the Piece Hall as prominent features, to the wooded Hebble valley and Southowram beyond. Dean Clough is an arts, business, design and education complex created by Sir Ernest Hall and his son Jeremy from the derelict Dean Clough Mills, once one of the world's largest carpet factories. The photograph on the right is a view across the town from the south with the 253ft (77m) high Wainhouse Tower in the foreground.

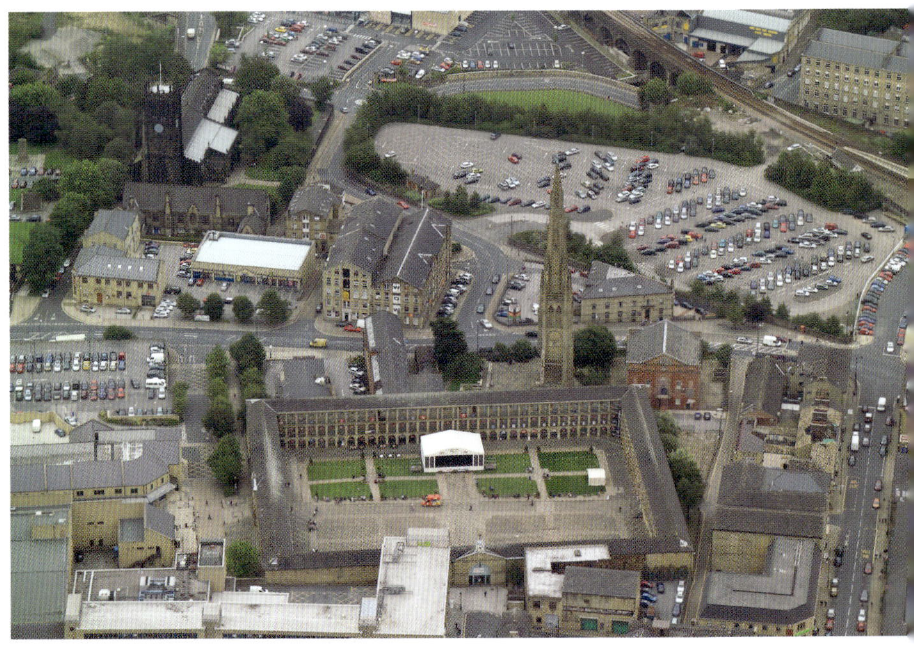

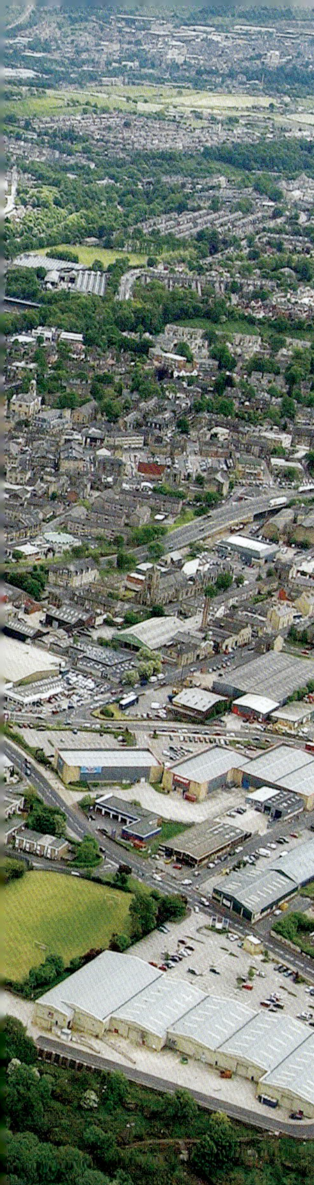

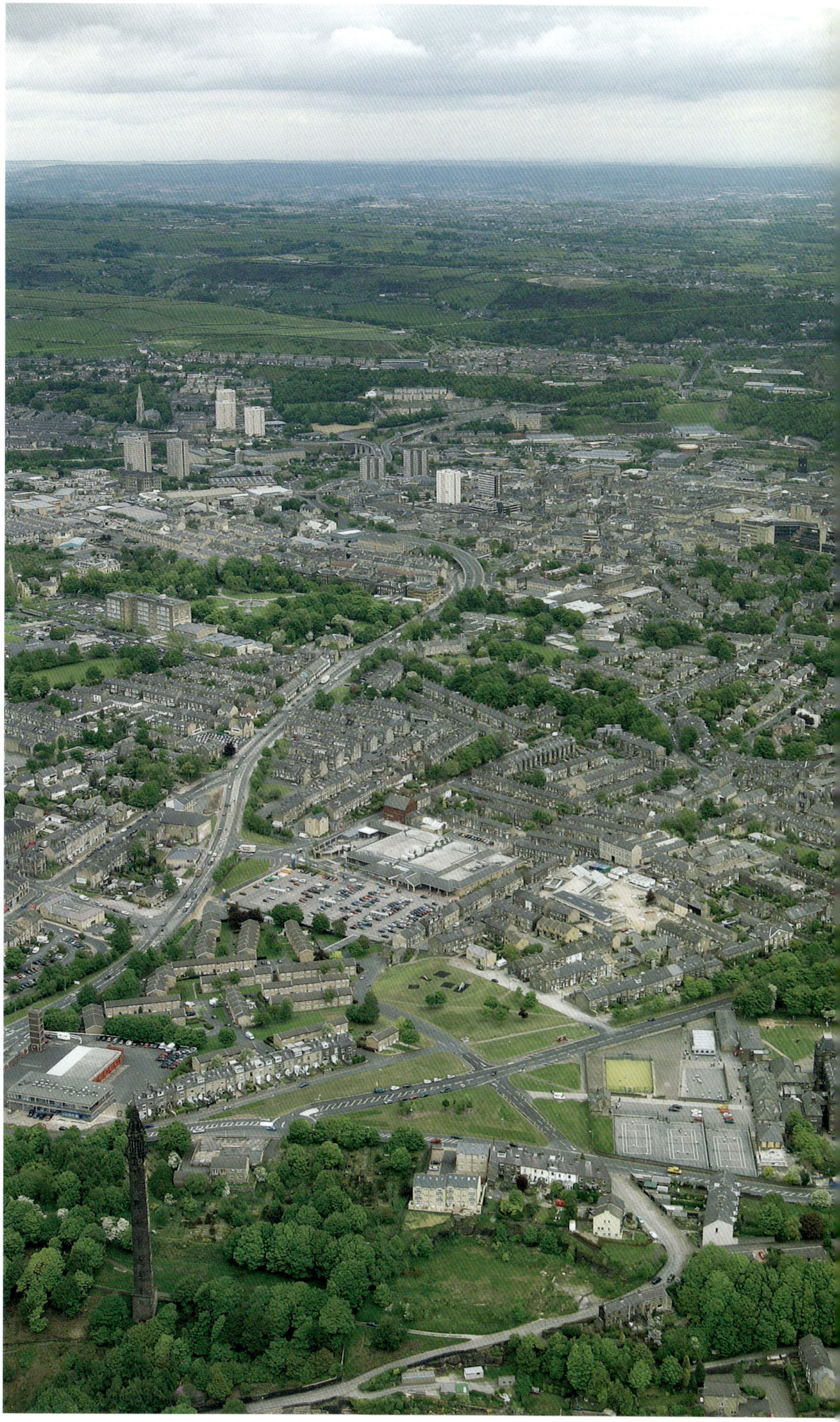

PIECE HALL, HALIFAX

(left)

This was a cloth hall, designed by John Hope of Liverpool, completed in 1779, to which handloom weavers brought their "pieces" of woollen cloth for sale, hence its name. The more than 300 rooms of the cloth hall are built around an open quadrangle which is entered through a grand archway. From the quadrangle, 90,000sq ft (8,361sq m) in size, on all sides rise the galleried arcades, with rusticated square pillars below and Tuscan columns above. The Piece Hall became a wholesale vegetable and fish market in the 1870s. It was renovated in 1976 and now contains a variety of shops and an art gallery, and the quadrangle is the venue for a weekly flea market and a general market.

HEADQUARTERS OF HALIFAX PLC *(below)*

Standing in Commercial Street is this unforgettable and, for many residents and visitors, visually unattractive, late 20th-century architectural monster. It was designed by the Building Design Partnership and completed in 1975 for the then Halifax Building Society. In the shape of a giant diamond it stands on concrete legs and dwarfs the town's earlier private and public buildings.

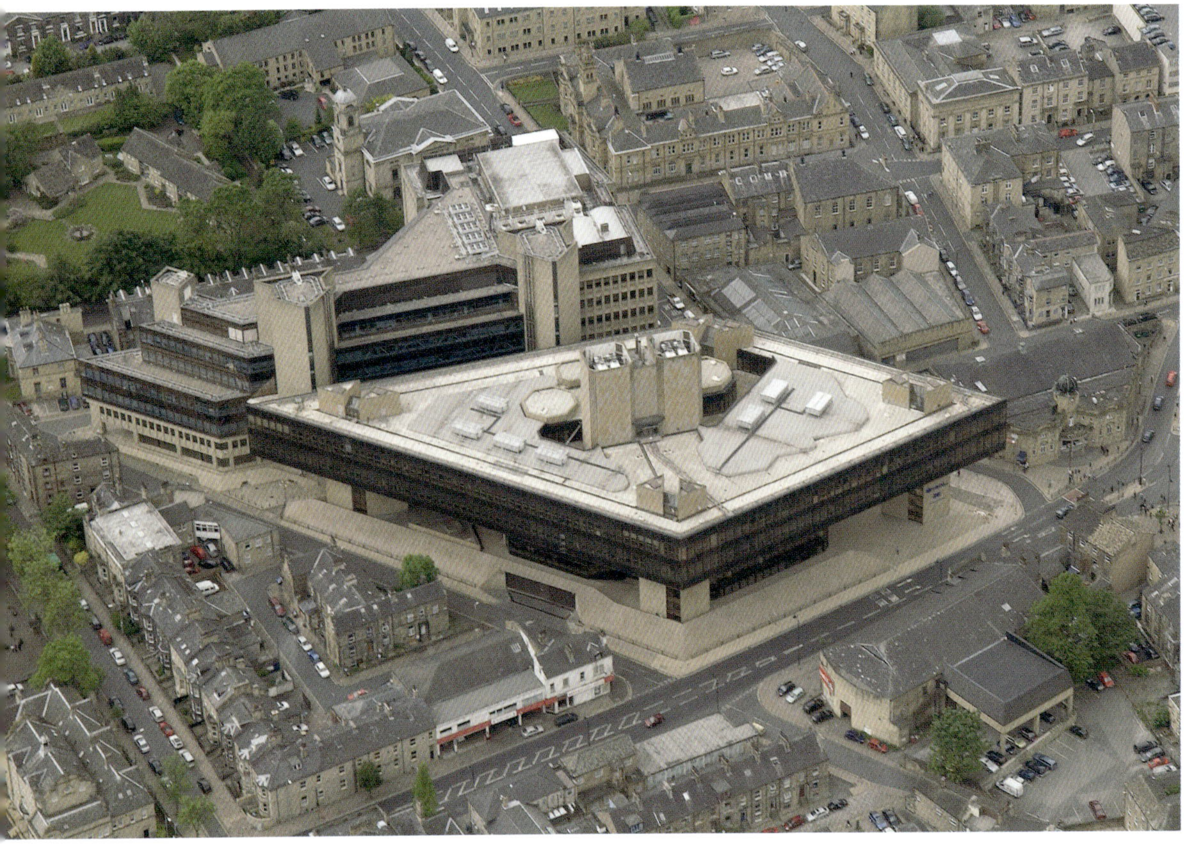

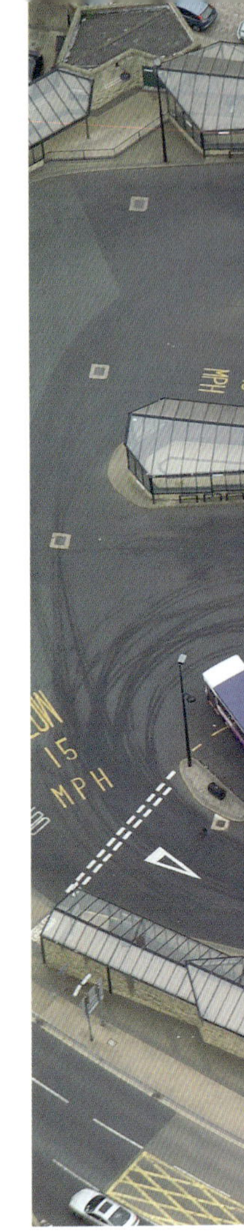

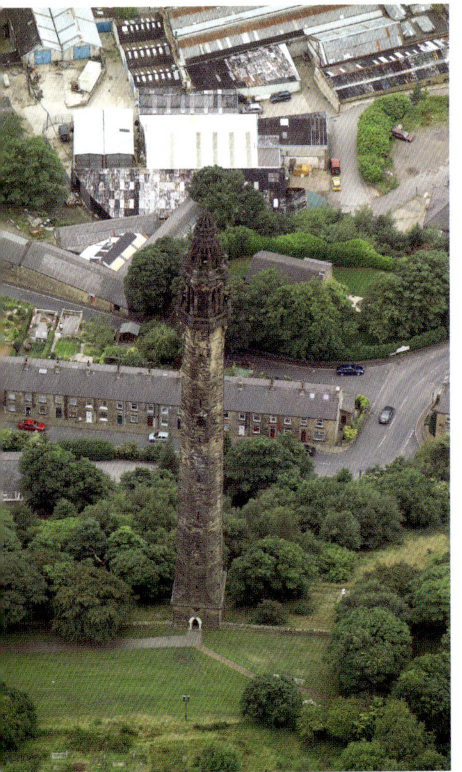

WAINHOUSE TOWER, HALIFAX

(left)

This tower is the product of the Smoke Abatement Act of 1870. It was built for John Edward Wainhouse, the wealthy owner of Washer Lane Dye Works. As a result of the Act it became necessary to construct a tall chimney to carry the smoke and fumes from the works out of the Calder valley. The chimney was to be connected to the works by means of a pipeline. Before it was completed Wainhouse sold the works but decided to keep the tower and turn it into an astronomical observatory. It is 253ft (77m) high and richly decorated at the top with balustrades, finials and other fantastical carvings. It is said that one reason why it was built was that Wainhouse was in dispute with his neighbour Sir Harry Edwards, who did not like chimneys, and it enabled him to anger Edwards and at the same time keep a close eye on what he was up to.

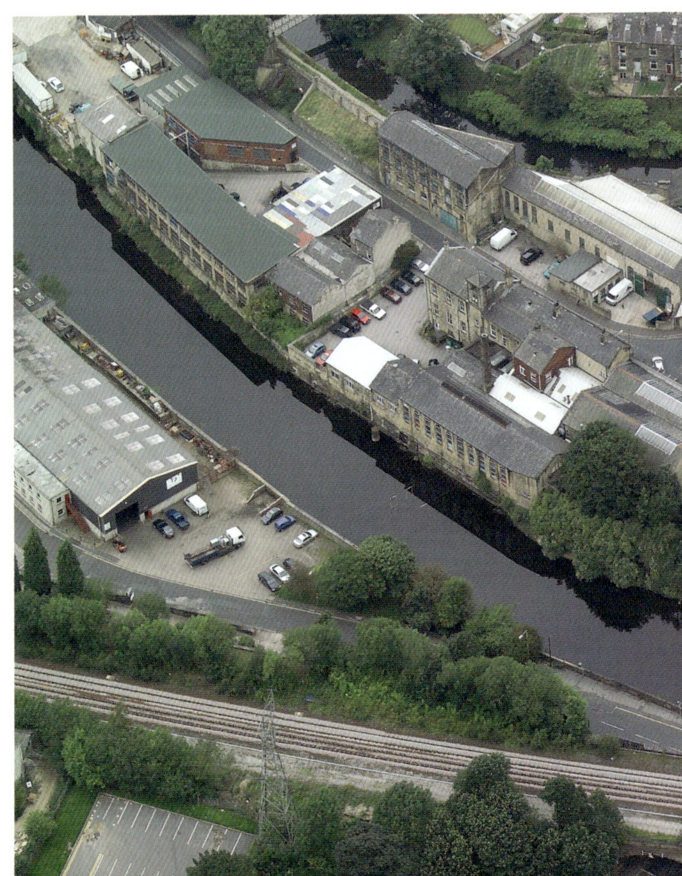

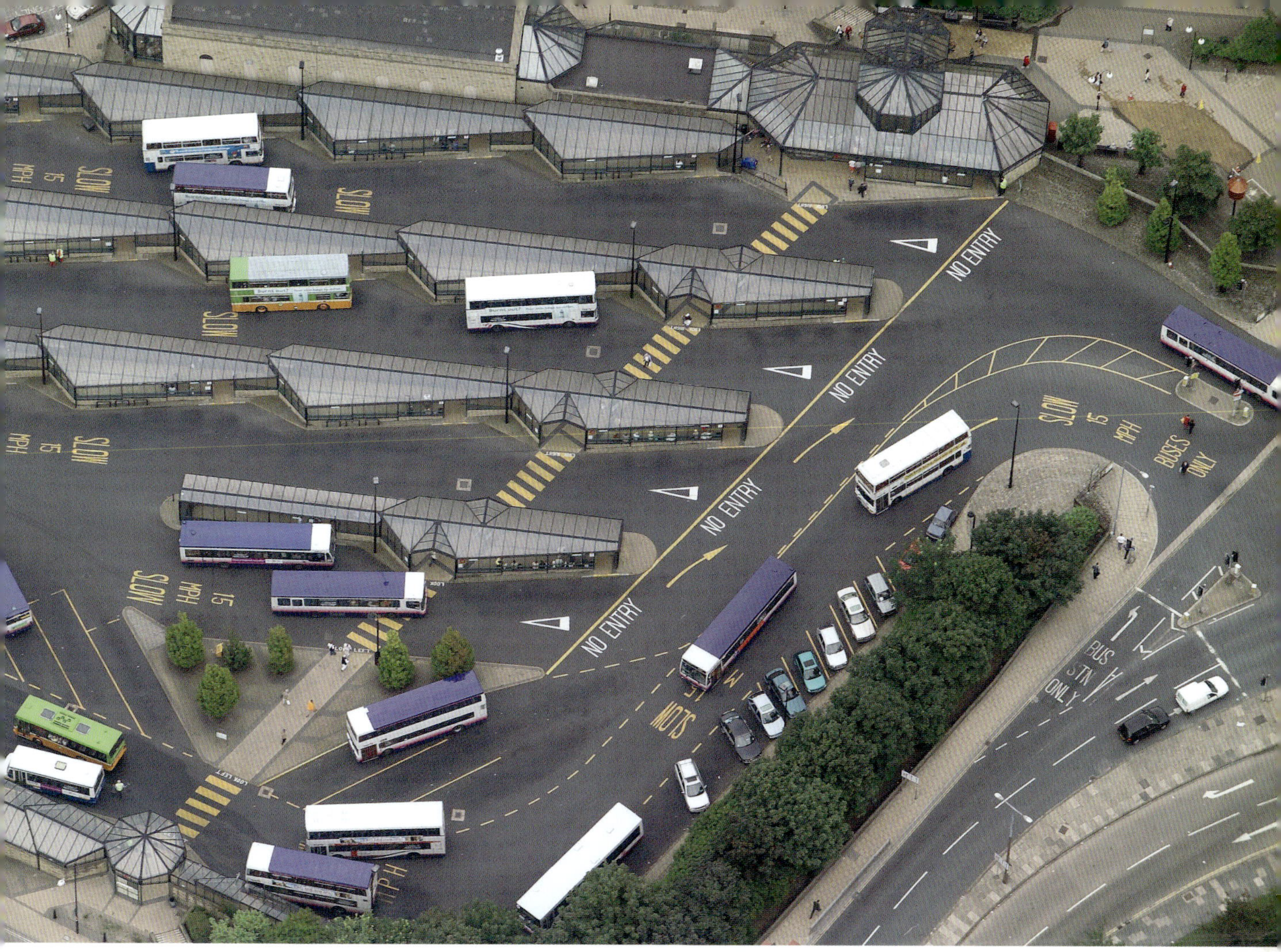

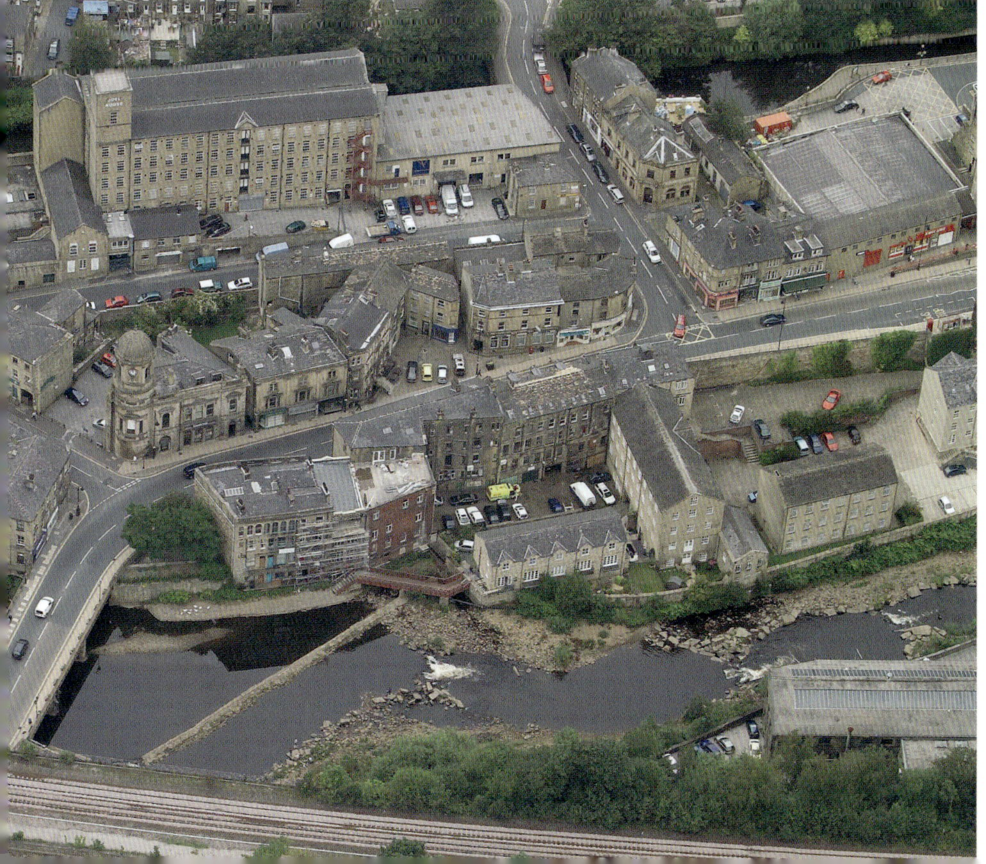

HALIFAX BUS STATION *(above)* AND SOWERBY BRIDGE *(left)*

Buses leave Halifax bus station for the surrounding towns and villages such as Mytholmroyd, Luddenden Foot, Hipperholme – and Sowerby Bridge. Originally the villages of the area grew up on shelves of grit above the valley floors and had the appearance of hill villages. Spinning and weaving were domestic processes carried out in the hill settlements. Two processes needed water-power – washing and beating the cloth to remove dirt and grease, and thickening and felting, both of which were carried out at a fulling mill in the river valley. All this changed in the 18th and 19th centuries when spinning and weaving were done by water power and then steam power and canals and railways came to the area through the valleys. The settlements around the fulling mills then expanded into manufacturing towns and the hill settlements became industrial museums. Sowerby Bridge is one of these creations of the Industrial Revolution. Others include Hebden Bridge (an offshoot of Heptonstall) and Brighouse (an offshoot from Raistrick). The photograph shows not only the bridge but also the river, the canal, the railway and a textile mill.

HUDDERSFIELD *(below, top right and bottom right)*

The product of the development of the woollen industry, Huddersfield occupies the valleys of the Calder, Colne and Holme and the surrounding hillsides and plateaus. But it was the river valleys that attracted the industrial development in the 18th and 19th centuries and led to the rapid expansion of the town. The initial attractions were the rivers themselves and the use of water-power. In the valleys canals were then built and later the railways, that brought coal to fuel the steam-engines that superseded water-wheels, and transported the raw material and the finished product. Below is the valley of the river Holme near Lockwood, looking towards the Calder valley and beyond to the centre of Huddersfield. In the background on the Leeds Road can be seen the distinctive shape of the McAlpine Stadium, the home of Huddersfield Town FC and Huddersfield Giants rugby league club. In the foreground can be seen the 36-arch Lockwood viaduct built in 1846-48 on the railway line to Sheffield. Dominating the town centre in the photographs immediately to the right is the railway station built in 1847-48 in the Classical Corinthian style. Opposite the railway station is the George hotel, the birthplace of rugby league in 1895.

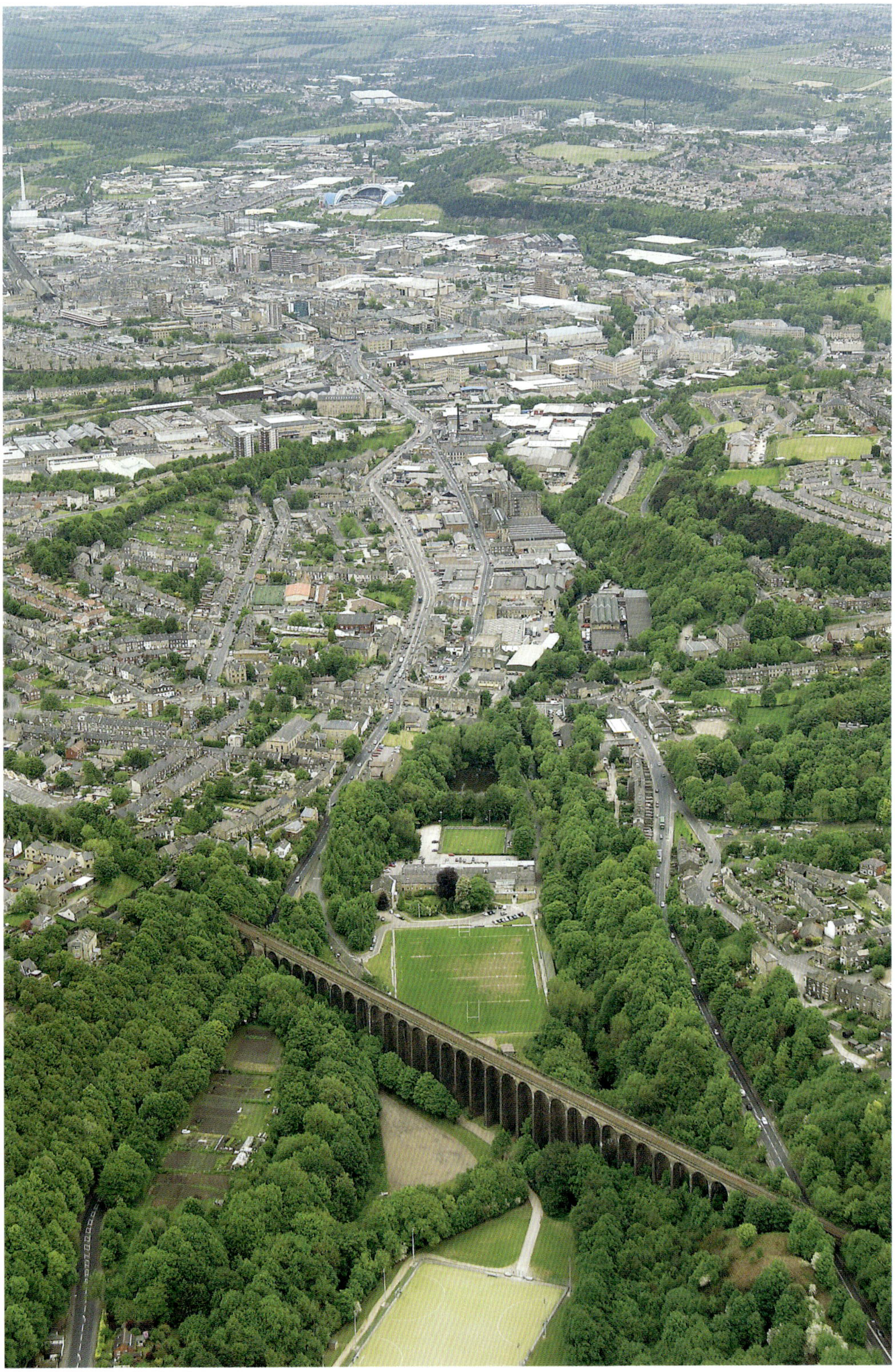

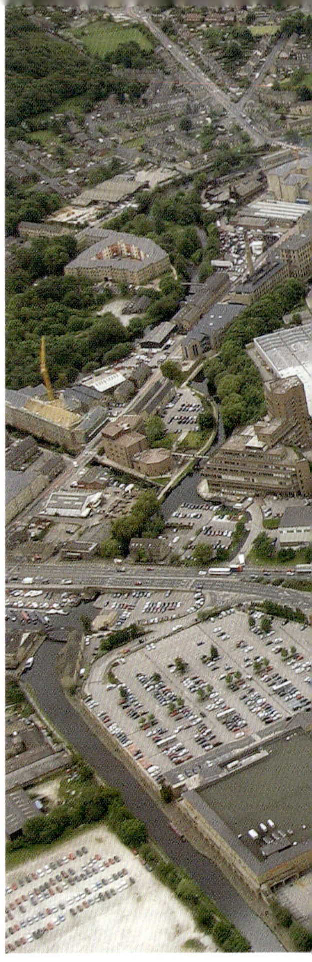

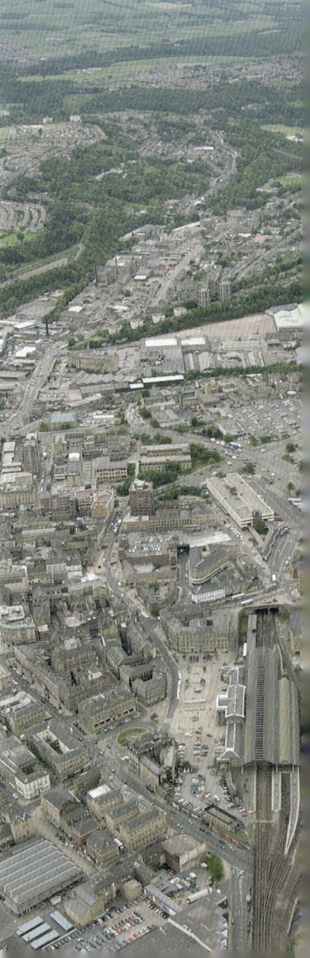

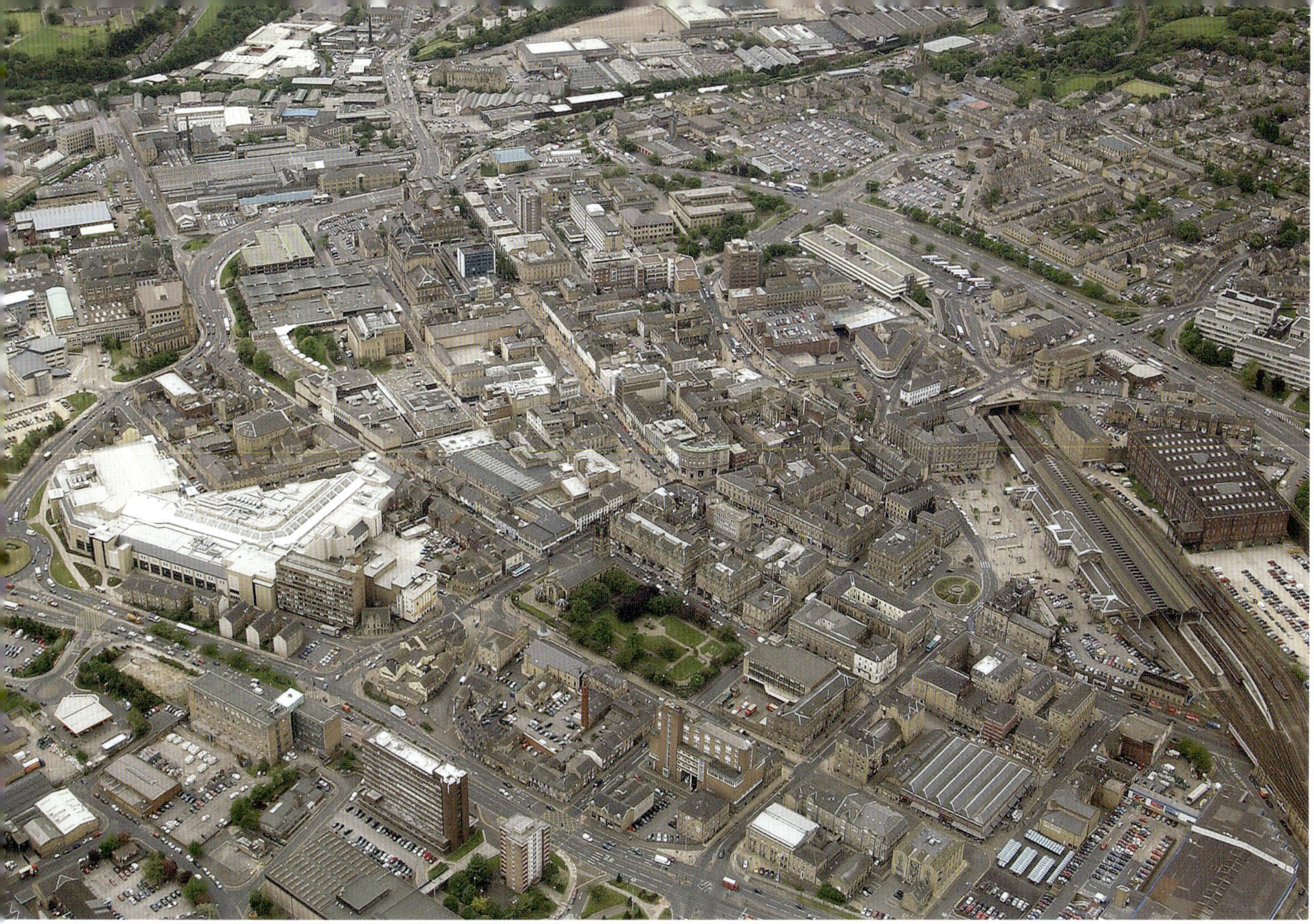

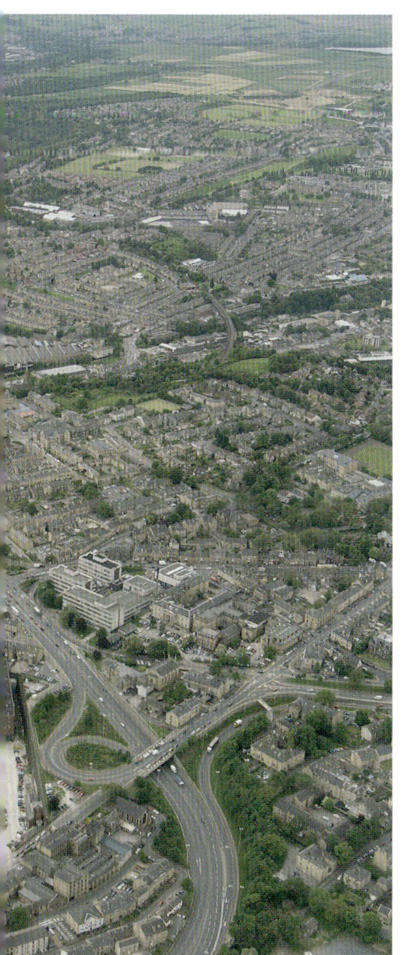

VICTORIA TOWER, ALMONDBURY

Crowning the gorse-covered Castle Hill, which is steep on three of its four sides and rises to 800ft (244m), is an Iron Age camp which is believed to have begun to be constructed in about 300BC by the Brigantian tribe. Originally it consisted of a single stone rampart, but this was later doubled and then a third outer rampart was added. It is assumed to have been abandoned with the coming of the Romans. In the reign of King Stephen (1135-1154) a stone keep was built on the hilltop that was later demolished by King Henry III (1216-1272). The top of Castle Hill is now occupied by the Victoria Tower built in 1897-98 to celebrate Queen Victoria's diamond jubilee. From its turreted rooftop at the top of a stairway of 165 steps can be seen the glorious views of the surrounding countryside which is typical "stone country": stone cottages, stone-walled fields and extensive woodlands. To the west the views stretch to the high Pennine moorlands and to the north over the industrialised Colne valley into central Huddersfield. On a windy day this is a wonderful place to get rid of the cobwebs!

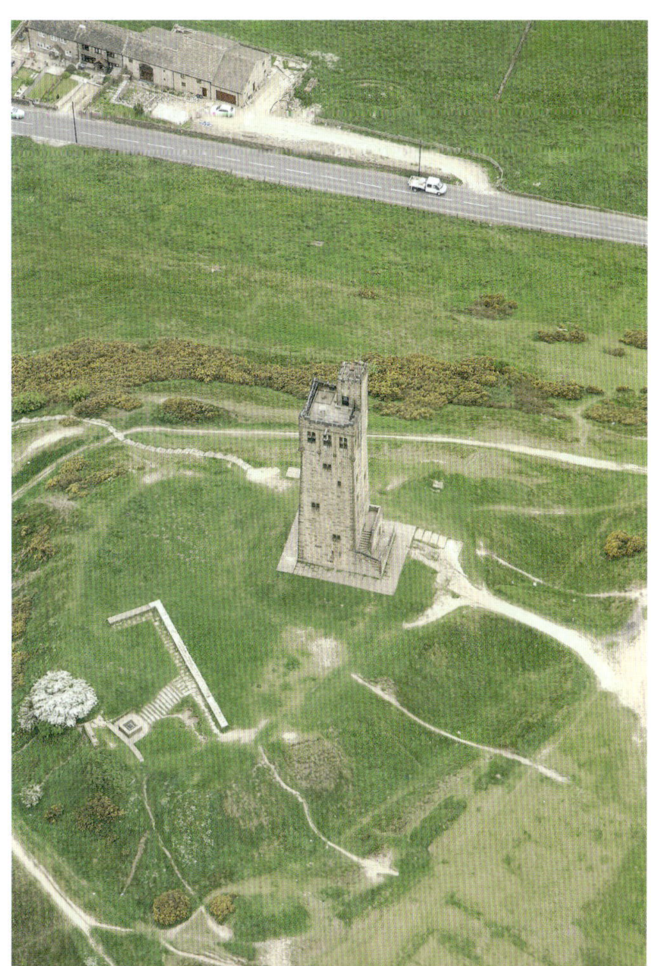

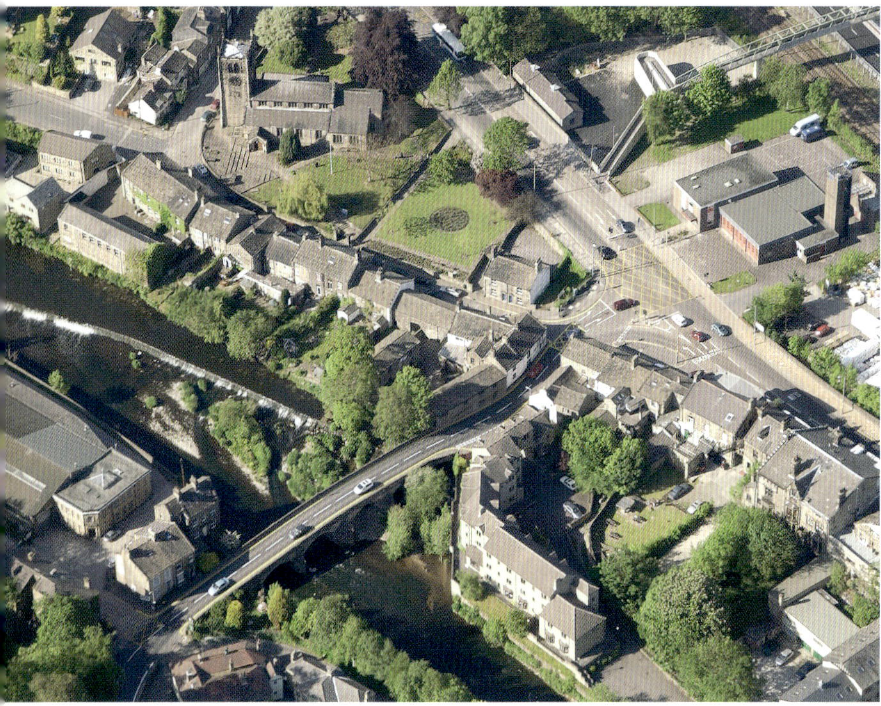

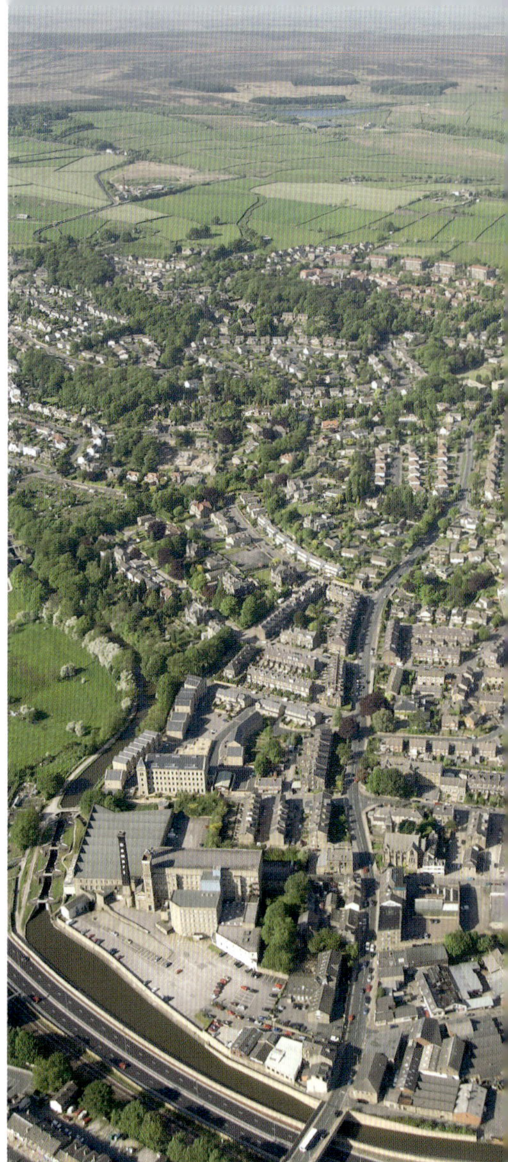

BINGLEY *(above, right and far right)*

Bingley was granted a market charter in 1212 by King John and after going through a long industrial phase is now a thriving commuter town for Bradford. The town was the place of residence of Sir Titus Salt's son – Titus Salt junior – who had his mansion built (now demolished) at Milner Field in 1873. The photograph on the far right shows a view over the town along the A650 and the Leeds and Liverpool Canal in the direction of Shipley and Bradford. The photograph on the right shows the Park Road bridge crossing of the railway, the A650 and the Leeds and Liverpool Canal on the southern edge of the town. The Prince of Wales Park can be seen in the background on the northern outskirts of the town. The photograph above shows Ireland Bridge over the river Aire. This stone bridge, built in 1686 and widened in 1776, replaced an earlier timber bridge.

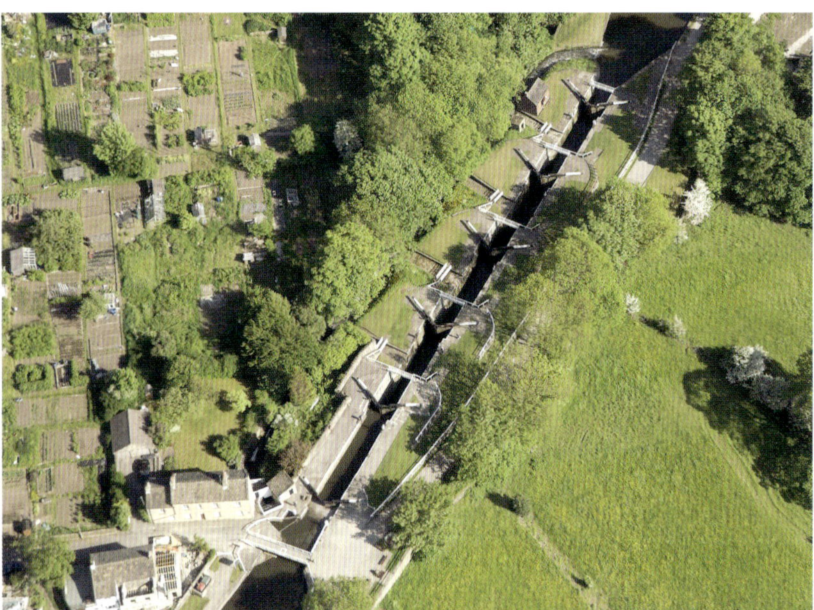

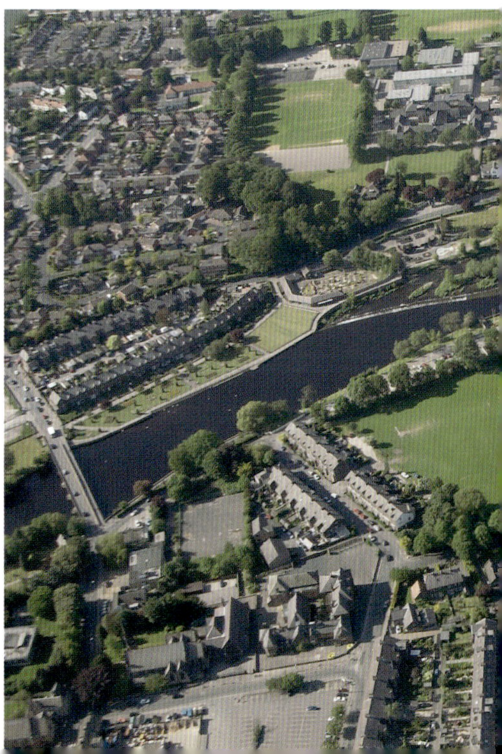

BINGLEY FIVE RISE LOCKS *(above)*

These locks are on the Leeds and Liverpool Canal which crosses the Pennines and therefore involved the frequent use of locks to ascend or descend steep slopes. On the Yorkshire side of the Pennines, as the canal rises out of Airedale there are, within a 16-mile stretch, three double locks, four staircase locks of three locks each and then the five-lock Bingley Rise. This set of locks, which raises the level of the canal by 59ft (18m), was originally called Bingley Great Lock. It was completed in 1777. In a staircase set of locks as at Bingley the top gate of one chamber acts as the bottom gate of the next chamber. Each chamber at Bingley can take a vessel 62ft (19m) long and just over 14ft (4.2m) wide.

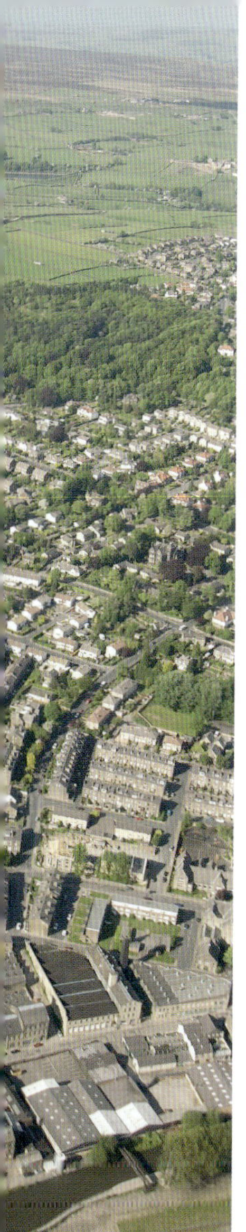

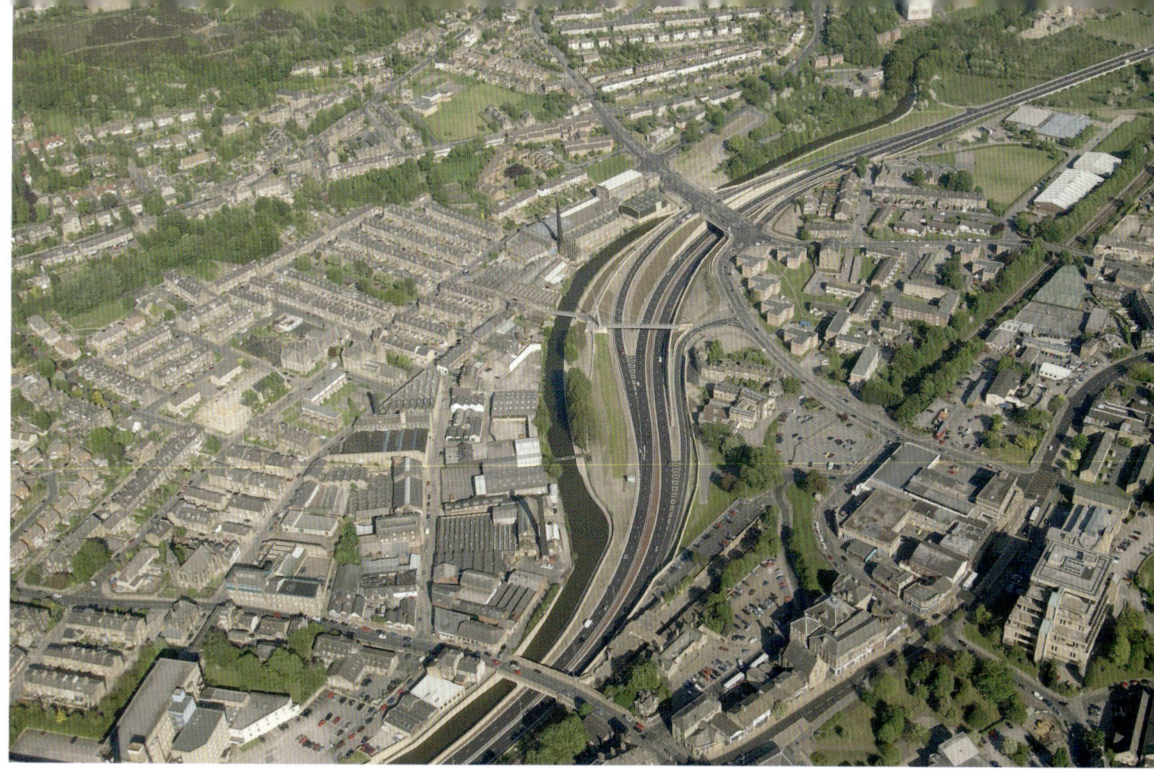

OTLEY *(below)*

Developed to the north and south of the river Wharfe halfway between Bradford and Ilkley, there are spectacular views of Otley from the Chevin, the gritstone escarpment to the south of the town that rises over 900ft (274m). Otley is a busy market town and the Otley Show began in 1796. It has two splendid churches, one medieval and the other late Victorian. The medieval church is All Saints parish church and the Victorian church is the Congregational church constructed in 1899. The photograph shows Otley Bridge over the river Wharfe.

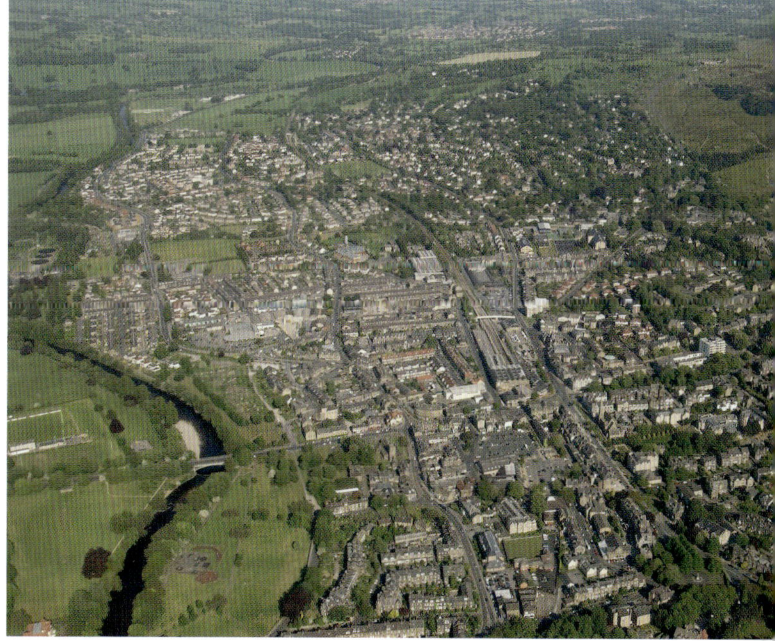

ILKLEY *(above)*

Ilkley is a pleasant commuter town in Wharfedale on the southern edge of the Yorkshire Dales. It hosts the Ilkley Literary Festival and the Ilkley Music Festival. It is also the starting point for the Dales Way long-distance footpath. The town rose to prominence in the 19th century as a spa town ("the Malvern of the north") and a number of purpose-built hydropathic hotels were built, the most well-known being Ben Rhydding, Craiglands, Troutbeck and Wells House. Wells House, which opened in 1856, was designed by Cuthbert Brodrick, the architect of Leeds Town Hall. One famous visitor to Ilkley in the autumn of 1859 was the naturalist Sir Charles Darwin awaiting the publication of his controversial *On the Origin of Species*, and suffering from stomach pains, swellings and boils. With the arrival of the railway in 1865 Ilkley entered its heyday as a fashionable resort and residential outpost for the successful industrialists, merchants and professional men of Leeds and Bradford. The town contains some notable Victorian and Edwardian buildings both public and private. These include the town hall in the Palladian style built between 1906-08; the railway station constructed in the Classical style in 1864; and private mansions by Richard Norman Shaw and Edwin Lutyens.

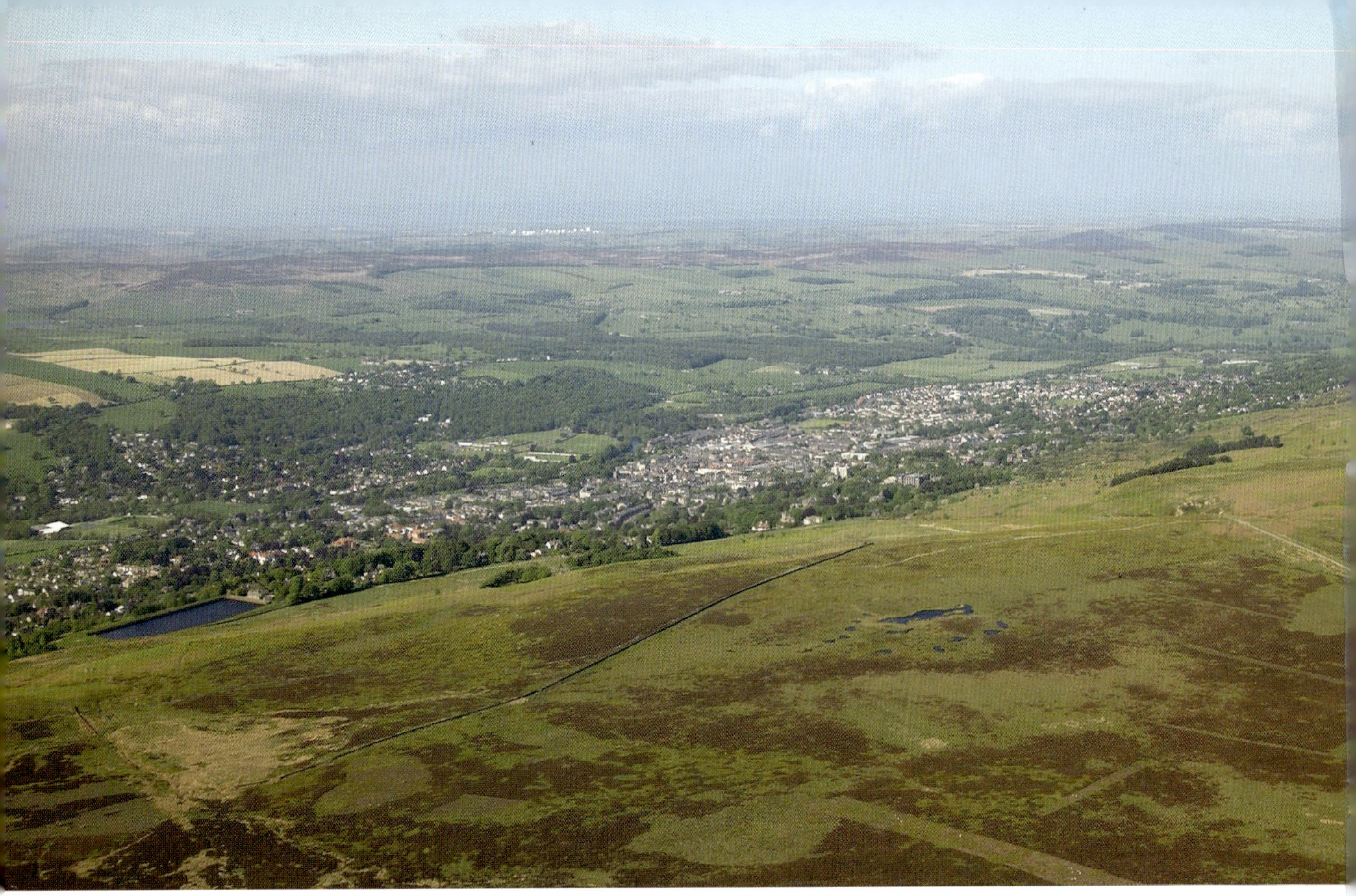

ILKLEY *(above)* AND THE COW AND CALF ROCKS ON ILKLEY MOOR *(right)*

Rising above the town of Ilkley to the south is Ilkley Moor, part of the much more extensive Rombalds Moor, rising to over 1,300ft (396m) with its gaunt millstone grit outcrops and glorious views of Wharfedale. It is also rich in prehistoric archaeological remains including cairns, barrows, hut circles and enigmatic "cup and ring" carvings in the millstone grit outcrops. Ilkley Moor has long been a mecca for excursionists, walkers and climbers from the industrial West Riding and the name is enshrined in the Yorkshire anthem *On Ilkla Mooar bah't 'at*. This is a tongue-in-cheek mocking song made up by members of a church choir outing about one of their members who had left the main party and gone out on the moor without his hat to court Mary Jane. It is sung to the hymn tune *Cranbrook* composed by Thomas Clark in 1808, but the words were not sung to the *Cranbrook* tune before the 1870s.

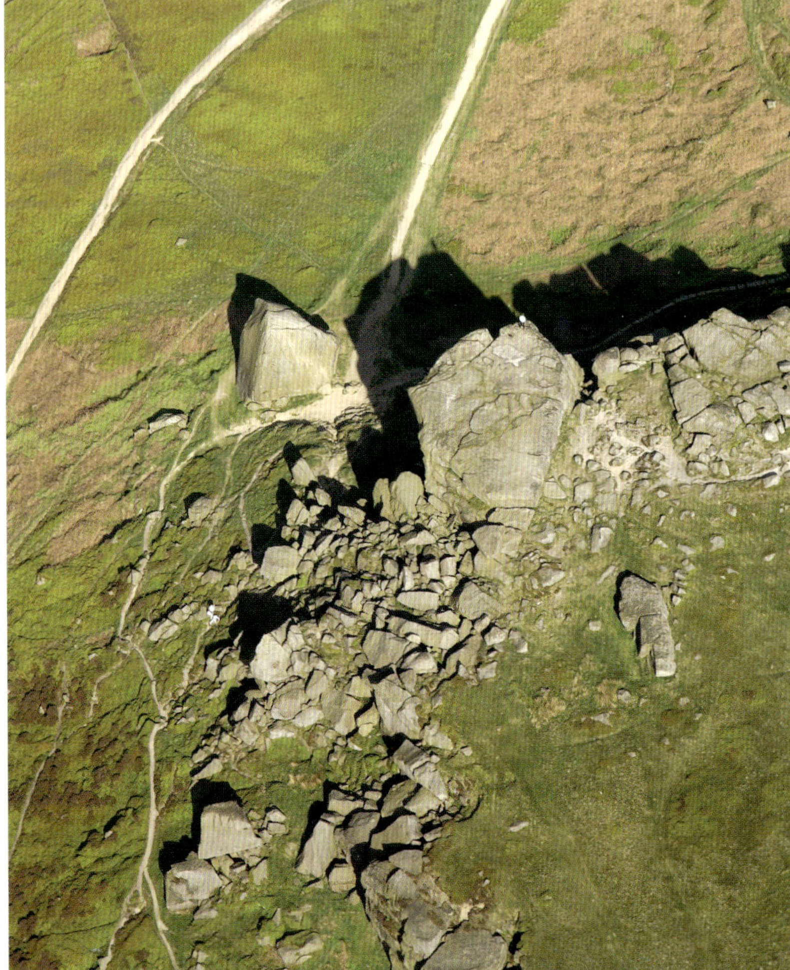

First published in 2009 by
Myriad Books Limited
35 Bishopsthorpe Road, London
SE26 4PA

ISBN 1 84746 236 7
EAN 978 1 84746 236 7

Designed by Jerry Goldie
Printed in China

www.myriadbooks.com

CUISINE COR

D'HIER
ET
D'AUJOURD'HUI

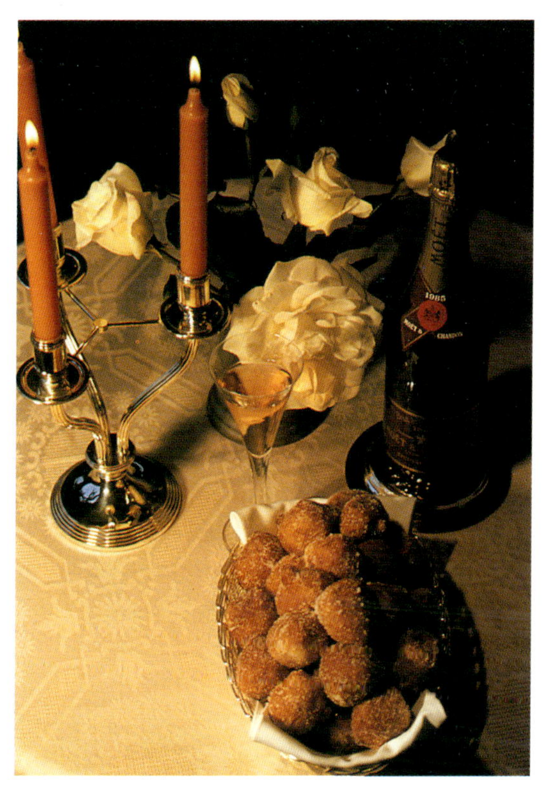

LA MARGE ÉDITIONS

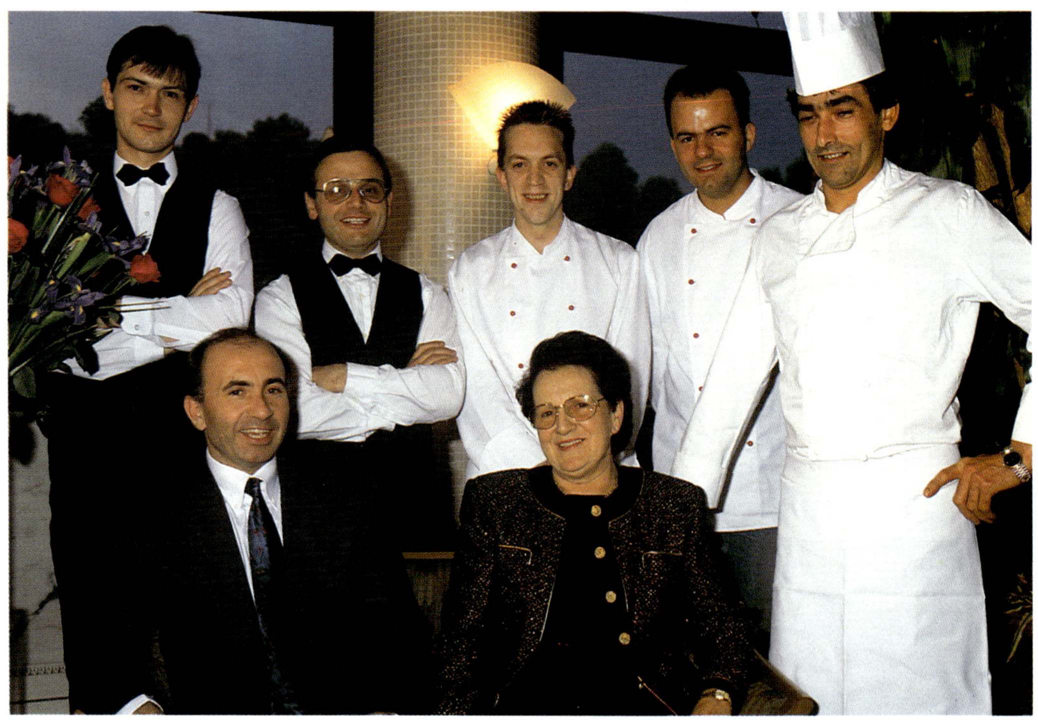

Paul SETA a le privilège d'allier la cuisine d'hier à celle d'aujourd'hui.

Son établissement moderne, l'une des grandes étapes de la gastronomie insulaire, a gardé la mémoire de l'auberge familiale créée en 1965 à Bastelicaccia (Corse du Sud) par ses parents, François et Toussainte SETA.

Paul SETA reste fidèle à une cuisine familiale conçue selon les recettes traditionnelles. Aussi sa carte très diversifiée garde-t-elle toute sa place à la cuisine insulaire. Ce restaurateur, loin de renier ses origines, cherche au contraire à les enrichir.

Une façon de maintenir l'identité de la Table Insulaire.

ACHEVÉ D'IMPRIMER 2e TRIMESTRE 1991 SUR LES PRESSES SPÉCIALES DE LA SEDAG - 5 RUE DE PONTOISE - 75005 PARIS
IMPRIMÉ EN ITALIE

SOMMAIRE

AVANT-PROPOS

Paraphrasant une apostrophe réputée, on pourrait écrire : ''Dis-moi ce que tu manges, je te dirai qui tu es''.

C'est donc presque un truisme que d'affirmer que le boire et le manger reflètent l'âme d'un pays, d'une région tant il est vrai que les produits d'un terroir sont liés à la vie, au travail des hommes qui l'habitent, à leurs habitudes, leurs traditions et coutumes.

La Corse, est-il besoin de le préciser, n'échappe pas à cette règle. Ici, les cultures agricoles ont épousé le relief du pays. Point de grandes étendues labourées comme dans certaines contrées du continent. Les parcelles travaillées s'accrochent au flanc des montagnes à l'exception peut-être de la plaine orientale.

Au fil des millénaires, chaque micro-région a adopté un ou plusieurs produits adaptés à la géologie et au relief local. Ainsi les Balanins se sont spécialisés dans l'olivier. En Castagniccia, le fruit des châtaigniers, ces arbres à pain, a nourri des générations de Corses. Les Cap corsins se sont tournés vers la vigne. Au cœur de l'île, les Niolins, bergers par nécessité, ont fabriqué les meilleurs fromages. Il est donc des endroits qui ont donné des spécialités, décrites dans cet ouvrage. Pourtant, au-delà de cette diversité, il est des mets que l'on retrouve partout dans l'île : la soupe corse, la polenta et, bien entendu, le produit de la chasse, activité presque consubstantielle de la culture locale : sanglier, merles, perdreaux, pigeons.

Il y a la nouvelle cuisine, il y a celle qui a évolué avec les mœurs, avec la société de consommation, mais comment pourrait-on oublier celle qui vient de loin et que nos anciens nous ont laissé en héritage.

Une cuisine directement inspirée du terroir. C'est ainsi que les habitants de l'île firent de la soupe corse un plat de base, tout comme la polenta.

La table corse a puisé sa richesse dans la châtaigne, la charcuterie, le fromage, l'huile d'olive, les produits de la chasse, ses poissons de mer et de rivière et dans ses vins d'un incomparable bouquet.

À travers les quarante-cinq recettes rassemblées dans ce livre, nous avons essayé de vous tracer l'authentique portrait de la cuisine corse dans toute sa vérité, dans toute sa simplicité, dans toute sa qualité.

Une cuisine qui parle autant au goût qu'au cœur.

C'est à partir de cette base très rurale, très proche de la vie quotidienne des hommes, que s'est bâtie une cuisine où la simplicité n'a jamais exclu la qualité.

Je me souviens avoir demandé un jour à une vieille dame de Pila Canale qui avait le secret de petits plats mijotés d'où elle tenait ses recettes. Je la revois encore me dire dans un sourire : "J'ai tout appris de ma mère. Lorsque mon père revenait de la chasse, il s'attablait à la maison avec tous ceux qui avaient participé aux battues et j'aidais à préparer le repas. Il n'était pas besoin alors de sortir d'une école hôtelière. Dans toutes les familles on avait des recettes bien à soi qui se transmettaient comme un héritage".

Même si elle est restée fidèle à ses sources, si elle a gardé le goût de ses produits de base, la cuisine insulaire a évolué, elle a cherché surtout à se diversifier, à ne pas se limiter à quelques plats. Il n'en reste pas moins vrai que la table corse nous est léguée comme un patrimoine. Une raison de plus pour la défendre et pour empêcher des recettes de toujours, celles qu'on appelle familièrement les recette de "grand-mère", de tomber dans l'oubli.

Comment ne pas apprécier une frittata à la brousse parfumée à la menthe ? Comment ne pas se laisser tenter par un tianu d'haricots bastiais à la viande de porc ? Que dire d'un cabri au feu de bois, de merles rôtis, de tripettes ?

Et n'oublions pas la fameuse bouillabaisse corse "l'Aziminu" qui rassemble les meilleurs poissons, de la rascasse au saint-pierre, de la dorade au congre.

Et que dire de ces fritelles au fromage frais ou au brocciu ?

Ce livre de recettes est allé d'une certaine manière à la recherche d'un passé. Elles portent en elles le souvenir d'une époque. Elles sont les témoins d'un mode de vie ; elles sont aussi des secrets de famille qu'on se transmettait de mère en fille et qu'on gardait jalousement au fond de sa mémoire.

Annebelle CHIOCCA

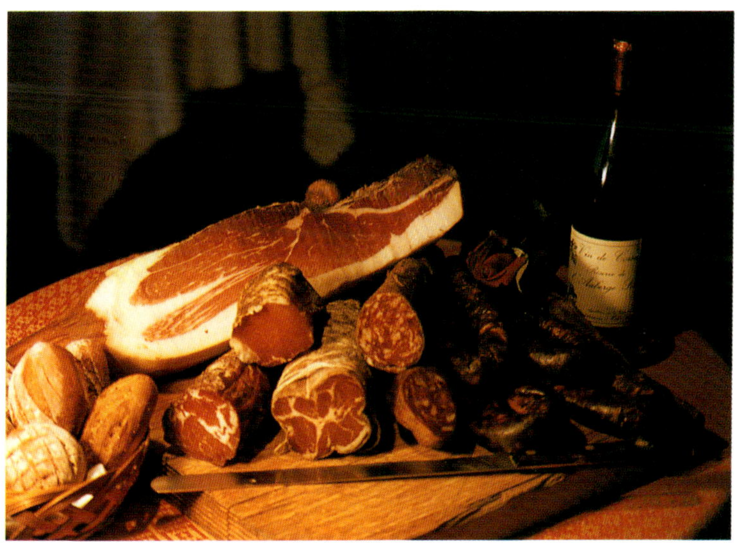

SOUPES

PRÉPARATION : 15 mn
CUISSON : 1 h 30

POUR 6 PERSONNES
250 g de haricots rouges
1 os de jambon
3 pommes de terre
1 petit chou frisé
200 g de blettes
1 oignon
2 gousses d'ail
Sel, poivre

Pour le coulis de tomates :
6 cuillerées à soupe d'huile d'olive
3 oignons
1 pincée de sucre en poudre
1 kg de tomates
4 gousses d'ail
1 cuillerées à soupe de basilic
Sel, poivre

NOTRE CONSEIL
Servir en soupière sur de fines tranches de pain rassis.

SOUPE PAYSANNE CORSE

La veille, faire tremper les haricots rouges dans de l'eau froide.

Le lendemain, les égoutter et les verser dans une grande casserole. Mouiller à hauteur et laisser bouillir 10 mn. Retirer une bonne moitié d'eau et remplacer la aussitôt par de l'eau froide.

Ajouter l'os de jambon.

Pendant ce temps, préparer le coulis de tomates : faire revenir les oignons émincés dans l'huile chaude en ajoutant une pincée de sucre, puis les tomates coupées en quatre, le sel et l'ail. Faire cuire 10 mn, en remuant fréquemment. Réduire à feu doux, et poursuivre la cuisson pendant encore 10 mn ; ajouter le poivre et le basilic.

A mi-cuisson, incorporer cette sauce au bouillon, et jetez-y un oignon haché, les gousses d'ail, le chou émincé, les blettes et les pommes de terre coupées en petits dés. Saler, poivrer.

Laisser cuire à feu doux.

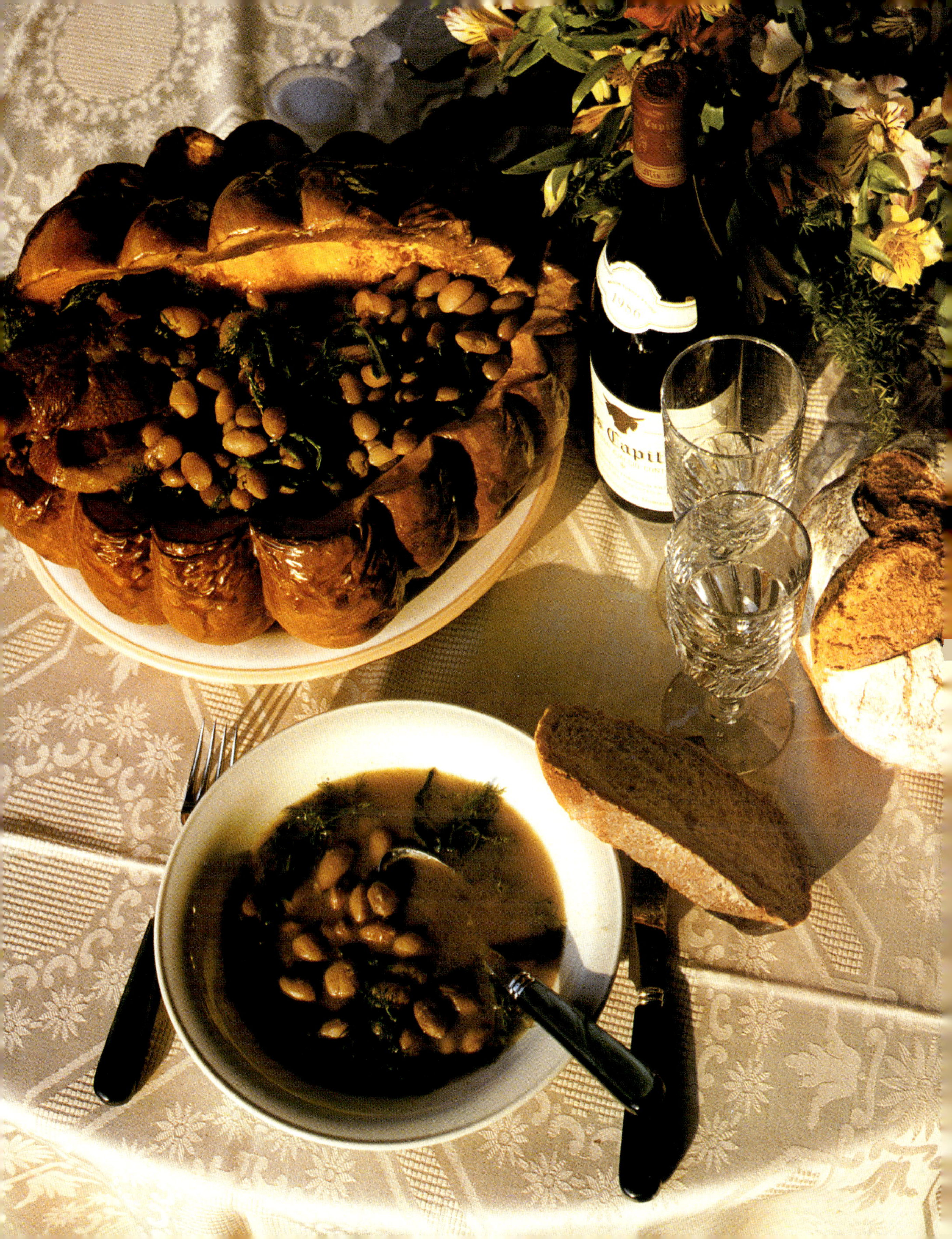
1986

SOUPES

PRÉPARATION : 15 mn
CUISSON : 1 h 15 mn

POUR 6 PERSONNES
1 kg de fèves fraîches
500 g de petits pois
5 pommes de terre nouvelles
2 oignons
1 gousse d'ail
1 tomate
Quelques feuilles de basilic
1 tranche de lard
1 cuillerée à soupe d'huile d'olive
Sel, poivre

NOTRE CONSEIL
Passer la soupe au moulin à légumes, elle n'en n'aura que plus de velouté.

SOUPE DE PRINTEMPS

Faire rissoler à l'huile d'olive les oignons hachés, puis mouiller avec 4 litres d'eau. Saler et porter à ébullition.

Ajouter les fèves, les pois écossés, et à mi-cuisson les pommes de terre entières, l'ail, la tomate, le basilic, et le lard haché.

Laisser cuire à feu moyen.

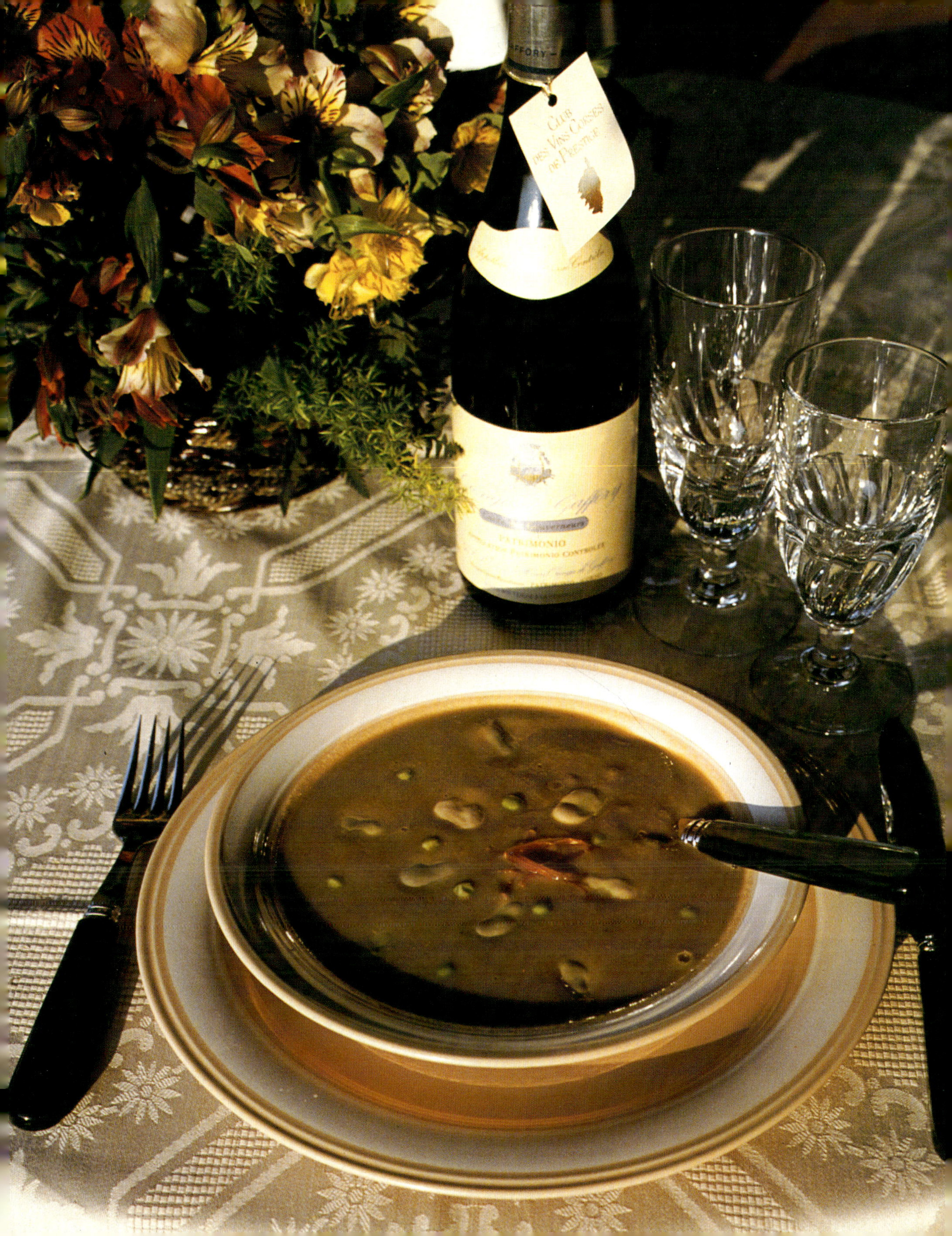
CLUB
DES VINS CORSES
DE PRESTIGE
PATRIMONIO

SOUPES

PRÉPARATION : 10 mn
CUISSON : 1 h

POUR 6 PERSONNES
250 g de haricots rouges
200 g de lard
1 gros oignon
5 pommes de terre
2 tomates
Sel, poivre
Herbes du maquis

NOTRE CONSEIL
Accompagner de tranches de pain grillé, aillé ou non

SOUPE AUX HERBES DU MAQUIS

Faire bouillir 250 g de haricots rouges préalablement trempés 2 h dans l'eau froide.

Jeter la première eau et ajouter les herbes : oseille, fenouil, faux pissenlit ainsi que 200 g de lard haché, un gros oignon coupé en morceaux, 2 tomates bien mûres, 5 pommes de terre, sel, poivre.

Faire bouillir à petit feu et laisser cuire pendant une heure.

Servir très chaud.

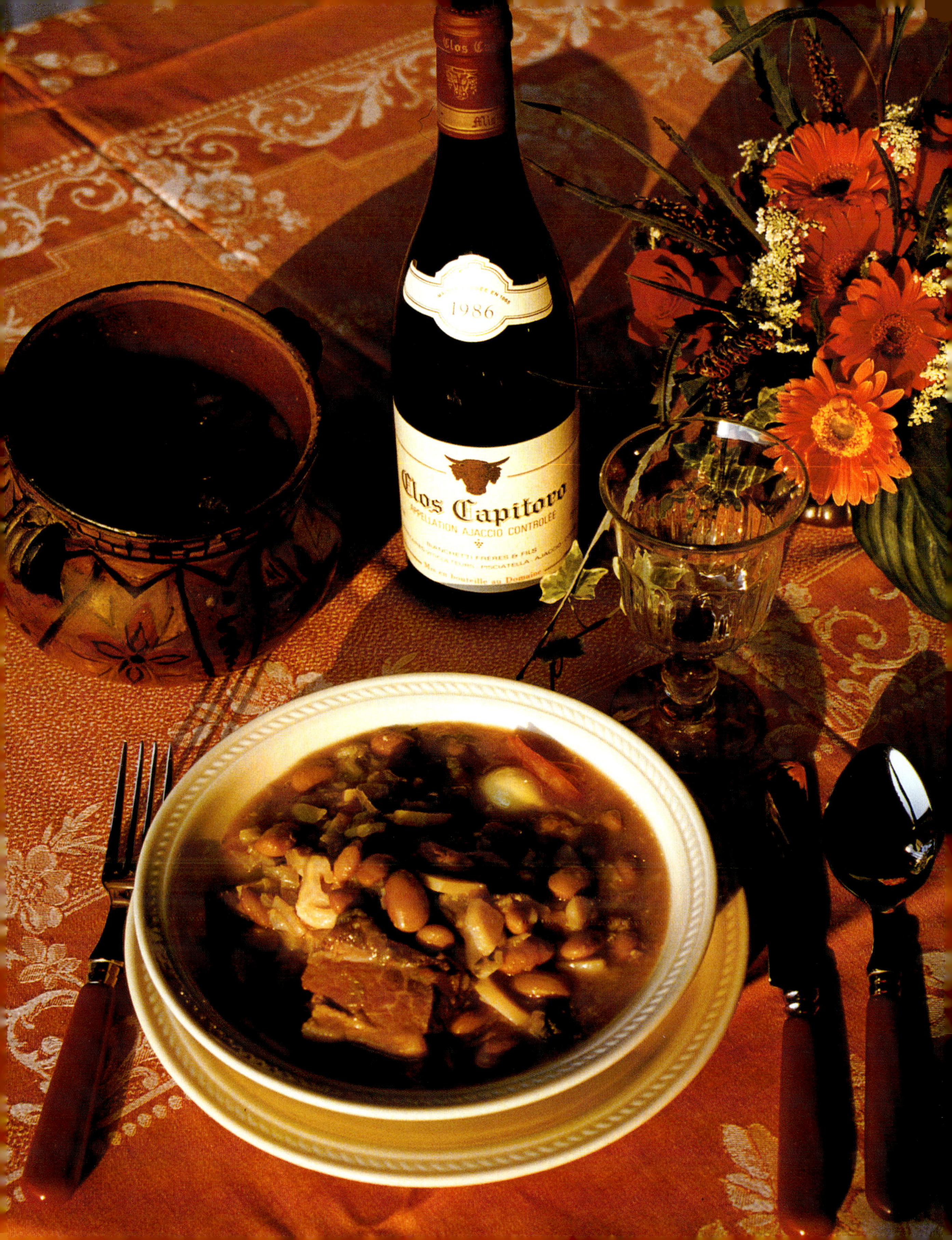
1986
Clos Capitoro
APPELLATION AJACCIO CONTROLEE

SOUPES

PRÉPARATION : 1 h
CUISSON : 2 h 30

POUR 6 PERSONNES
Poisson :
200 g petits poissons de roche
100 g congre
100 g rascasse
100 g rouget
100 g pagre (≃ dorade)
200 g étrille
Garniture :
100 g oignons
100 g carottes
50 g de céleri
50 g de fenouil
150 g poireaux
2 kg tomates
3 c. à soupe de concentré de tomates
3 gousses ail
5 dl de vin blanc
20 cl d'huile d'olive
Safran
Thym, laurier
Sel, poivre

NOTRE CONSEIL
Accompagner cette soupe de croûtons de pain grillé, de parmesan et de rouille.

SOUPE DE POISSONS

Faire chauffer l'huile d'olive, y ajouter les oignons, carottes, céleri, fenouils et poireaux préalablement lavés à l'eau courante et taillés grossièrement.

Les laisser suer 10 mn environ.

Ajouter les tomates, le concentré de tomates, l'ail, le safran, le thym et le laurier et faire mijoter 10 mn.

Y jeter les poissons coupés en petits morceaux (que vous avez fait nettoyer par votre poissonnier) et laisser cuire 10 mn.

Mouiller au vin blanc et faire réduire 3 mn.

Additionner d'eau jusqu'à 10 cm au-dessus des poissons. Saler et poivrer.

Laisser cuire 2 heures.

Mixer la soupe, cuire à nouveau 15 mn.

Servir brûlant.

Note : Pour la préparation de la rouille, écraser 2 gousses d'ail et 2 petits piments rouges, ajouter 2 tranches de mie de pain trempées dans le bouillon et exprimées, une pincée de safran. Incorporer progressivement 2 cuillerées à soupe d'huile d'olive, comme pour une mayonnaise. Allonger d'une cuillerée à soupe de bouillon.

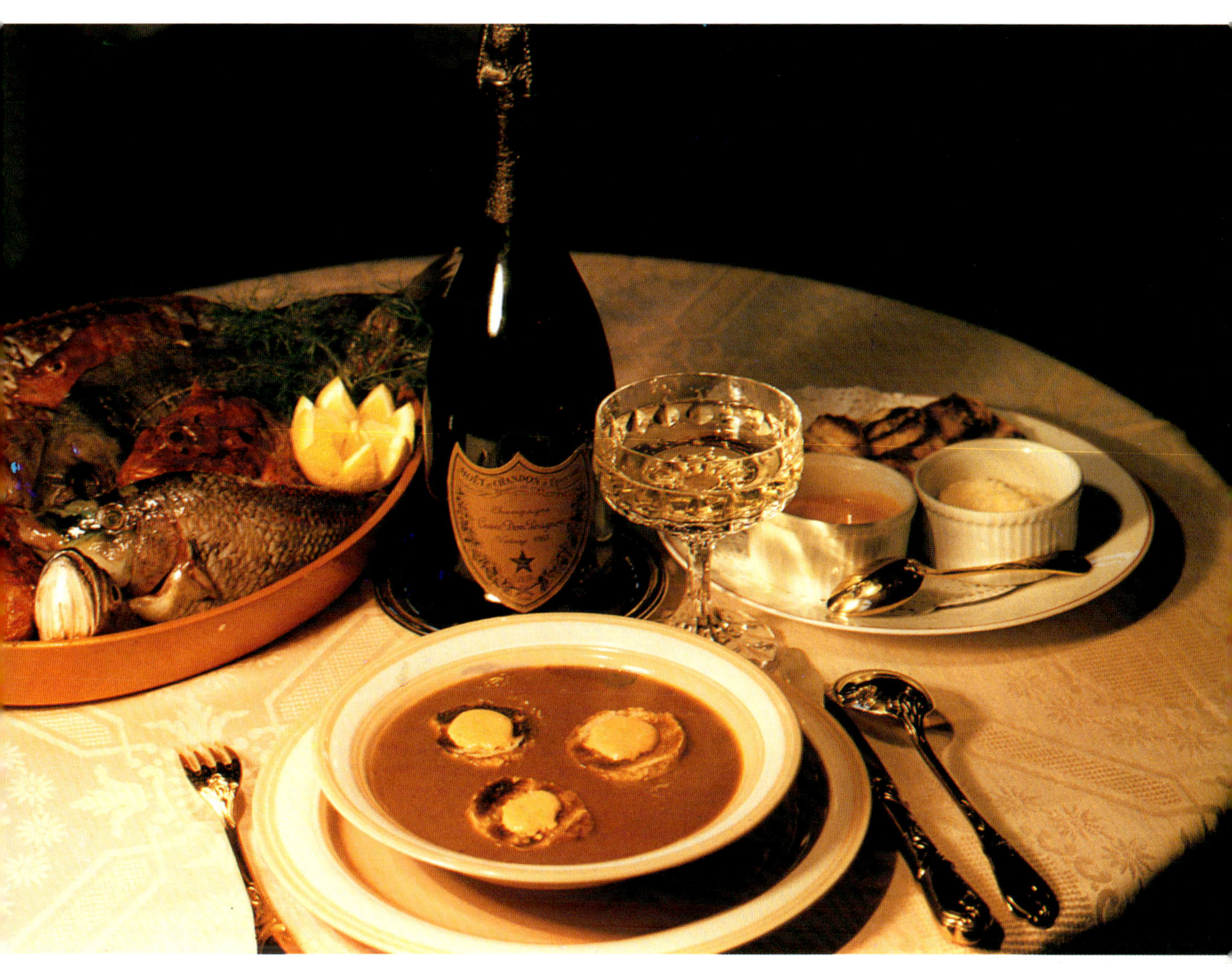
MOËT et CHANDON

SOUPES

PRÉPARATION : 5 mn
CUISSON : 50 mn

POUR 6 PERSONNES
500 g de châtaignes sèches
3 litres d'eau
1 cuillerée à soupe d'huile d'olive
Sel

NOTRE CONSEIL
Vous pouvez également ajouter 1/2 litre de lait bouillant aux châtaignes préalablement écrasées en purée.
Laissez alors mijoter à feu doux pendant 15 mn.

SOUPE DE CHÂTAIGNES

Mettre les châtaignes à tremper toute la nuit.

Le lendemain, les vérifier une à une. Il faut qu'elles soient débarrassées de toutes traces de peaux.

Porter à ébullition 3 l d'eau salée et jetez-y les châtaignes épluchées.

Laisser cuire pendant 1 h après avoir ajouté 1 cuillerée à soupe d'huile d'olive.

Servir les châtaignes avec le bouillon.

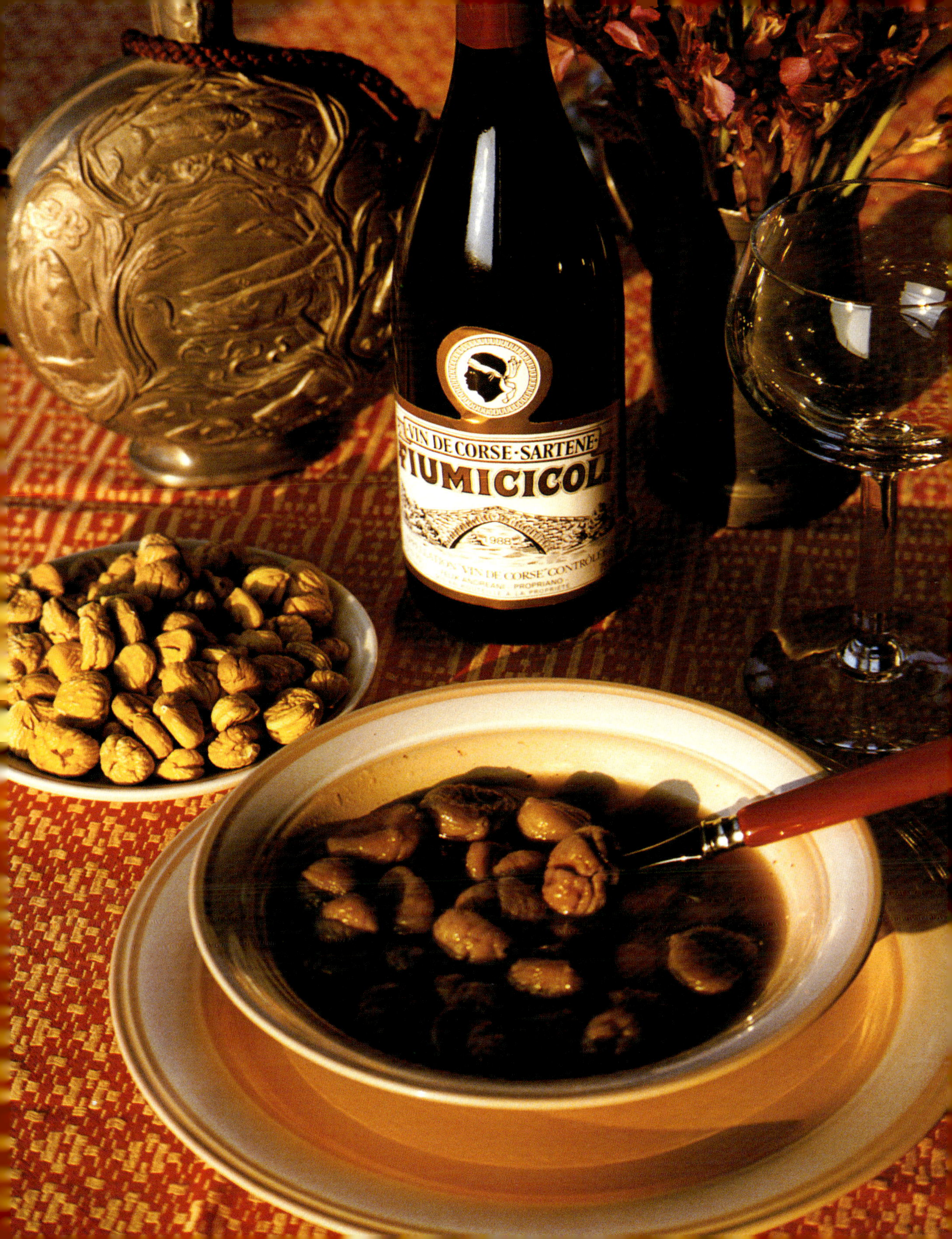
VIN DE CORSE·SARTENE·
1988

PRÉPARATION : 25 mn
CUISSON : 20 mn

POUR 6 PERSONNES
1 kg pâte feuilletée
1 kg d'oignons
700 g de courges
700 g de blettes
8 c. à soupe d'huile d'arachide

NOTRE CONSEIL
Acheter la pâte feuilletée, vous gagnerez du temps.

CHAUSSONS AUX BLETTES, À LA COURGE ET AUX OIGNONS

Préparer les légumes la veille :

Faire légèrement suer à l'huile les oignons émincés très fins. Saler et poivrer.

Couper en petits morceaux les blettes et la courge et les faire revenir à l'huile. Saler et poivrer.

Égoutter les légumes dans une passoire.

Le lendemain étaler la pâte feuilletée. Couper de grands rectangles et faire des chaussons avec ces différentes préparations. Dorer au jaune d'œuf et cuire à four chaud.

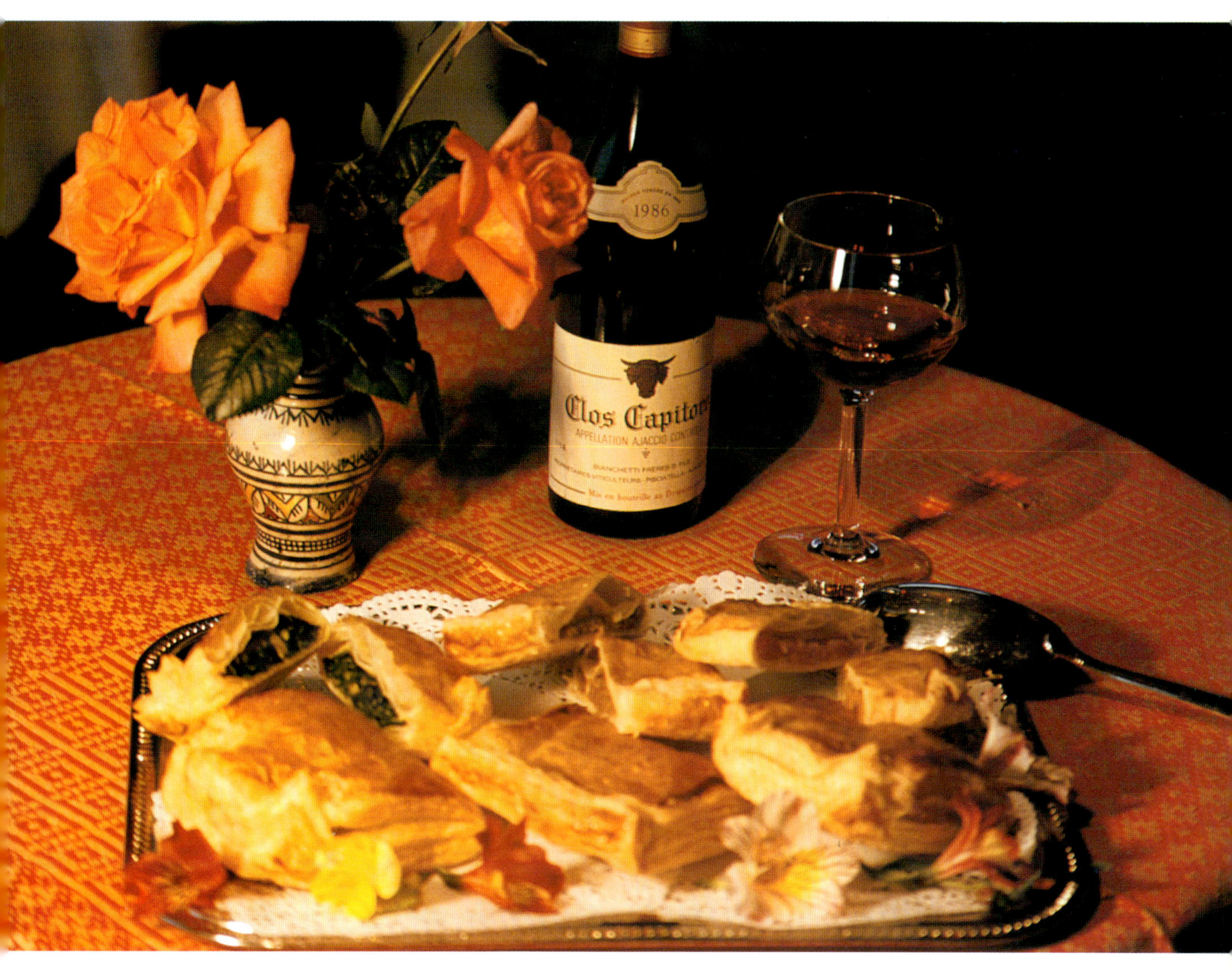
1986
Clos Capito
APPELLATION AJACCIO

PRÉPARATION : 5 mn
CUISSON : 5 mn

POUR 6 PERSONNES
600 g de brocciu
12 œufs
Quelques feuilles de menthe fraîche
Sel, poivre

NOTRE CONSEIL
À défaut de brocciu, vous pouvez utiliser du fromage de brebis à pâte molle (Ricotta)

OMELETTE AU BROCCIU ET À LA MENTHE

Battre les œufs en omelette.

Ajouter le sel, le poivre et la menthe coupée finement.

Travailler à la fourchette le brocciu, et l'incorporer aux œufs battus.

Verser cette préparation dans une poêle contenant de l'huile chaude. Laisser saisir.

Tourner doucement pour que l'omelette n'attache pas.

Retourner l'omelette à l'aide d'une assiette, et la recouvrir avec la poêle pour la laisser cuire un peu.

Servir l'omelette baveuse.

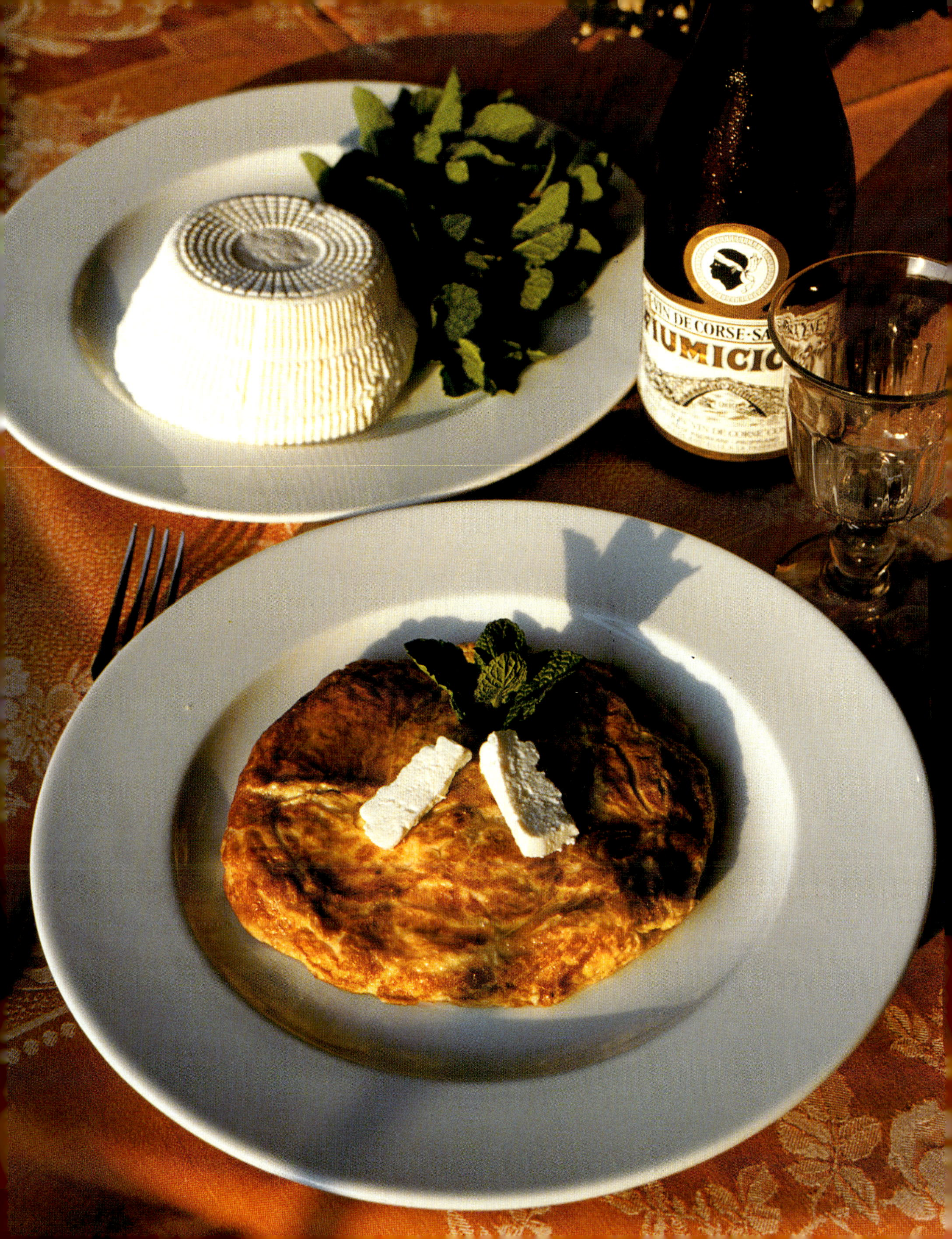
VIN DE CORSE

PRÉPARATION : 5 mn
CUISSON : 10 mn

POUR 6 PERSONNES
600 g de brocciu
12 œufs
1 botte d'asperges sauvages
2 cuillerées à soupe d'huile d'olive
Sel, poivre

NOTRE CONSEIL
À défaut d'asperges sauvages, vous pouvez utiliser des pointes d'asperges en boîte.

OMELETTE AUX POINTES D'ASPERGES SAUVAGES

Couper les pointes d'asperges.

Les faire dorer dans une poêle avec un peu d'huile d'olive.

Battre les œufs en omelette. Ajouter le sel, le poivre et le brocciu écrasé.

Remettre la poêle contenant les asperges à chauffer, y verser les œufs et le brocciu.

Cuire à feu doux puis retourner l'omelette, et laisser la cuisson s'achever hors du feu.

Servir l'omelette baveuse.

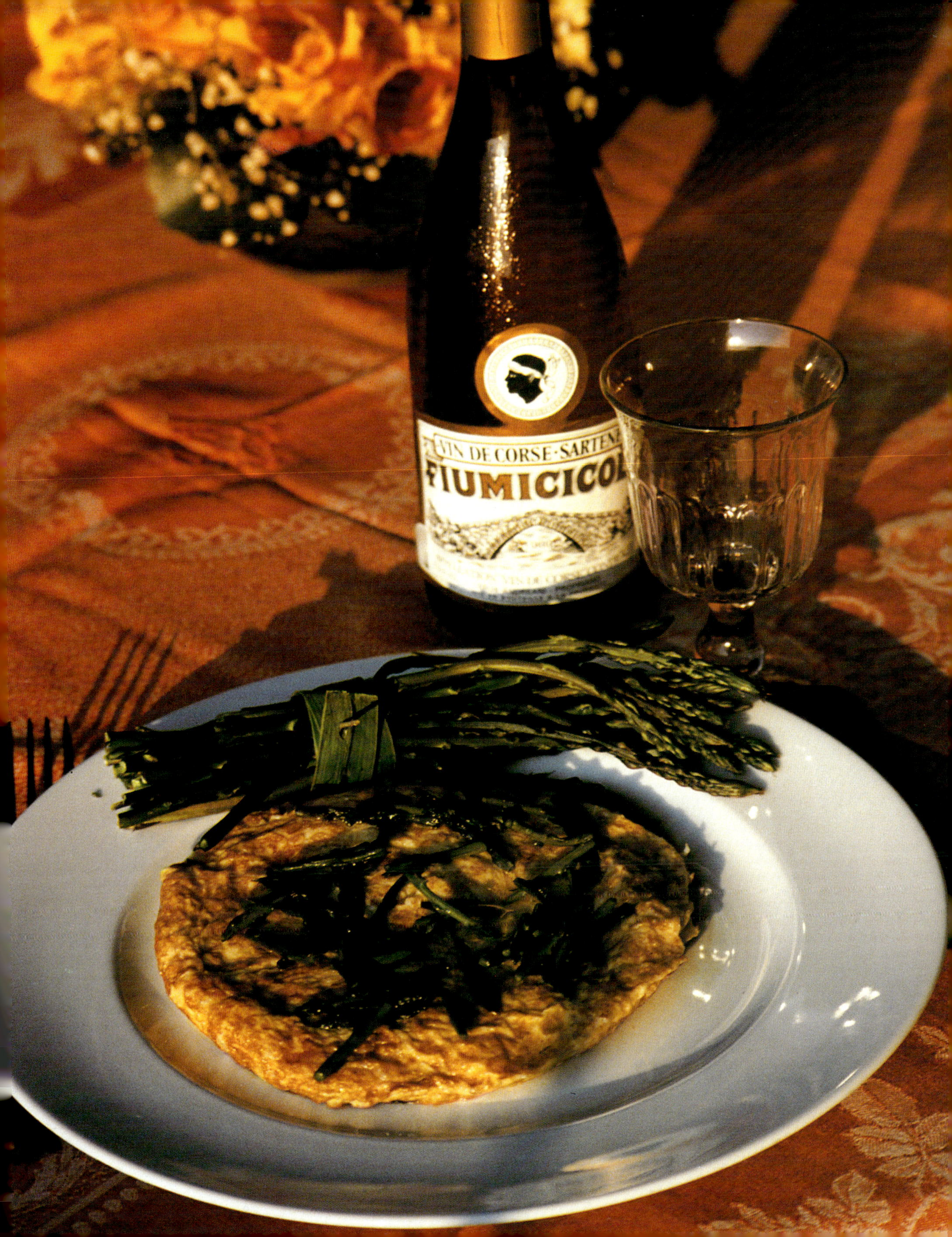
VIN DE CORSE·SARTENA
FIUMICICOL

PRÉPARATION : 20 mn
CUISSON : 10 mn

POUR 6 PERSONNES
Pâte à beignets
500 g de farine
4 dl d'eau
4 œufs
10 g de sel
6 cl d'huile d'arachide
5 dl de bière
6 blancs d'œufs
Garniture
1 kg de poireaux
150 g de beurre
Sel, poivre

NOTRE CONSEIL
Mettre la friture chaude à feu doux, pour donner le temps aux poireaux de se fondre dans la pâte.

BEIGNETS DE POIREAUX

Laver les poireaux à l'eau courante, prélever la partie blanche et l'émincer finement. Faire suer ce blanc dans le beurre fondu 15 mn environ. Laisser refroidir.

Préparer la pâte : Mettre dans un saladier la farine. Creuser un puits pour y mettre le sel, l'huile, les œufs et l'eau. Les mélanger à l'aide d'une spatule en bois en y incorporant un peu de farine. Ajouter la bière en mélangeant progressivement le tout jusqu'à ce que ce soit parfaitement homogène. Laisser reposer 1 h au frais.

Monter en neige les 6 blancs d'œufs, les incorporer délicatement à la pâte.

Bien presser les poireaux et en faire de petites boules. Les plonger dans la pâte, puis dans l'huile de friture très chaude jusqu'à ce qu'elles prennent une couleur dorée. Les égoutter sur un papier absorbant.

Servir immédiatement.

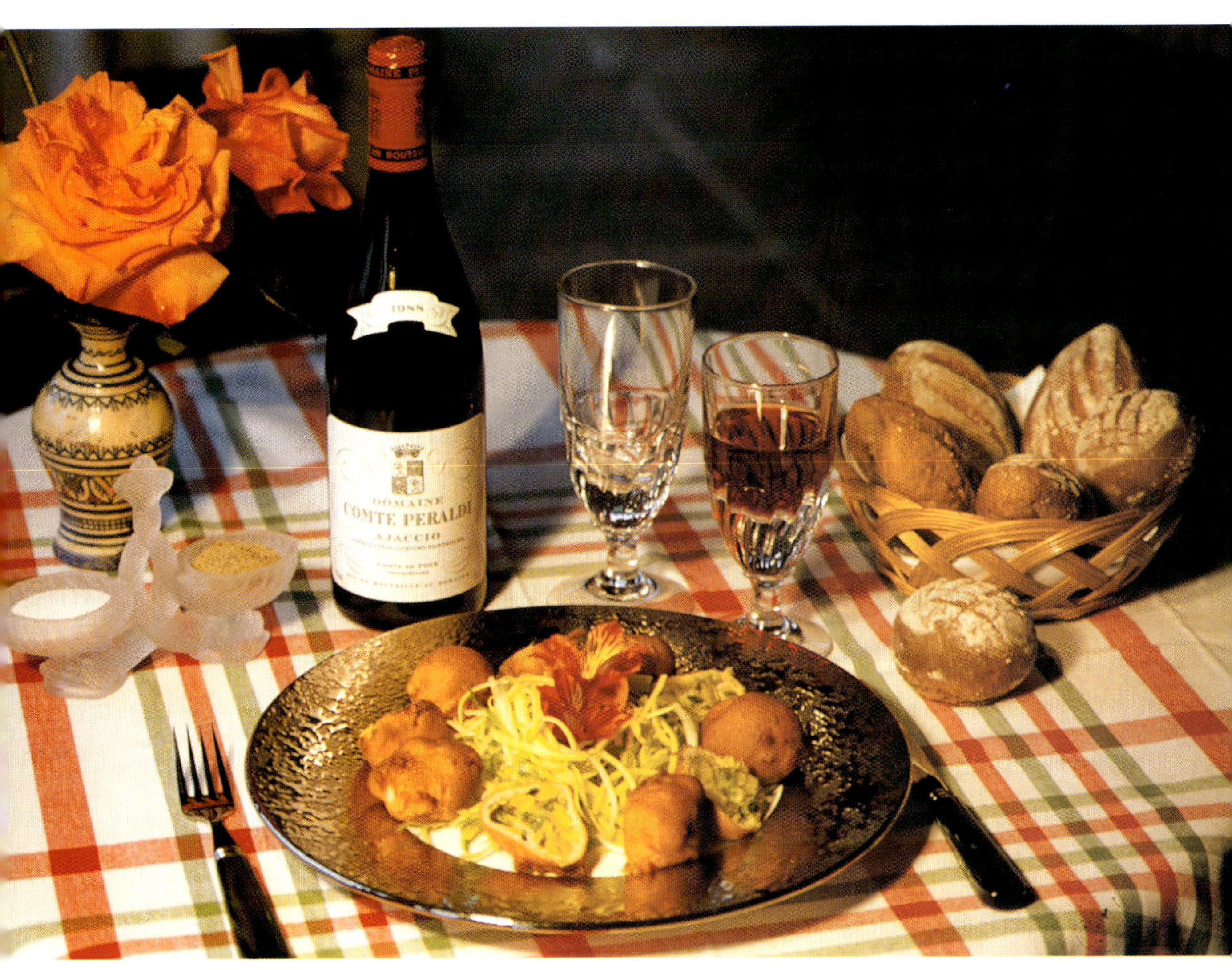
1988
DOMAINE
COMTE PERALDI
AJACCIO

ENTRÉES

PRÉPARATION : 30 mn
CUISSON : 35 mn

POUR 6 PERSONNES
6 douzaines d'escargots gris
1 oignon
4 ou 5 tomates
1/2 verre d'eau de vie
1/2 l. de vin blanc ou rosé
Thym, laurier
6 anchois
2 gousses d'ail
Huile d'olive

NOTRE CONSEIL
Pour gagner du temps vous pouvez utiliser des escargots en boîte.

ESCARGOTS À LA MODE CORSE

Laisser jeûner les escargots pendant 5 à 6 jours, puis les laver à l'eau vinaigrée et salée en changeant l'eau plusieurs fois.

Faire bouillir les escargots dans de l'eau additionnée de sel, thym et laurier durant 1/4 h environ. Les égoutter.

Faire revenir l'oignon émincé dans de l'huile mise à chauffer dans une cocotte puis ajouter les escargots. Incorporer les tomates épépinées et hachées. Verser l'eau de vie chaude et flamber. Mouiller avec le vin blanc ou rosé et ajouter le thym, laurier, sel et poivre.

Piler les anchois, l'ail dans un peu d'huile d'olive jusqu'à obtention d'une pommade que l'on incorpore à la sauce quelques minutes avant de retirer du feu.

Servir brûlant dans des assiettes chaudes.

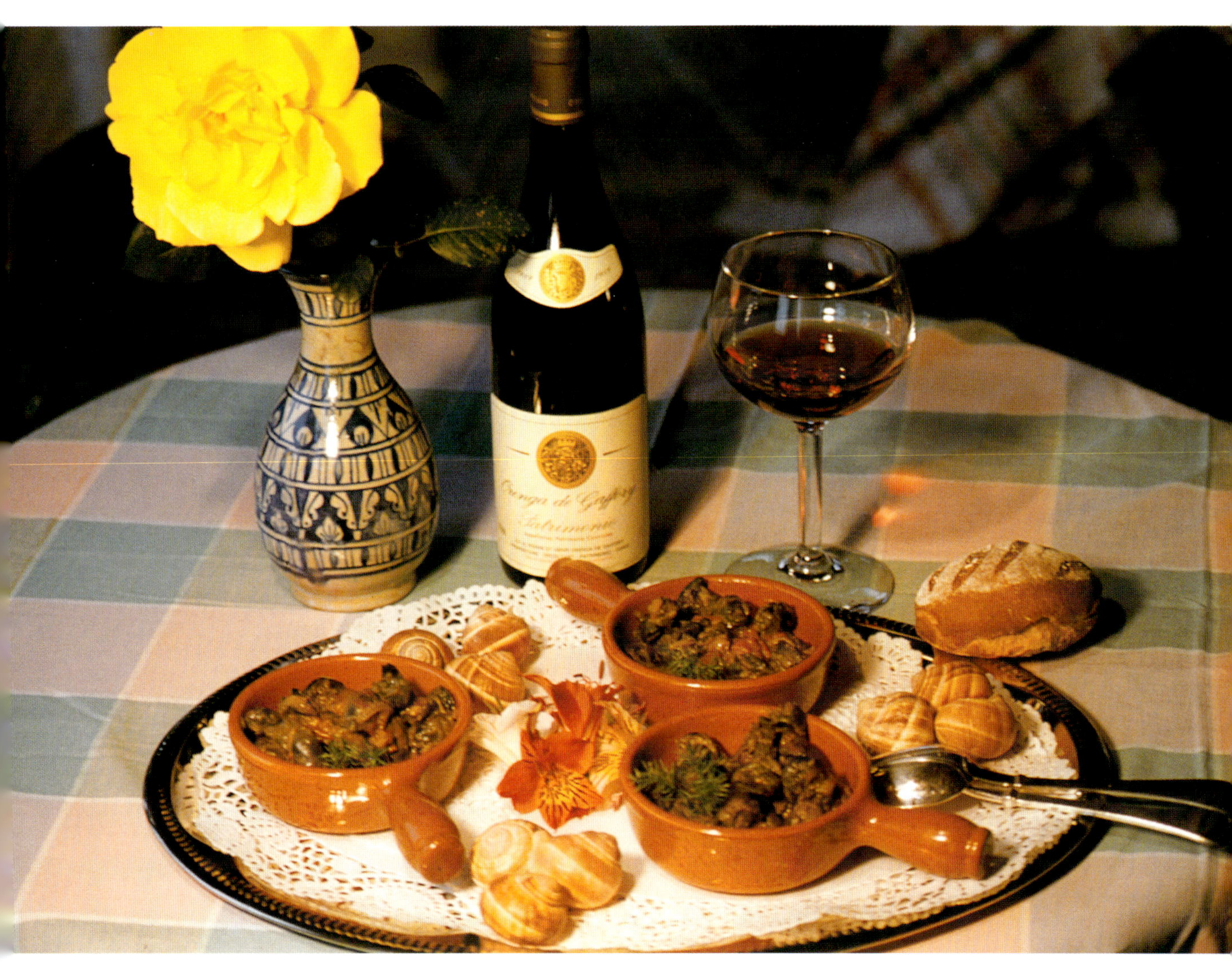

PRÉPARATION : 35 mn
CUISSON : 20 mn

POUR 6 PERSONNES
3 langoustes de 800 g

Pour le court-bouillon :
2 carottes
2 oignons
1 poireau
3 l d'eau
3 dl de vin blanc
1 bouquet de persil
Thym, laurier
Sel, poivre

NOTRE CONSEIL
Servir les langoustes avec une saucière d'aïoli.

LANGOUSTES AU COURT-BOUILLON

Dans un fait-tout, préparer le court-bouillon avec les légumes coupés en morceaux, le bouquet de persil, les aromates, l'eau et le vin blanc.

Porter à ébullition, écumer, puis saler et poivrer.

Laisser cuire 20 mn, à feu vif puis plonger les langoustes dans ce court-bouillon.

Couvrir et cuire à feu moyen pendant une vingtaine de minutes.

Une fois la cuisson terminée, égoutter les langoustes, les laisser refroidir, puis les fendre en deux.

Note : Pour la préparation de l'aïoli, écraser 8 gousses d'ail pelées au pilon dans un mortier, ajouter un jaune d'œuf, du sel et du poivre.

Verser l'huile goutte à goutte, comme pour une mayonnaise avec 30 cl d'huile d'olive.

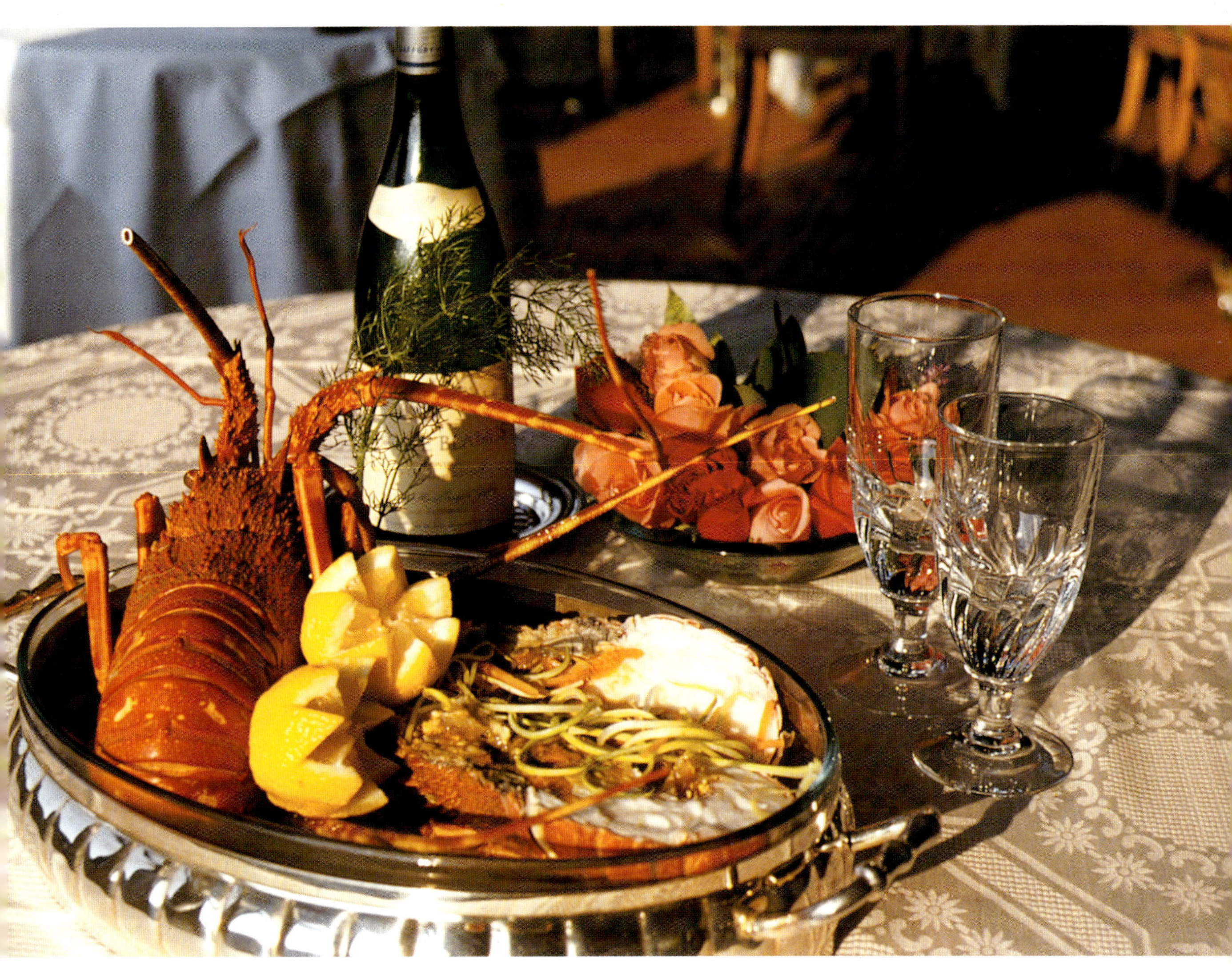

PRÉPARATION : 10 mn
CUISSON : 20 mn

POUR 6 PERSONNES
1 kg de congre
2 oignons
5 dl de coulis de tomates (voir p. 6)
1 dl de vin rosé
60 g de câpres
Laurier
Huile d'olive
Farine
Sel, poivre

NOTRE CONSEIL
Servir avec des pommes vapeur et accompagner d'un blanc de blanc.

CONGRE AUX CÂPRES

Couper le congre en tronçons de 2 cm environ. Les fariner.

Les faire dorer à la poêle, dans un peu d'huile d'olive.

Ajouter les oignons hachés, et les laisser cuire quelques minutes.

Verser ensuite le coulis de tomates et le vin blanc avant d'y jeter le laurier et les câpres.

Saler, poivrer.

Laisser mijoter 15 mn.

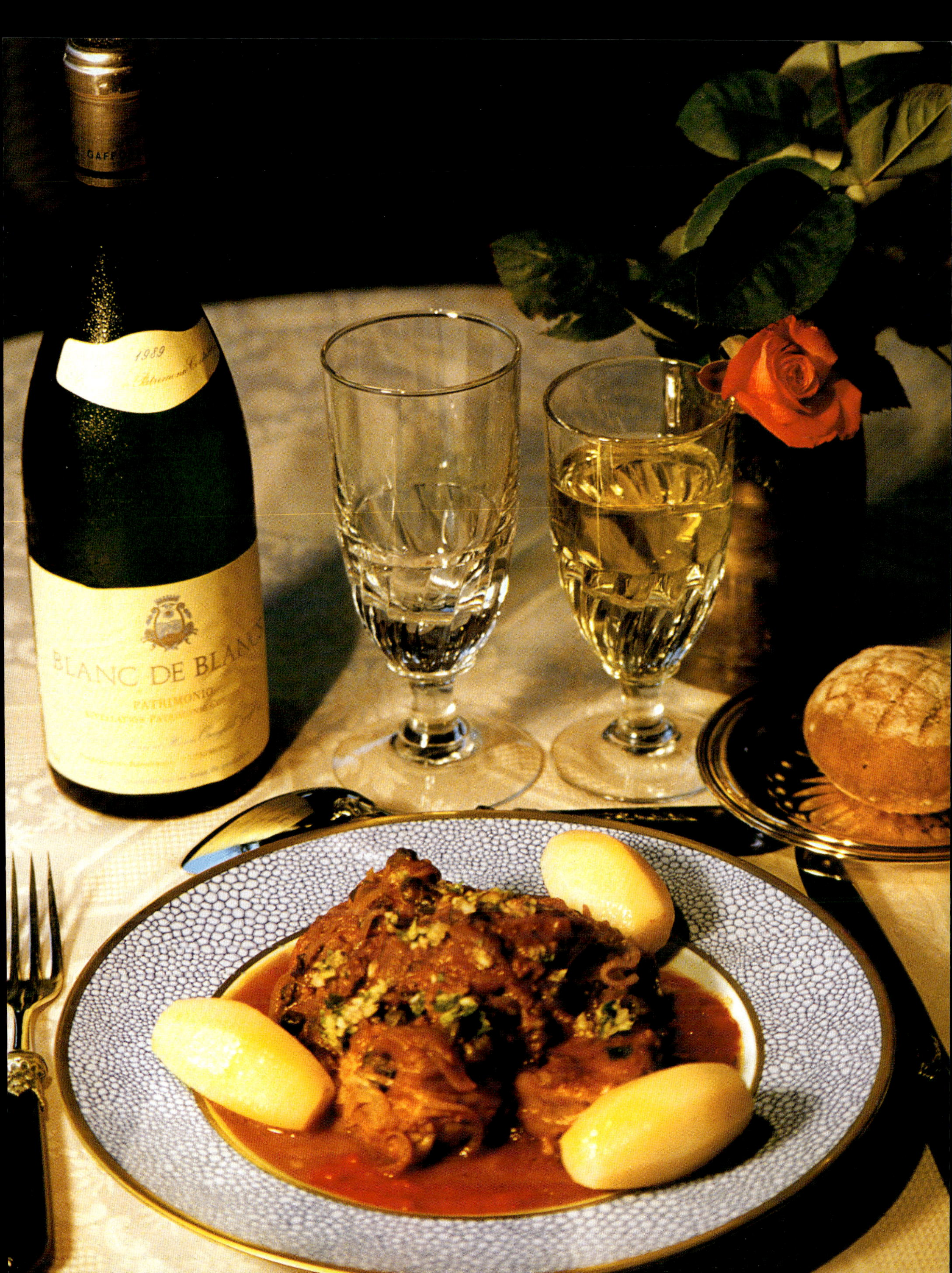
1989
BLANC DE BLAN
PATRIMONIO

PRÉPARATION : 40 mn
CUISSON : 15 mn

POUR 6 PERSONNES
6 chapons
1 poireau
3 oignons
3 carottes
6 champignons de Paris
1 fenouil
1 tige de céleri
1 branche d'estragon
Thym, laurier
Sel, poivre en grains

NOTRE CONSEIL
Napper le plat avec le bouillon additionné de crème fraîche et légèrement réduit.

CHAPON POCHÉ AUX PETITS LÉGUMES

Dans une marmite mettre 3 l d'eau et 1 l de vin blanc. Saler, poivrer. Porter à ébullition.

Pendant ce temps éplucher et laver soigneusement les légumes, les émincer finement, les mettre dans la marmite avec les herbes et laisser cuire 20 mn. Plonger alors les chapons dans ce bouillon, couvrir et faire mijoter 15 mn.

Égoutter les chapons avec précaution ainsi que les légumes et dresser sur un plat.

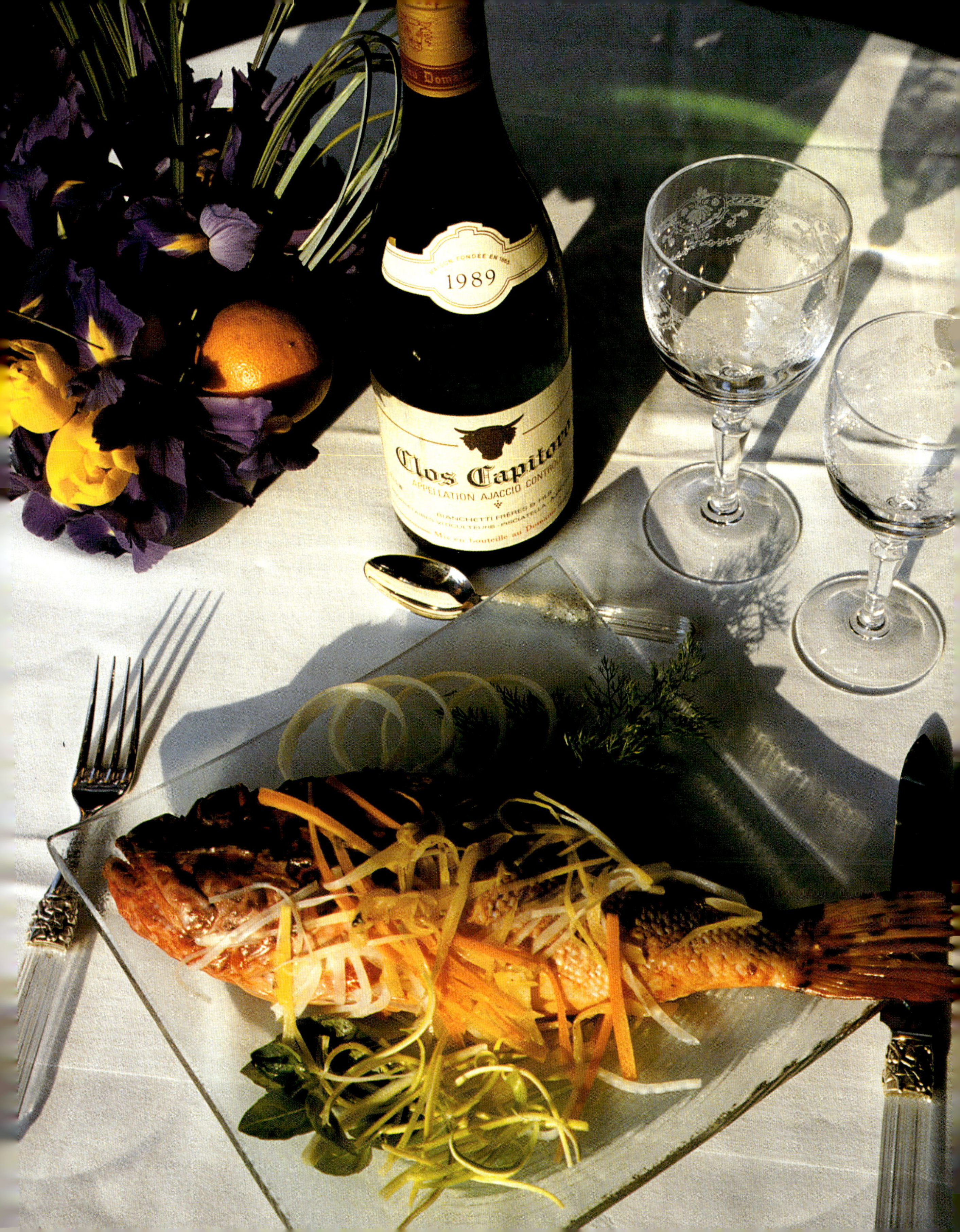
1989
Clos Capitoro

POISSONS ET CRUSTACÉS

PRÉPARATION : 15 mn
CUISSON : 40 mn

POUR 6 PERSONNES
1 kg 200 de cabillaud
2 oignons
5 dl de coulis de tomates (voir p. 6)
1 dl de vin blanc
12 pommes de terre
1 feuille de laurier
24 olives noires
Huile d'olive
Sel, poivre

NOTRE CONSEIL
Accompagner d'un vin blanc sec.

RAGOÛT DE MORUE AUX POMMES DE TERRE

Couper le cabillaud en darnes de 200 g environ.

Les rouler dans la farine et les faire dorer dans une poêle contenant de l'huile chaude. Une fois la cuisson terminée, les retirer, mais conserver l'huile de friture. Y faire dorer les pommes de terre coupées en fines lamelles.

Dans une sauteuse, verser le vin blanc, le coulis de tomates additionné d'une feuille de laurier, et l'huile de friture. Faire cuire à feux doux, et laisser réduire 20 mn.

Saler et poivrer.

Enlever les arêtes des darnes. Les concasser et les incorporer à la sauce tomate réduite.

Ajouter les pommes de terre et les olives noires ; laisser cuire 10 mn.

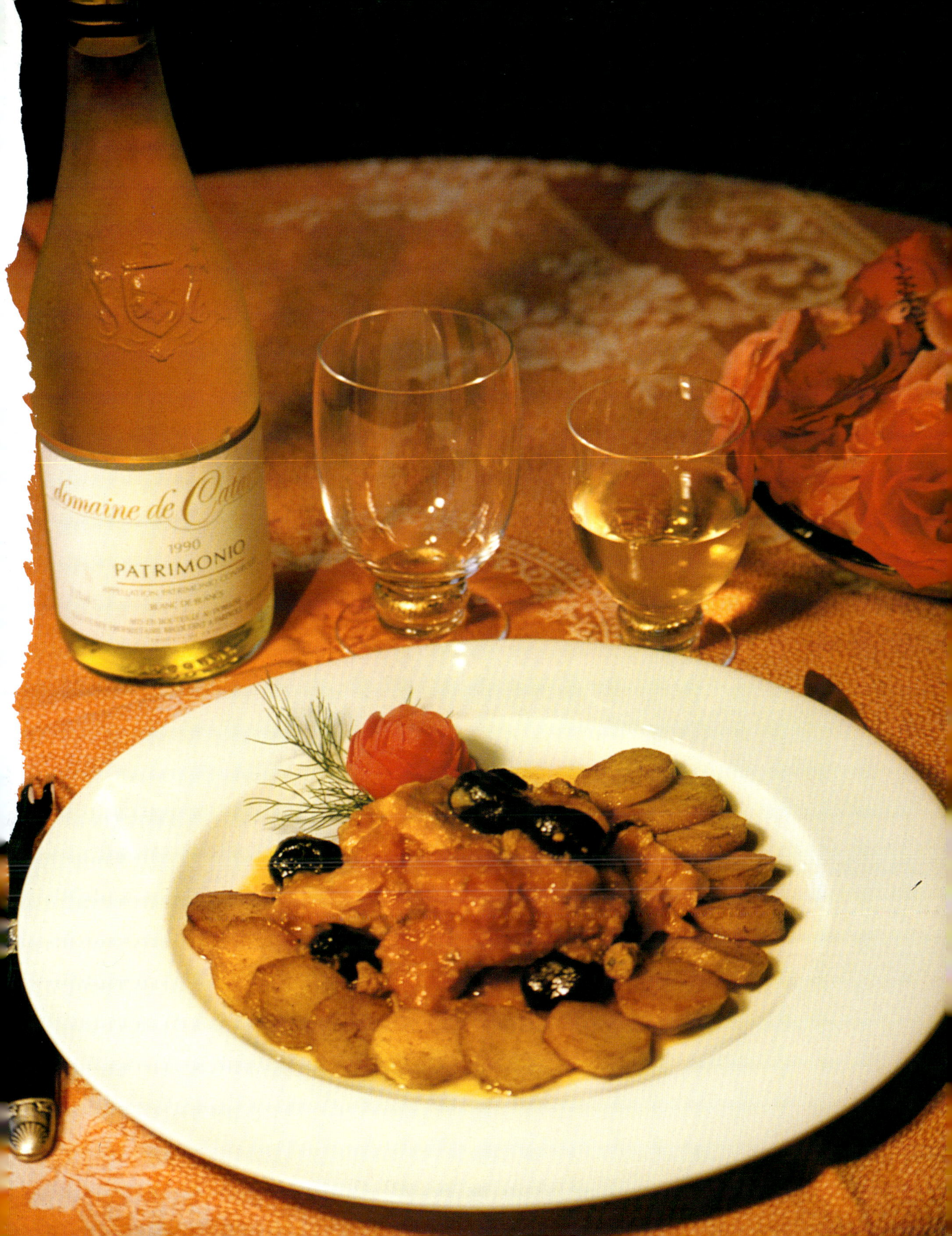
domaine de
1990
PATRIMONIO

POISSONS ET CRUSTACÉS

PRÉPARATION : 10 mn
CUISSON : 20 mn

POUR 6 PERSONNES
12 rougets
7 anchois
4 gousses d'ail
1 petit bouquet de persil
2 verres de chapelure
Huile d'olive
Sel, poivre

NOTRE CONSEIL
Garnir de rondelles de citron avant de servir.

ROUGETS À LA BONIFACIENNE

Écailler, vider et laver soigneusement les rougets.

Les essuyer avec du papier absorbant.

Piler les anchois bien égouttés avec l'ail épluché, ajouter le persil ciselé.

Placer cette farce dans un plat légèrement huilé. Déposer les rougets dessus, saler et poivrer.

Couvrir avec de la chapelure et arroser de 2 cuillerées à soupe d'huile d'olive.

Faire cuire au four th. 6 (220°) 15 mn environ.

Servir très chaud.

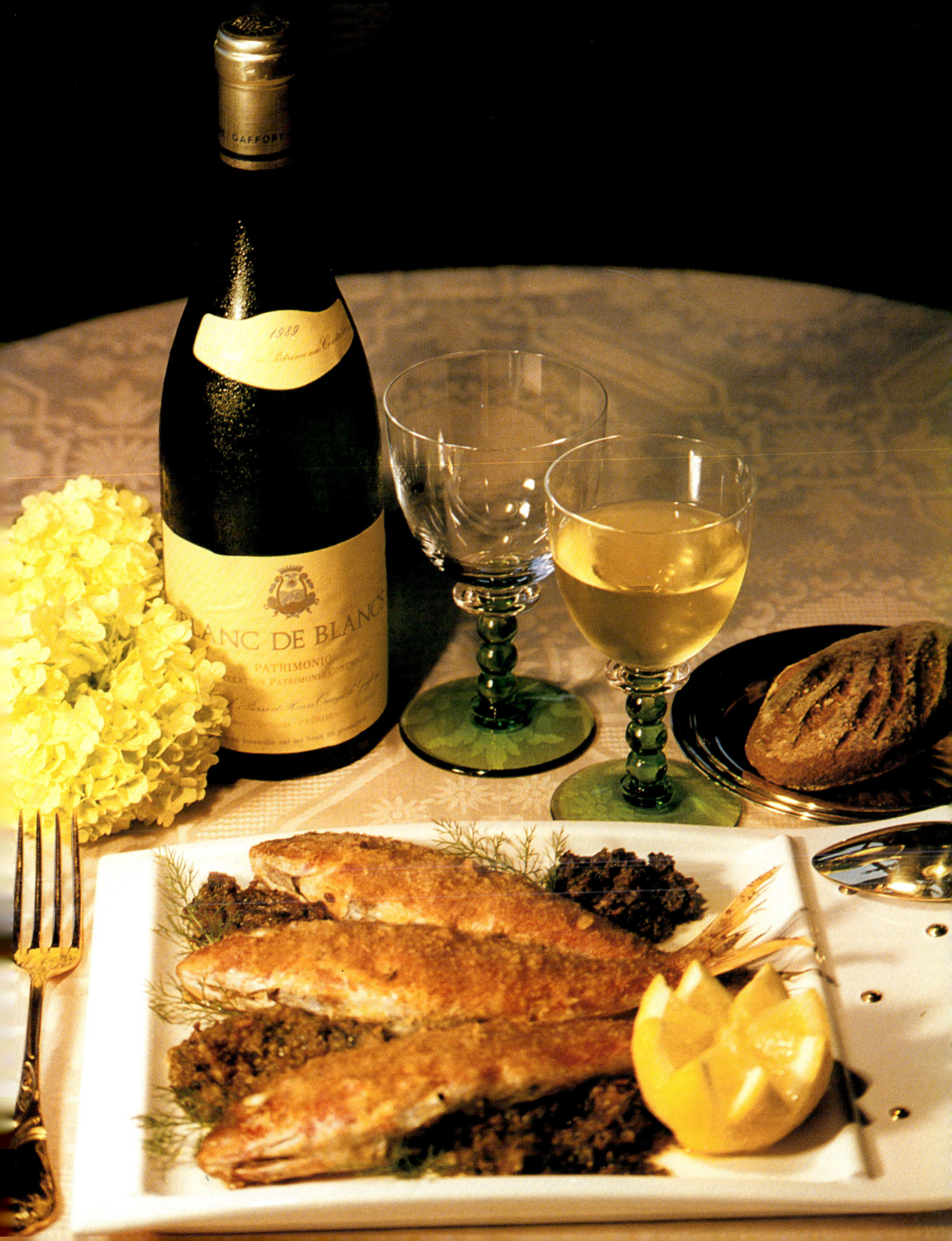
1989
LANC DE BLANCS
PATRIMONIO

POISSONS ET CRUSTACÉS

PRÉPARATION : 10 mn
CUISSON : 10 mn

<u>POUR 6 PERSONNES</u>
6 truites
Farine
1 filet de vinaigre
Ail
Huile d'olive
Sel

<u>NOTRE CONSEIL</u>
Servir les truites avec des pommes de terre cuites à la vapeur et un blanc sec.

TRUITES DE MONTAGNE À L'AIL

Vider, laver et essuyer les truites avant de les saler des deux côtés.

Les rouler dans la farine, les faire dorer à l'huile chaude et les dresser sur un plat de service.

Faire revenir l'ail dans la poêle de cuisson, déglacer avec un filet de vinaige.

En arroser les truites et servir aussitôt.

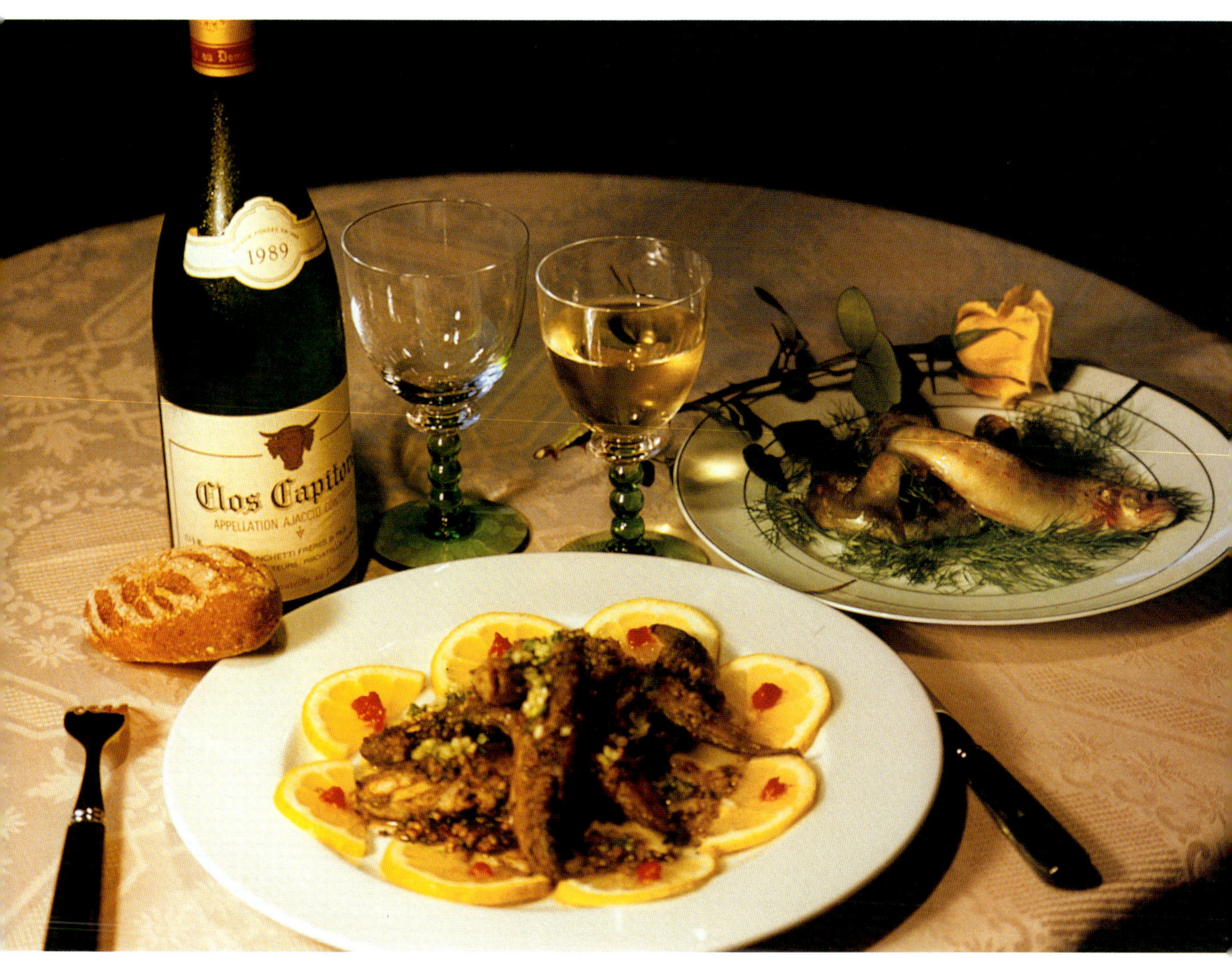
1989
APPELLATION AJACCIO

ANGUILLES FRITES À L'AIL

PRÉPARATION : 10 mn
CUISSON : 10 mn

POUR 6 PERSONNES

6 anguilles (jeunes de préférence)
Huile d'olive
Sel, poivre
1 filet de vinaigre
Ail, persil

NOTRE CONSEIL

Il n'est pas utile de dépouiller les anguilles lorsqu'elles sont jeunes.

Après avoir vidé les anguilles, les couper en tronçons d'environ 5 cm. Les laver et sécher.

Faire rissoler dans de l'huile bien chaude.

Une fois cuites, dresser sur un plat de service.

Faire dorer l'ail dans la poêle de cuisson, déglacer avec un filet de vinaigre et arroser les anguilles. Saupoudrer de persil haché.

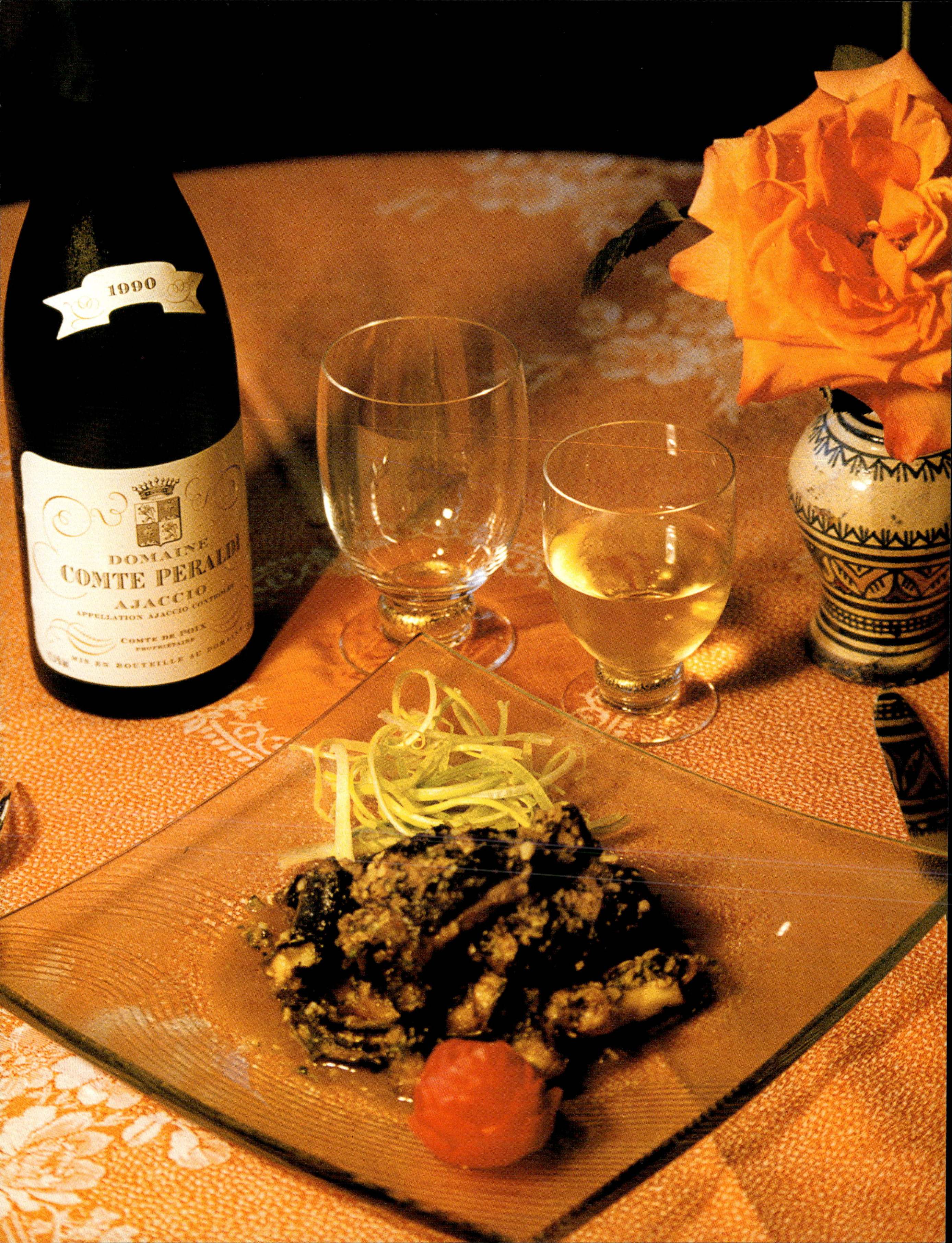
1990
DOMAINE
COMTE PERALDI
AJACCIO
APPELLATION AJACCIO CONTROLEE
COMTE DE POIX
PROPRIETAIRE
MIS EN BOUTEILLE AU DOMAINE

PRÉPARATION : 5 mn
CUISSON : 1 h

POUR 6 PERSONNES
1 gigot d'agneau
4 gousses d'ail
3 c. à soupe d'huile d'olive
1 c. à soupe de vinaigre
Sel, poivre

NOTRE CONSEIL
Accompagner le gigot de pommes de terre sautées

GIGOT D'AGNEAU GRILLÉ AU FEU DE BOIS

Faire rôtir à la braise, ou à la broche, un gigot d'agneau de lait.

Le retourner souvent.

Saler, poivrer.

Pendant la cuisson, l'arroser fréquemment avec une préparation à base d'huile d'olive, de vinaigre, de sel et de poivre.

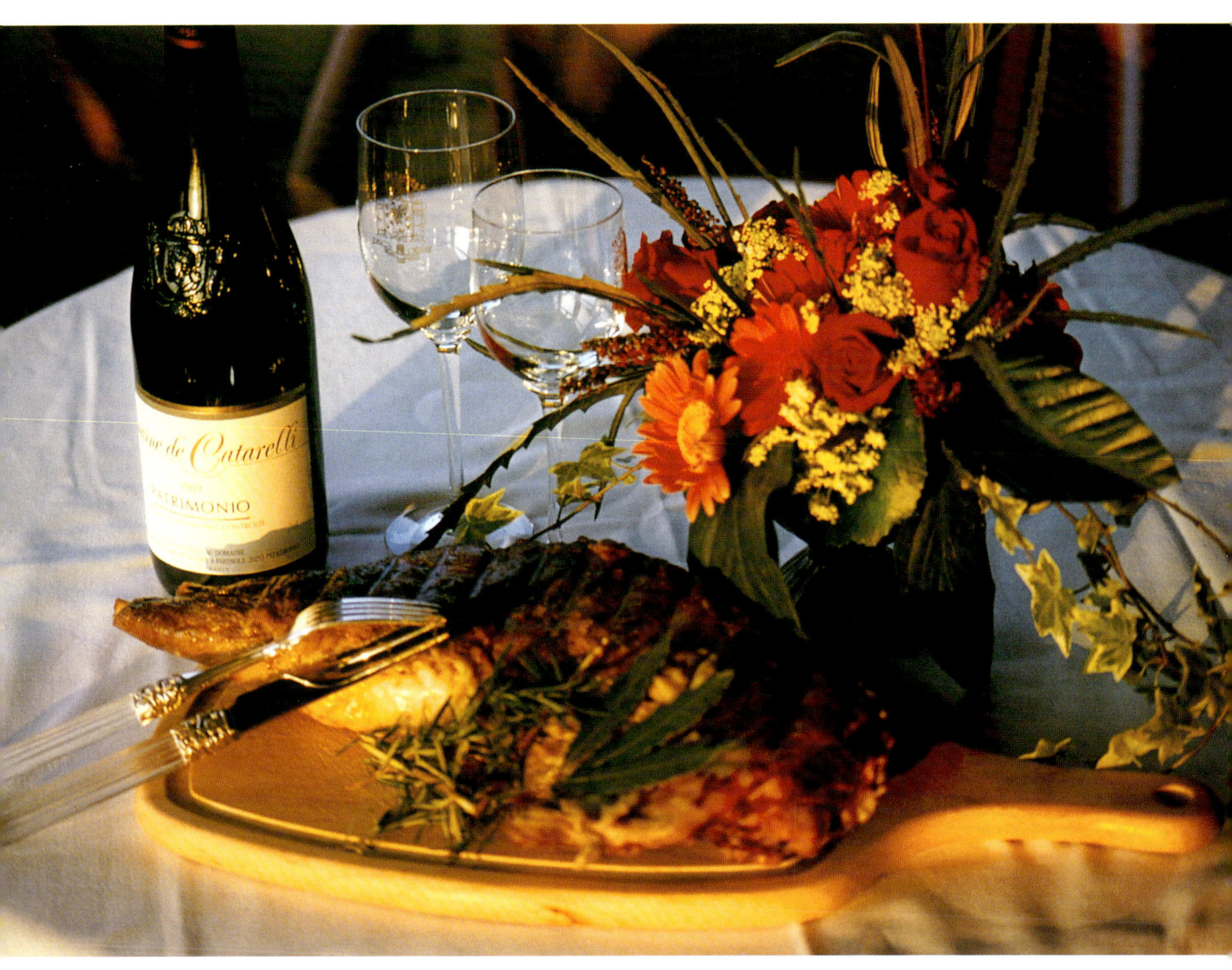
Catarelli
PATRIMONIO

PRÉPARATION : 10 mn
CUISSON : 1 h 20

POUR 6 PERSONNES
1 kg de veau
3 oignons
Ail, romarin, laurier
Sel, poivre
2 dl de vin rosé
Coulis de tomates (p. 6)
24 olives vertes

NOTRE CONSEIL
Les pâtes fraîches sont l'accompagnement idéal de ce sauté de veau aux olives.

SAUTÉ DE VEAU AUX OLIVES

Couper la viande en dés et la faire rissoler dans du saindoux.

Dans une cocotte faire revenir les oignons hachés, ajouter les gousses d'ail écrasées, le coulis de tomates, 2 verres de vin rosé, la viande et mouiller largement d'eau. Saler, poivrer, mettre une feuille de laurier, un brin de romarin.

À mi-cuisson ajouter les olives dénoyautées.

Laisser mijoter une 1 h environ.

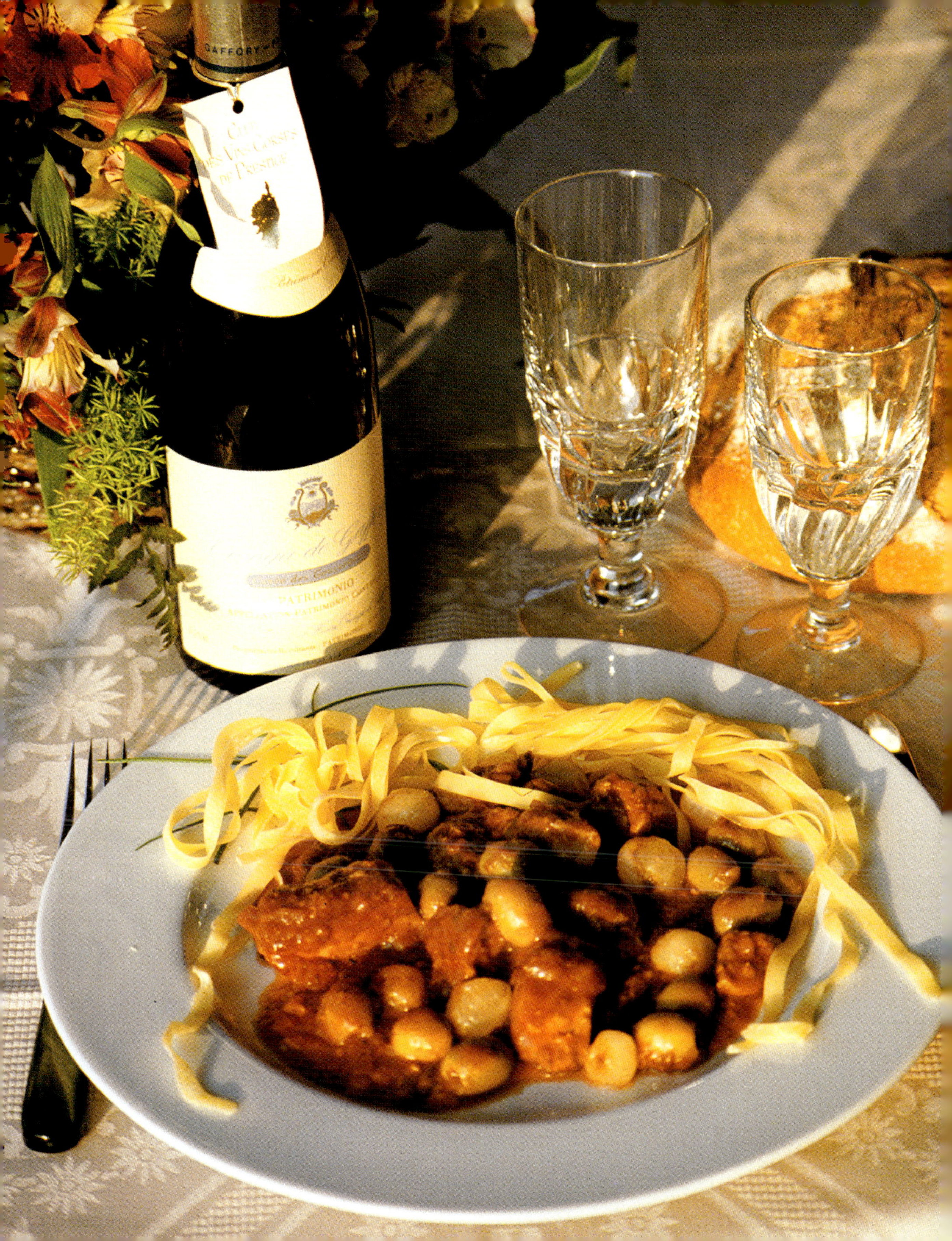

DES VINS CORSES
DE PRESTIGE
PATRIMONIO

ABATS ET VIANDES

PRÉPARATION : 20 mn
CUISSON : 1 h 20

POUR 6 PERSONNES
1 kg 200 épaule de porc en morceaux
3 oignons
Coulis de tomates (p. 6)
Sel, poivre, laurier
6 artichauts
12 pommes de terre
100 g de fèves fraîches écossées
Huile d'olive

NOTRE CONSEIL
Varier le temps de cuisson suivant les différentes sortes de légumes.

SAUTÉ DE PORC PRINTANIER

Dans un poêlon, faire rissoler les morceaux de viande. Ajouter les oignons hachés, le laurier et le coulis de tomates.

Saler, poivrer, couvrir d'eau.

Cuire à feu doux 30 mn.

Prendre des petits artichauts bien tendres, enlever les premières feuilles et couper les artichauts en deux.

Éplucher les pommes de terre, les mettre dans le ragoût avec les artichauts ainsi que les fèves préalablement blanchies.

Laisser cuire encore 30 mn, puis ajouter les petits pois et cuire encore 1/4 d'heure.

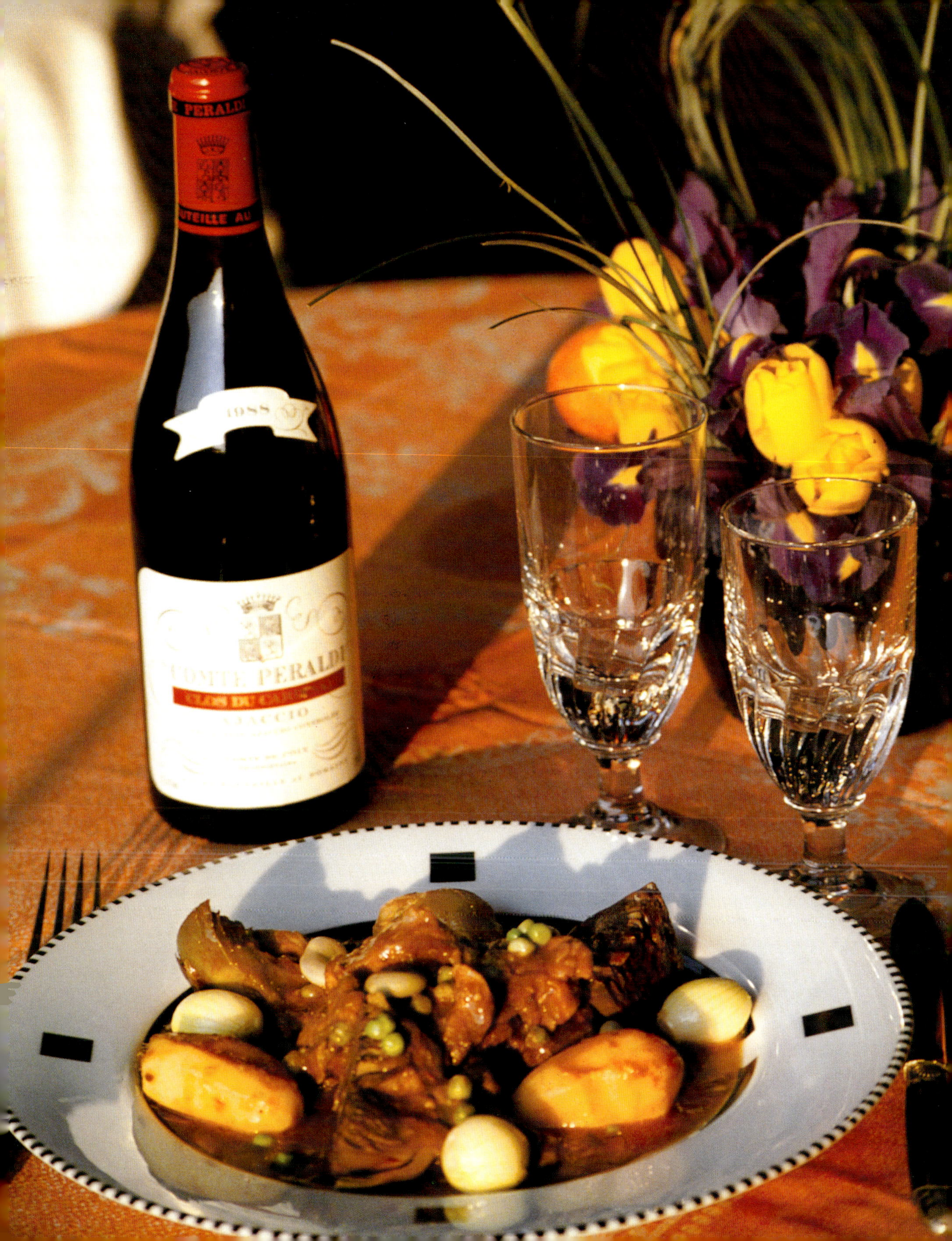
PERALDI
1988
PERALDI

PRÉPARATION : 15 mn
CUISSON : 1 h 30

POUR 6 PERSONNES
1 kg 200 de bœuf
100 g de lardons
2 oignons
2 gousses d'ail
Persil
Laurier
1 c. à soupe d'huile d'olive
1 c. à soupe de farine
Coulis de tomate (p. 6)
1 l de vin rouge
Sel, poivre

NOTRE CONSEIL
Servir chaud avec un plat de macaronis.

DAUBE DE BŒUF

Faire revenir le bœuf coupé en morceaux dans un poêlon contenant un peu d'huile d'olive.

Ajouter le lard coupé en dés et les oignons émincés. Les faire rissoler.

Saupoudrer le tout d'une cuillerée de farine, puis verser le coulis de tomates. Y ajouter l'ail, le laurier et le persil. Bien mélanger et laisser cuire 5 mn.

Mouiller avec le vin rouge, et compléter d'eau jusqu'à hauteur.

Couvrir et laisser cuire à feu doux.

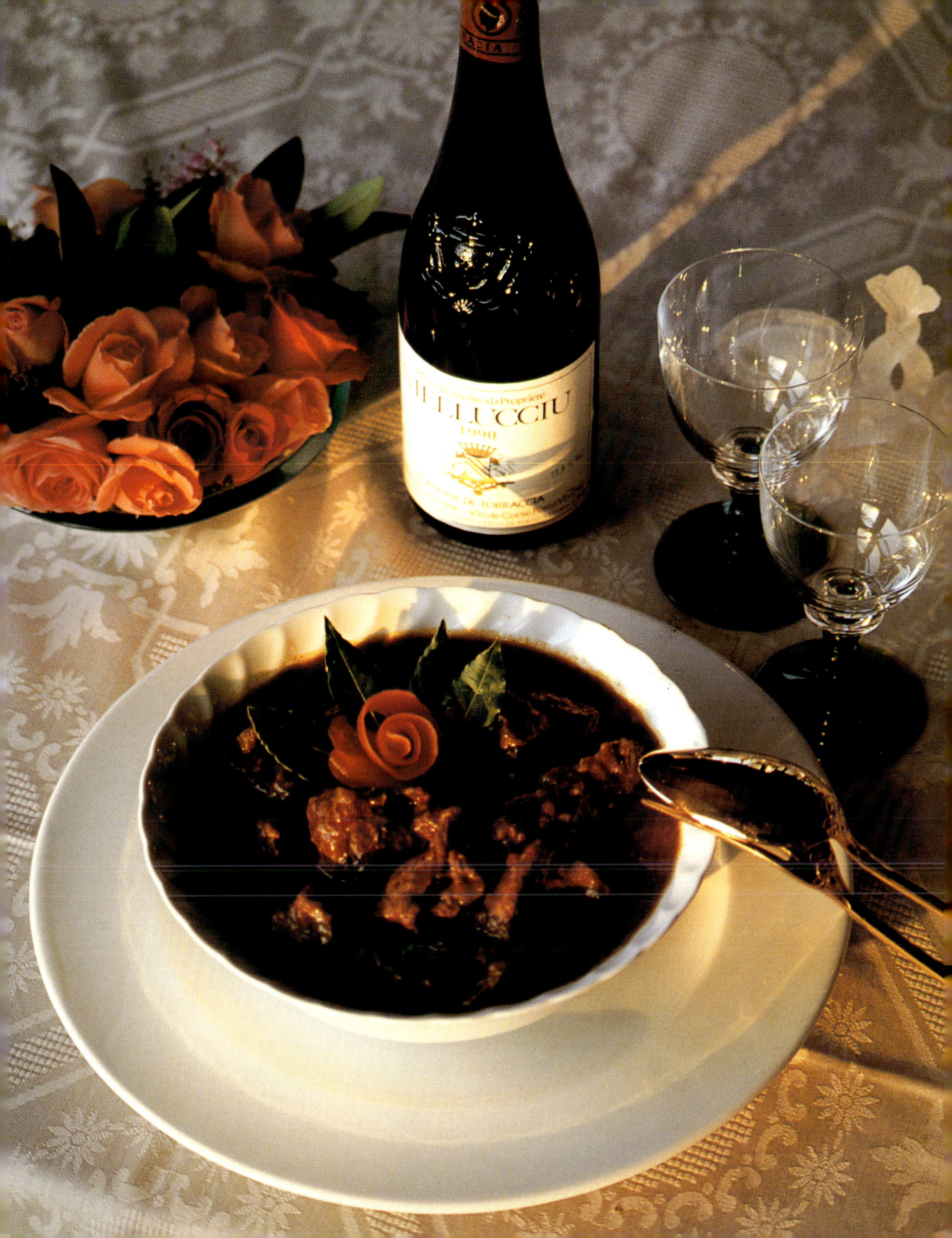

Bouteille à la Propriété
1990
TORRACCIA
Vin de Corse

ABATS ET VIANDES

PRÉPARATION : 1 h
CUISSON : 30 mn

POUR 6 PERSONNES
1/2 agneau de lait
4 oignons
2 gousses d'ail
Persil haché, romarin
Coulis de tomates (p. 6)
1 l de vin rosé
Huile
Petits légumes : carottes, pommes de terre, courgettes, navets
Gousses d'ail

NOTRE CONSEIL
Profiter des légumes du printemps, très tendres : ils donneront à votre sauté d'agneau un goût savoureux.

SAUTÉ D'AGNEAU AUX PETITS LÉGUMES

Détailler l'agneau en le dégraissant au maximum, le faire rissoler à l'huile.

Ajouter les oignons hachés, les gousses d'ail, le persil haché, le romarin. Bien mélanger.

Mouiller avec le coulis de tomtes et le vin rosé.

Cuire 30 mn à feu doux.

Saler, poivrer.

Cuire les petits légumes séparément, à l'eau bouillante salée puis les incorporer au sauté d'agneau.

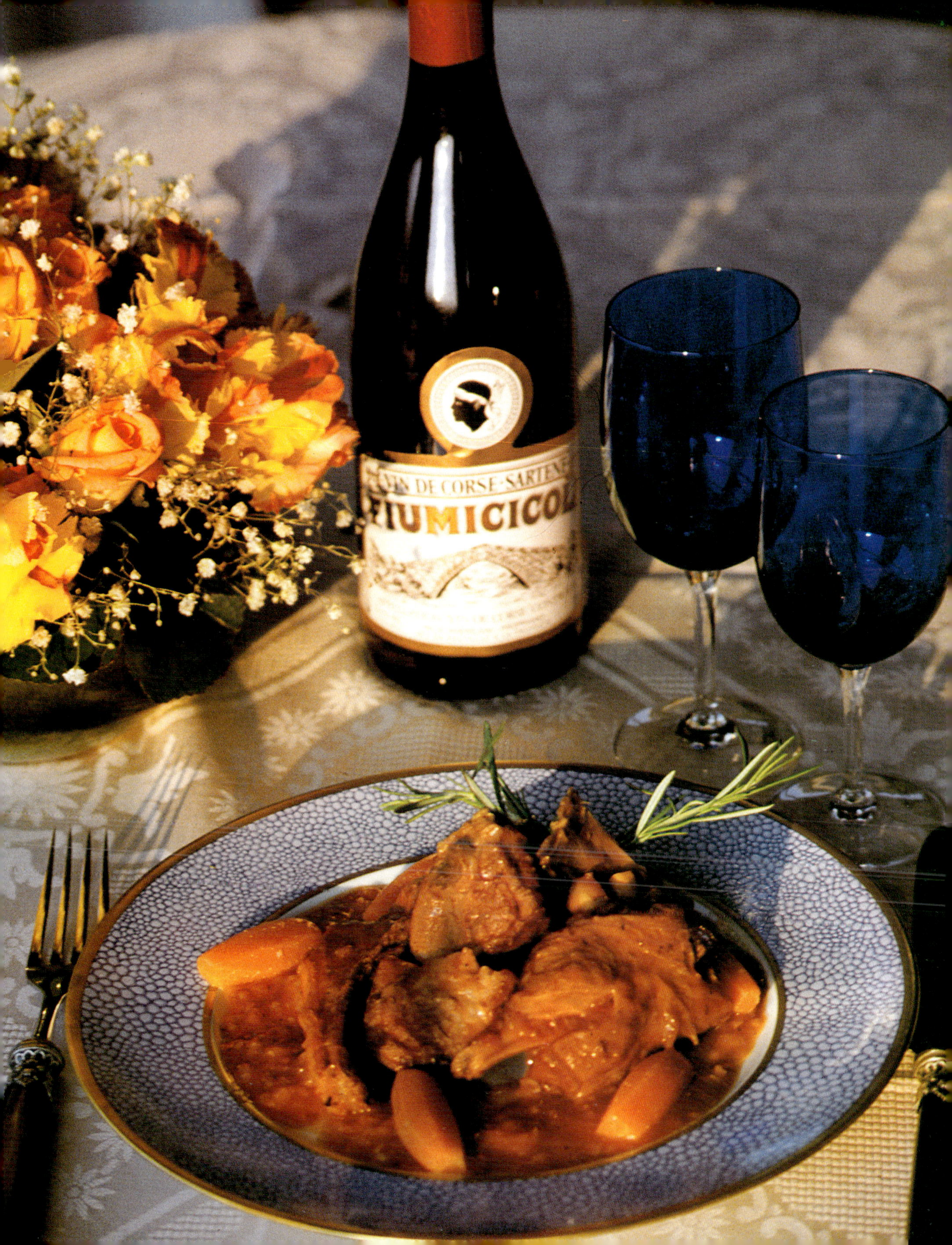
VIN DE CORSE·SARTENE
FIUMICICOL

ABATS ET VIANDES

PRÉPARATION : 30 mn
CUISSON : 4 h

POUR 10 PERSONNES
3 kg de tripettes de veau
1 dl d'huile d'olive
1 l de vin blanc
coulis de tomates (p. 6)
3 oignons
4 gousses d'ail
Laurier
Sel, poivre

NOTRE CONSEIL
Servir avec des pommes de terre cuites à la vapeur.

TRIPETTES À LA MODE CORSE

Laver soigneusement les tripettes à l'eau courante.

Les faire blanchir 15 mn à l'eau bouillante.

Les rafraîchir et les égoutter.

Couper les tripettes en lanières de 2 cm de large sur 5 cm de long et les faire rissoler à l'huile d'olive.

Faire revenir les oignons hachés et les gousses d'ail.

Mélanger le tout et cuire pendant 10 mn.

Ajouter le vin blanc, le coulis de tomates, et le laurier.

Assaisonner généreusement.

Laisser mijoter pandant 4 h, en prenant soin de remuer souvent.

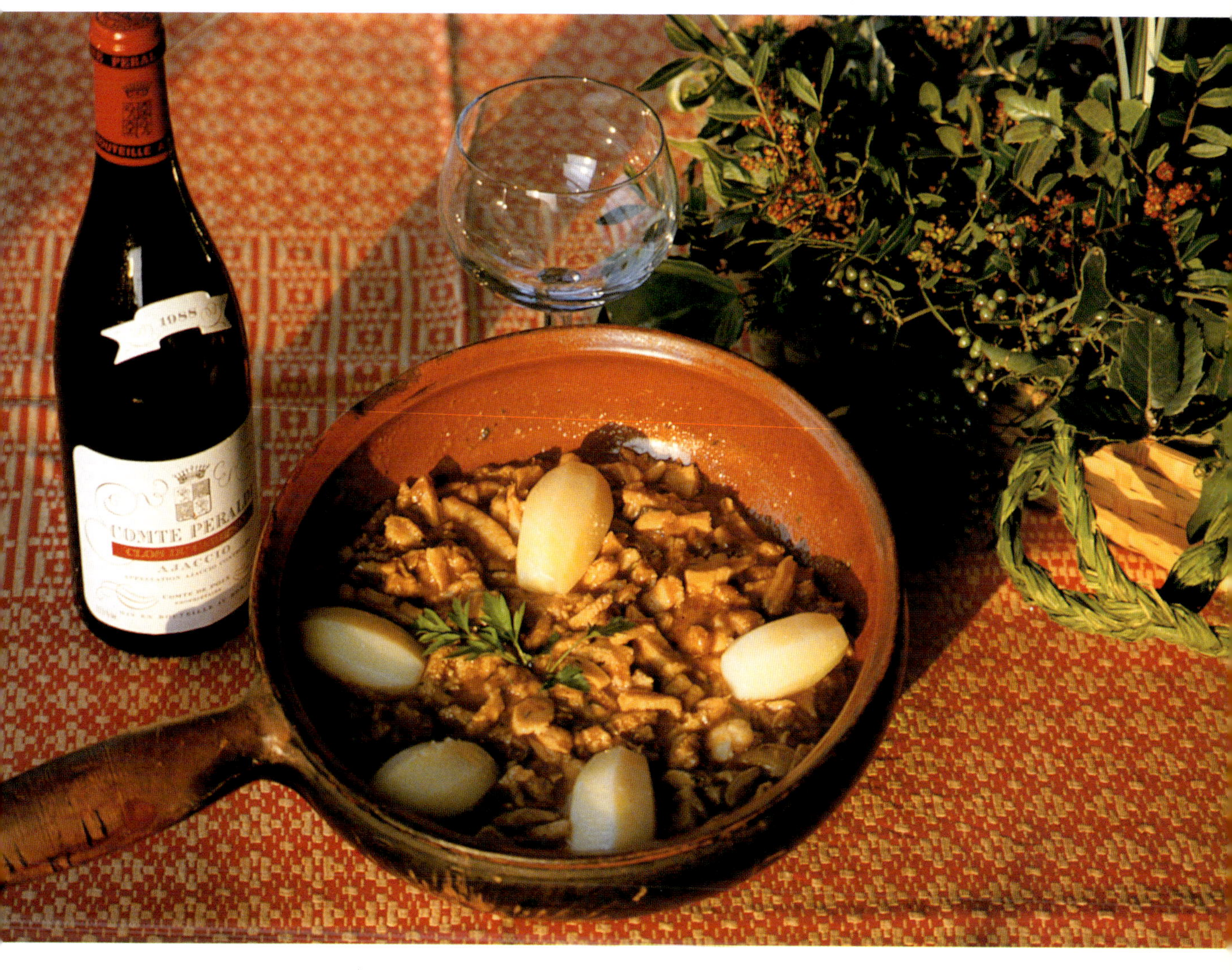
1988
AJACCIO

PRÉPARATION : 5 mn
CUISSON : 10 mn

POUR 6 PERSONNES
- 2 foies d'agneau
- 2 cœurs d'agneau
- Ris d'agneau
- Vin blanc
- 1 c. à soupe d'huile d'olive
- Ail
- Persil
- Sel, poivre

NOTRE CONSEIL
Accompagner de pommes vapeur.

FRESSURE D'AGNEAU OU DE CABRI

Couper en dés les foies, cœurs et ris d'agneaux, et les faire revenir à l'huile bien chaude.

En fin de cuisson, saupoudrer d'un hachis d'ail et de persil.

Bien mélanger.

Saler, poivrer.

Déglacer avec un verre de vin blanc.

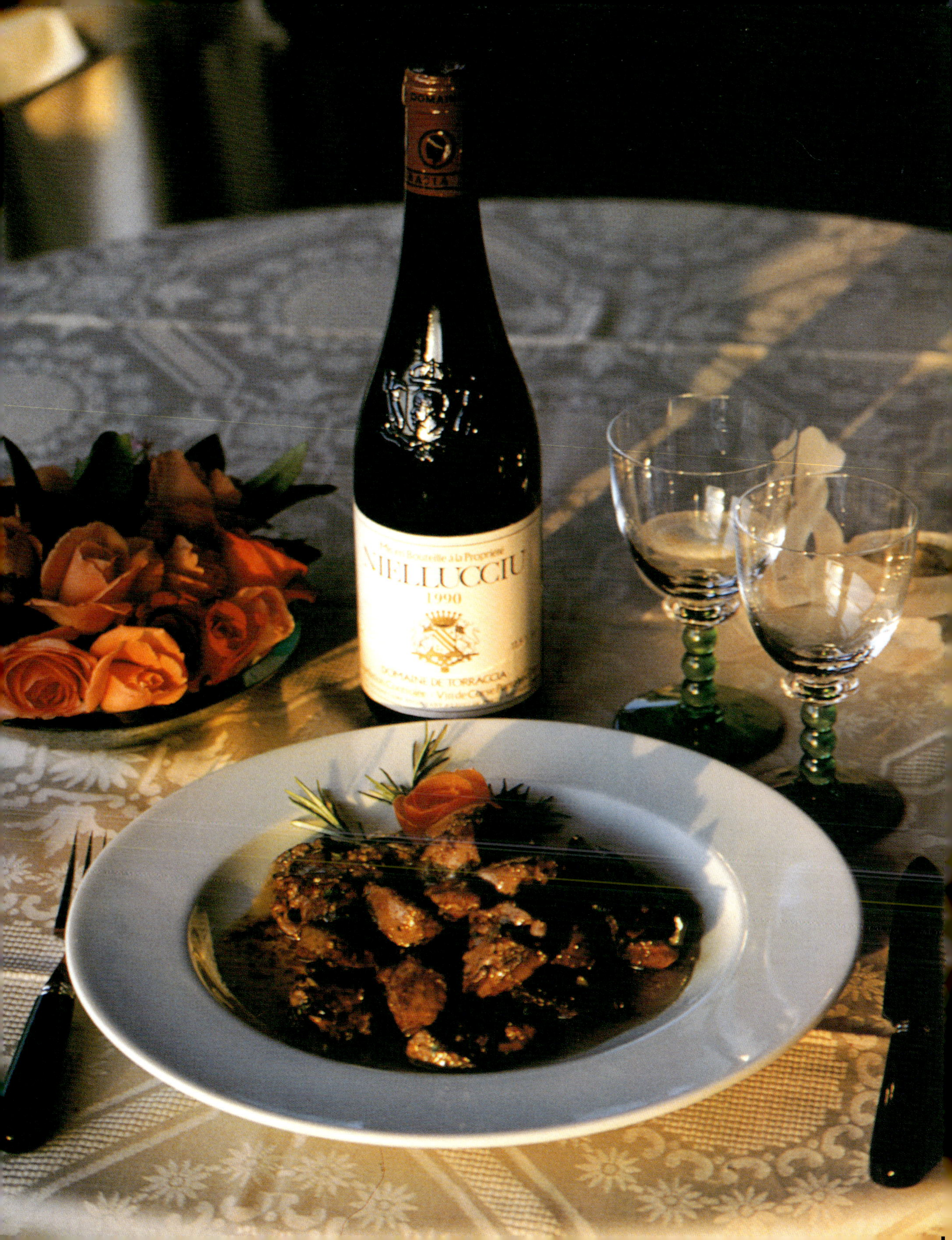
MELLUCCIU
1990
DOMAINE DE TORRACCIA

VOLAILLES ET GIBIERS

PRÉPARATION : 10 mn
CUISSON : 50 mn

POUR 6 PERSONNES
12 merles
200 g riz
Coulis de tomates (p. 6)
Huile d'olive
Oignon
Eau
Sel, poivre

NOTRE CONSEIL
Dresser le riz sur un plat, disposer les merles autour avec une garniture de croûtons grillés.

MERLES AU RIZ

Plumer, vider les merles, couper les pattes et le bec. Faire rissoler dans un peu d'huile avec sel et poivre. Les retirer et les garder au chaud.

Dans cette même huile faire rissoler les oignons hachés et mouiller au coulis de tomates.

Remettre les merles et couvrir d'eau à hauteur des merles.

Laiser mijoter 30 mn, retirer les merles et faire cuire le riz dans cette préparation, environ 18 mn.

Ajouter les merles en fin de cuisson et servir.

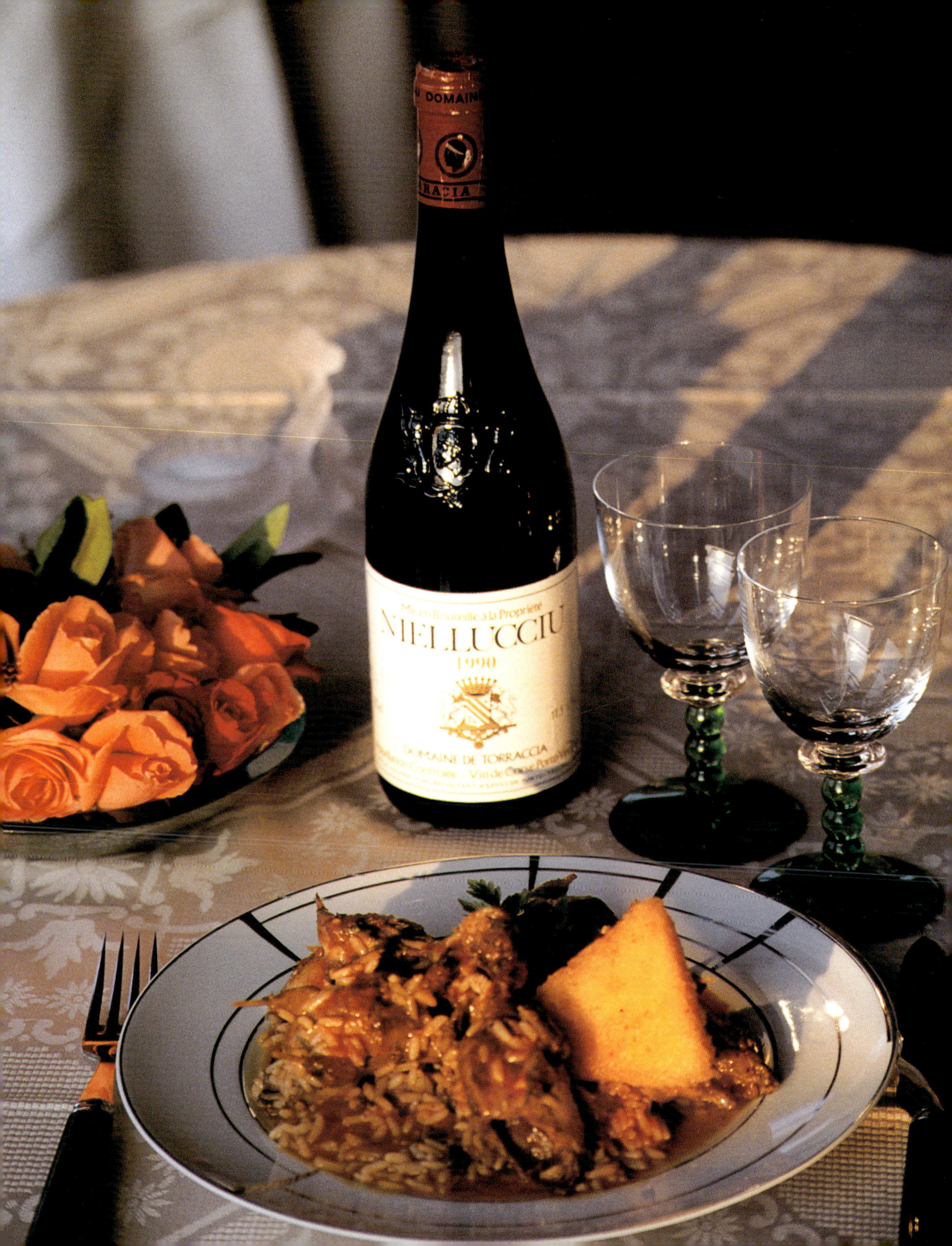
Mis en Bouteille à la Propriété
NIELLUCCIU
1990
DOMAINE DE TORRACCIA

VOLAILLES ET GIBIERS

PRÉPARATION : 5 mn
CUISSON : 15 mn

POUR 6 PERSONNES
18 merles
Lard ou gras de jambon
Sel, poivre

NOTRE CONSEIL
Accompagner de pommes paille.

MERLES GRILLÉS AU FEU DE BOIS

Plumer les merles sans les vider.

Les embrocher et les faire griller à la braise, au-dessus d'un feu de sarments. Les tourner fréquemment. Saler, poivrer.

Envelopper un morceau de lard dans du papier absorbant.

Au moment de servir, faire rôtir le lard, et faire couler le jus de cuisson sur les merles.

Servir chaud.

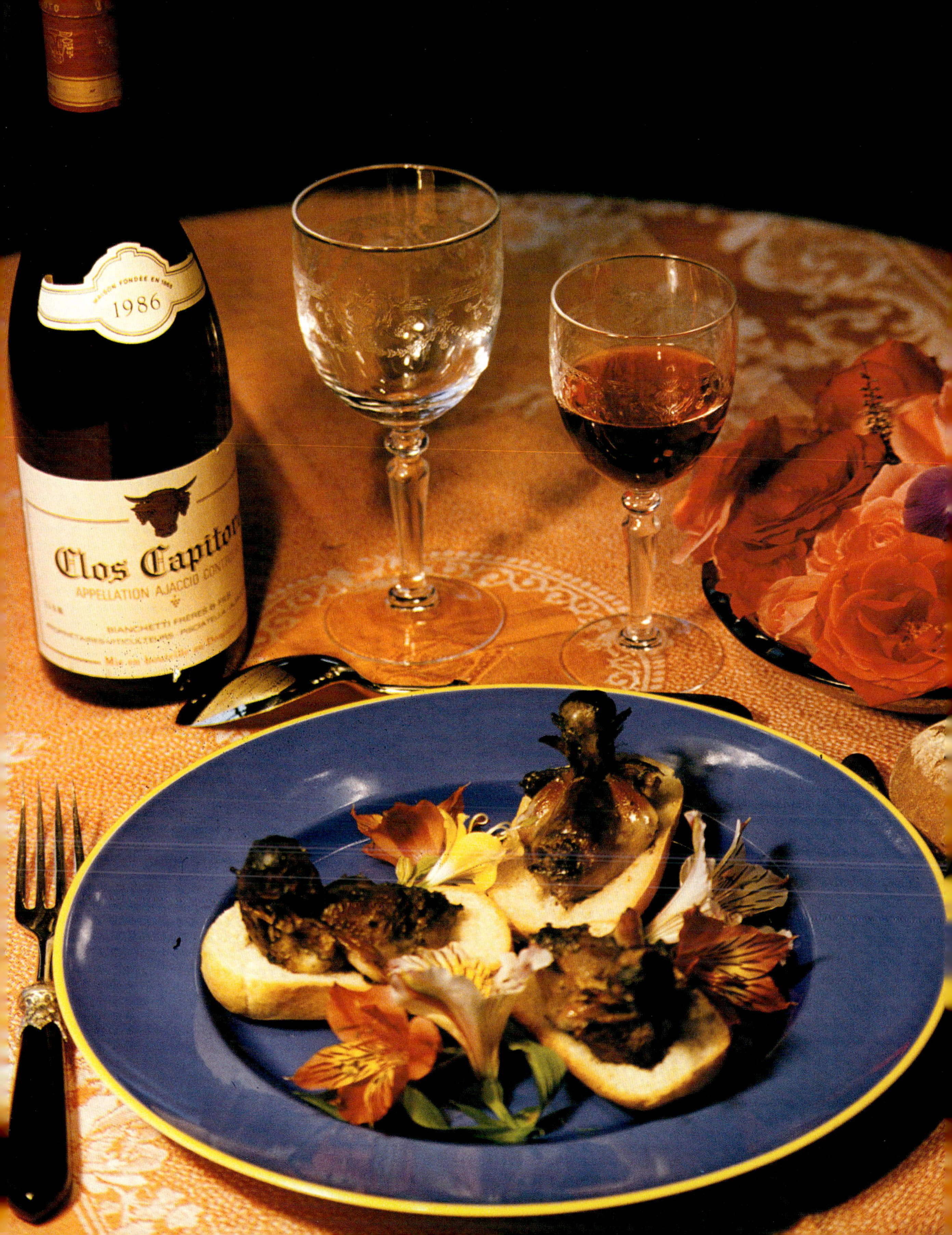
1986
APPELLATION AJACCIO

VOLAILLES ET GIBIERS

MARINADES : 2 JOURS
PRÉPARATION : 40 mn
CUISSON : 2 à 3 h

POUR 6 PERSONNES
1 kg 800 sanglier
4 oignons
4 carottes
Thym, laurier, genièvre, romarin
3 l de vin
Coulis de tomates (p. 6)
4 gousses d'ail
Sel, poivre

NOTRE CONSEIL
Servir avec des pâtes fraîches.

CIVET DE SANGLIER

Prendre un sanglier frais coupé en morceaux un peu épais.

Préparer une marinade avec du bon vin rouge, de l'oignon émincé, des feuilles de laurier, du romarin, du thym, du genièvre et quelques carottes coupées en dés. Laisser mariner au moins 2 jours.

Mettre les morceaux de sanglier marinés dans une passoire, bien égoutter.

Les faire rissoler dans une cocotte avec de l'huile, puis les disposer dans un plat.

Faire dorer de l'oignon, un peu d'ail haché et ajouter les morceaux de sanglier, sel, poivre, sauce tomate, et enfin la marinade passée au tamis.

Laisser cuire 2 à 3 h à petit feu.

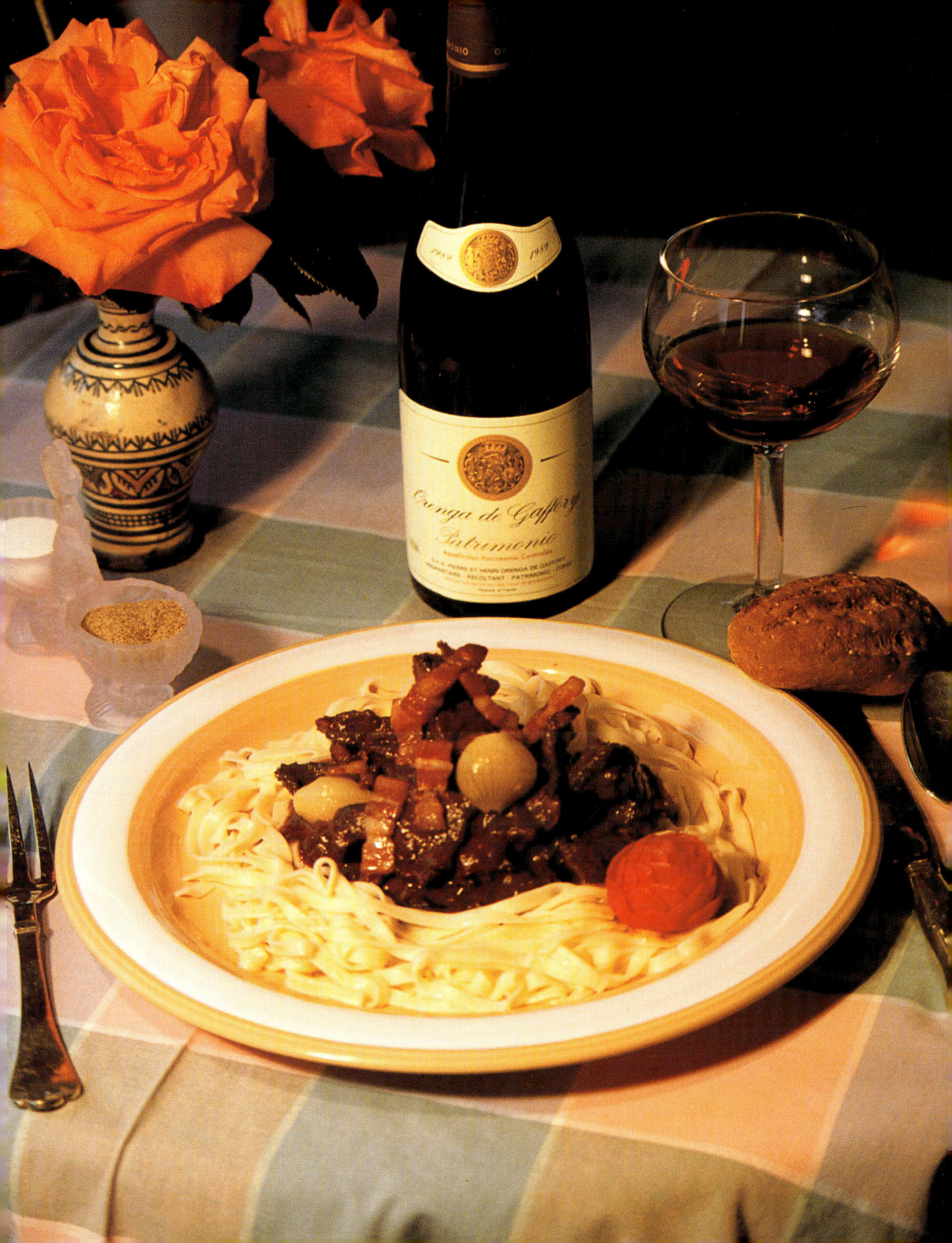
1989
1989
Orenga de Gaffory
Patrimonio

VOLAILLES ET GIBIERS

PRÉPARATION : 15 mn
CUISSON : 2 h

POUR 6 PERSONNES
6 pigeons ramiers
4 l d'eau
3 poireaux
12 carottes
3 gousses d'ail
1 oignon
2 tomates
Thym, laurier, 1 branche de céleri
Sel, poivre

NOTRE CONSEIL
Pigeons entourés de leurs légumes et le bouillon à part.

POT AU FEU DE PIGEONS RAMIERS

Mettre les pigeons dans une marmite en terre contenant 4 l d'eau froide.

Porter à ébullition, en écumant fréquemment.

Saler, et ajouter les légumes, les aromates.

Écumer à nouveau.

Couvrir et laisser mijoter au coin du feu pendant 2 h.

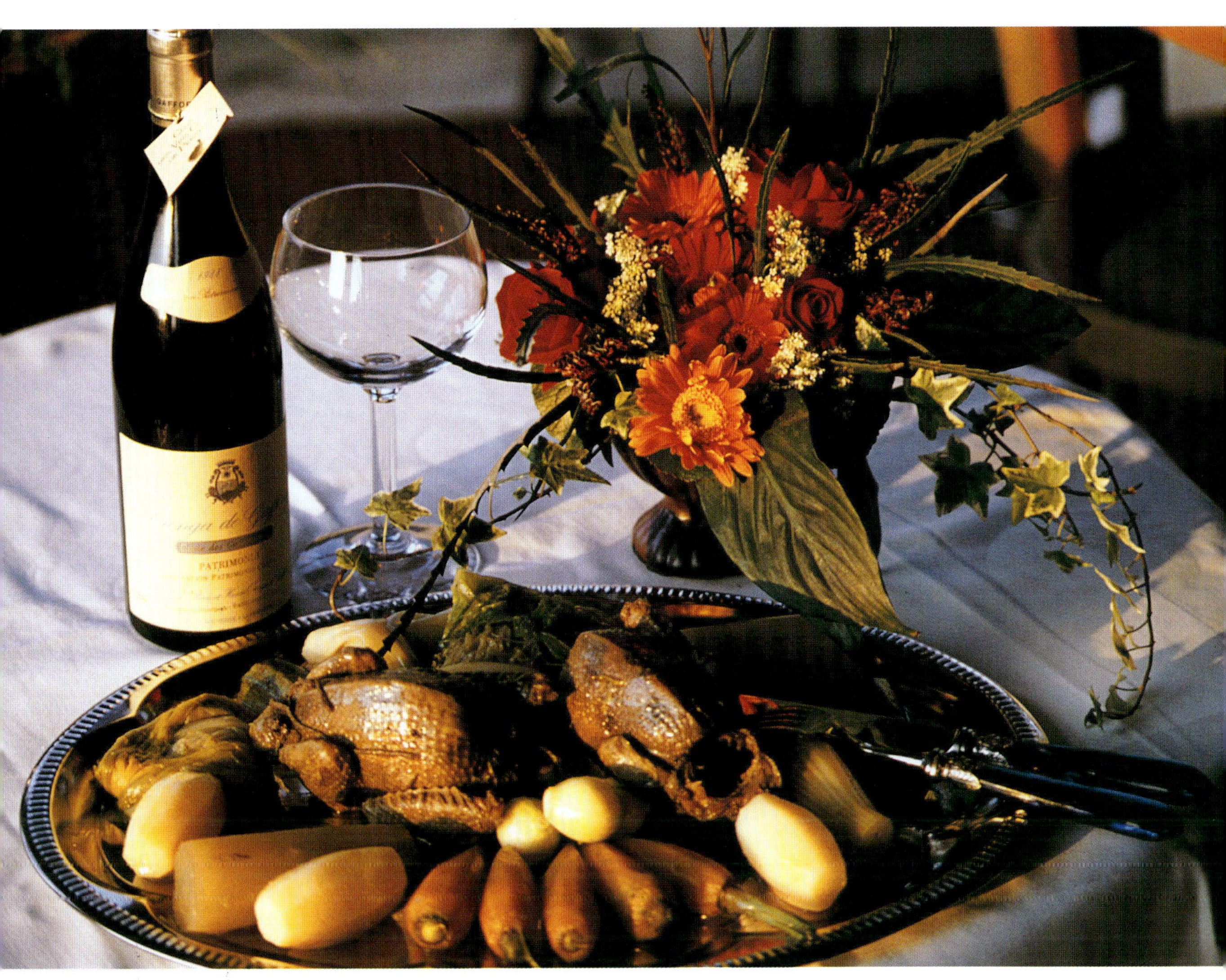

PRÉPARATION : 30 mn
CUISSON : 1 h 20

POUR 6 PERSONNES
1 coq de 1 kg à 2 kg
200 g de petits oignons
120 g de lardons
2 gousses d'ail
Laurier, thym, romarin
Huile, sel, poivre
Cèpes de montagne (1 poignée)
1 l de vin rouge
1 verre d'eau de vie

NOTRE CONSEIL
Verser en plat creux et garnir de croûtons frits au beurre.

COQ AU VIN

Détailler le coq en 8 morceaux, et faire bien revenir à l'huile dans une poêle. Retirer la viande et la mettre à égoutter. Dans la même huile, faire dorer les lardons et les petits oignons. Égoutter avec la viande.

Dans un sautoir, placer la viande, les lardons et les petits oignons. Verser l'eau de vie et flamber.

Déglacer la poêle avec 1 l de vin rouge et porter à ébullition. Verser dans le sautoir avec l'ail haché, le laurier, thym, romarin. Saler et poivrer. Ajouter 3 dl d'eau et laisser mijoter 1 h 15.

Ajouter les cèpes de montagne, préalablement blanchis 1/4 d'heure avant la fin de la cuisson.

Note : un sautoir est une sauteuse. Les deux expressions s'utilisent.

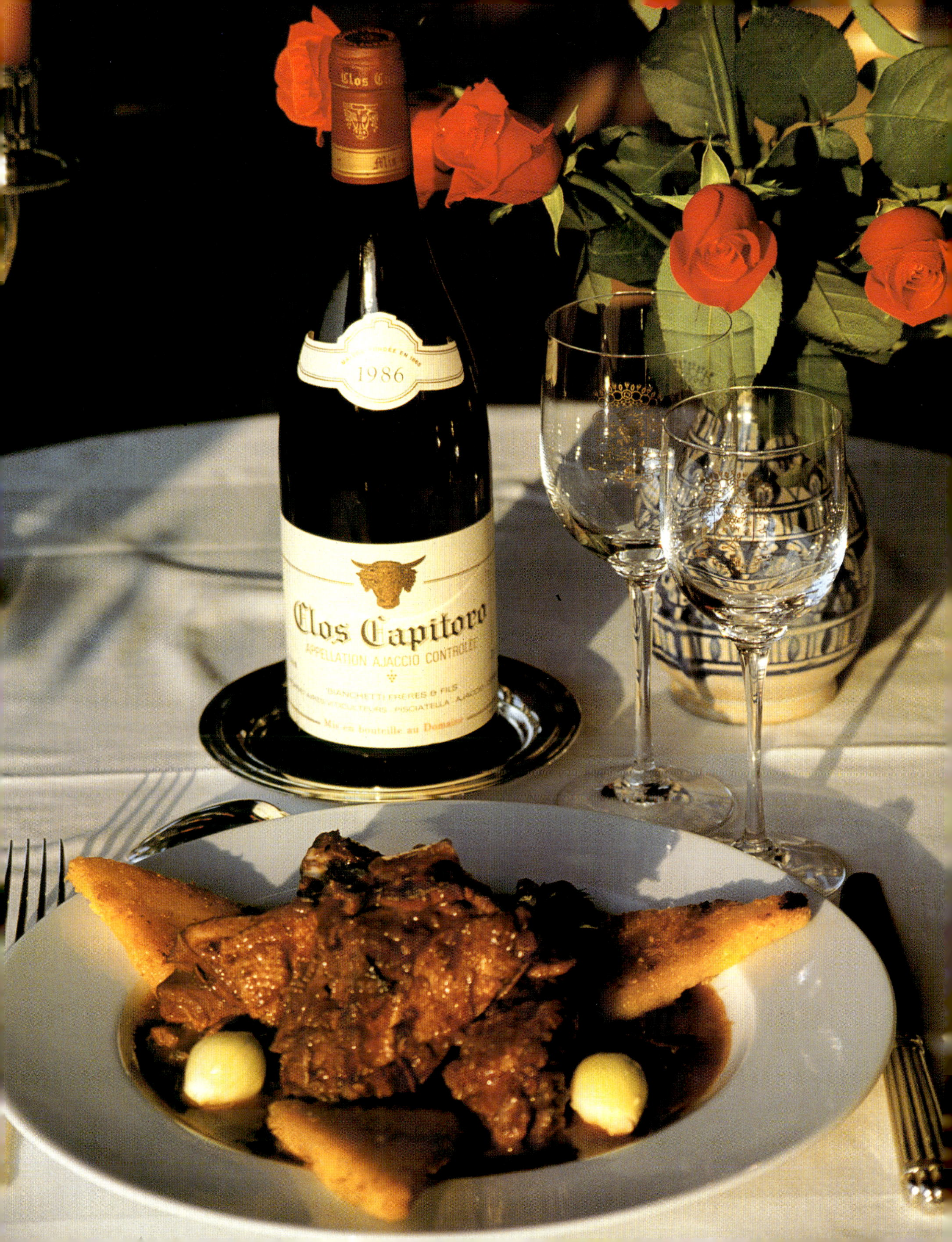
1986
Clos Capitoro
APPELLATION AJACCIO CONTROLÉE
Mis en bouteille au Domaine

PRÉPARATION : 1 h
CUISSON : 50 mn

POUR 6 PERSONNES
12 artichauts
1 kg de brocciu (fromage frais de brebis)
Sel, poivre, chapelure
Persil haché, ail
Coulis de tomates

NOTRE CONSEIL
On peut faire cuire ce plat au four.

ARTICHAUTS FARCIS AU BROCCIU

Parer les artichauts enlevant quelques feuilles. Couper les pointes. Retirer le foin. Les blanchir, refroidir et égoutter.

Préparer la farce.

Mettre le brocciu dans une terrine. À l'aide d'une spatule en bois, battre la pâte, y incorporer le persil haché, l'ail, le sel et le poivre.

Farcir les artichauts jusqu'à hauteur, les rouler dans la chapelure et les faire dorer côté farce dans un peu d'huile. Les placer dans une cocotte légèrement huilée.

Ajouter la sauce tomate et couvrir d'eau jusqu'à mi-hauteur.

Laisser cuire 45 mn à feu doux.

Servir chaud.

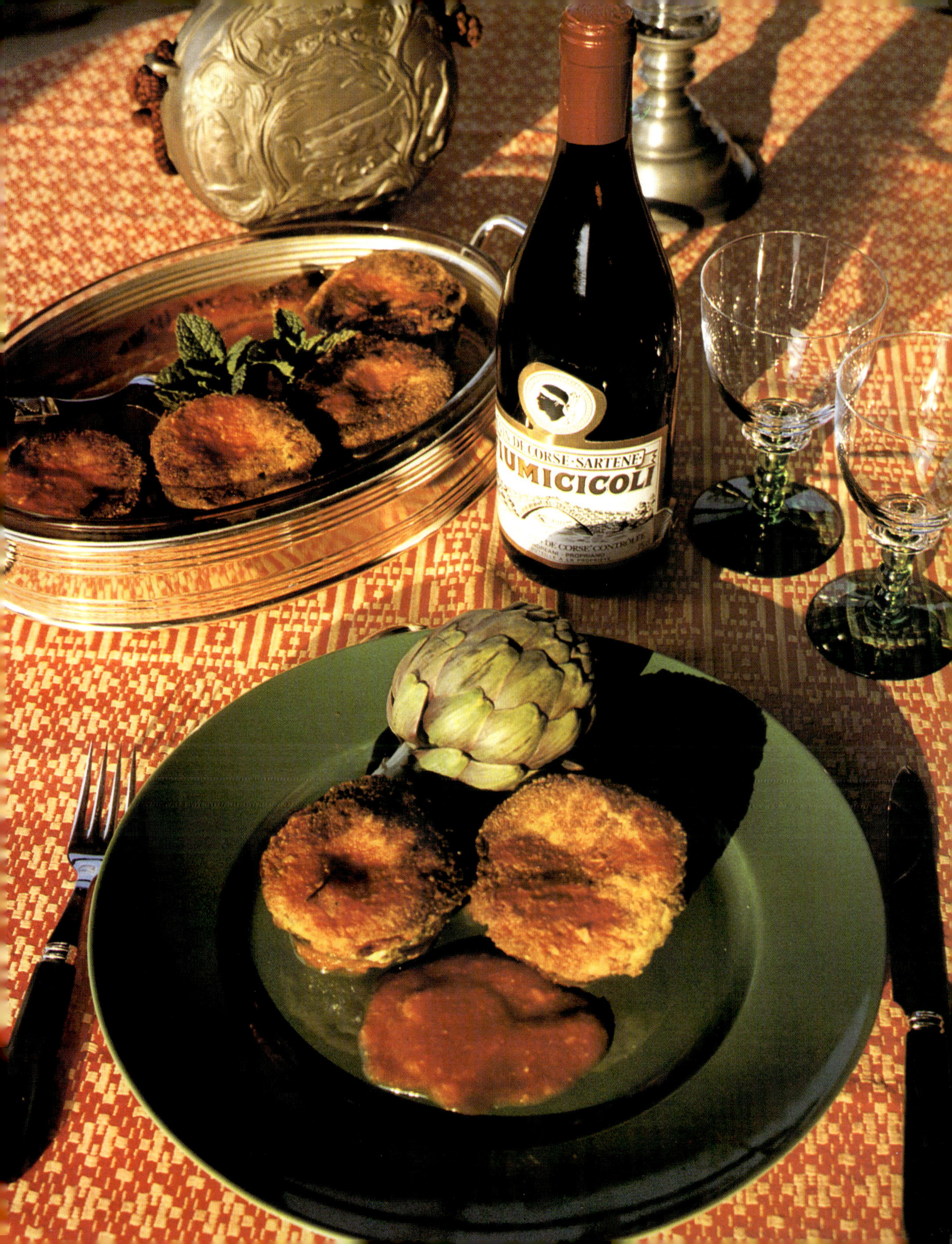
DE CORSE·SARTENE·
UMICICOLI
DE CORSE CONTROLEE
PROPRIANO

PRÉPARATION : 20 mn
CUISSON : 35 mn

POUR 6 PERSONNES
4 tomates
4 poivrons
4 oignons

POUR LA FARCE
600 g de viande hachée (moitié porc moitié veau)
Sel, poivre
Mie de pain trempée dans du lait
2 œufs
Persil
2 gousses d'ail hachées
Huile d'olive

NOTRE CONSEIL
On peut servir en même temps une sauce tomate bien relevée.

PETITS LÉGUMES FARCIS À LA VIANDE

Couper les tomates, faire un chapeau, les vider et faire de même avec les poivrons et les oignons.

Préparer la farce : Mettre dans une terrine la viande hachée, la mie de pain trempée dans le lait, sel, poivre, l'ail, le persil.

Bien mélanger.

Farcir les légumes. Les disposer sur une plaque huilée, puis faire cuire à feu doux.

Servir chaud.

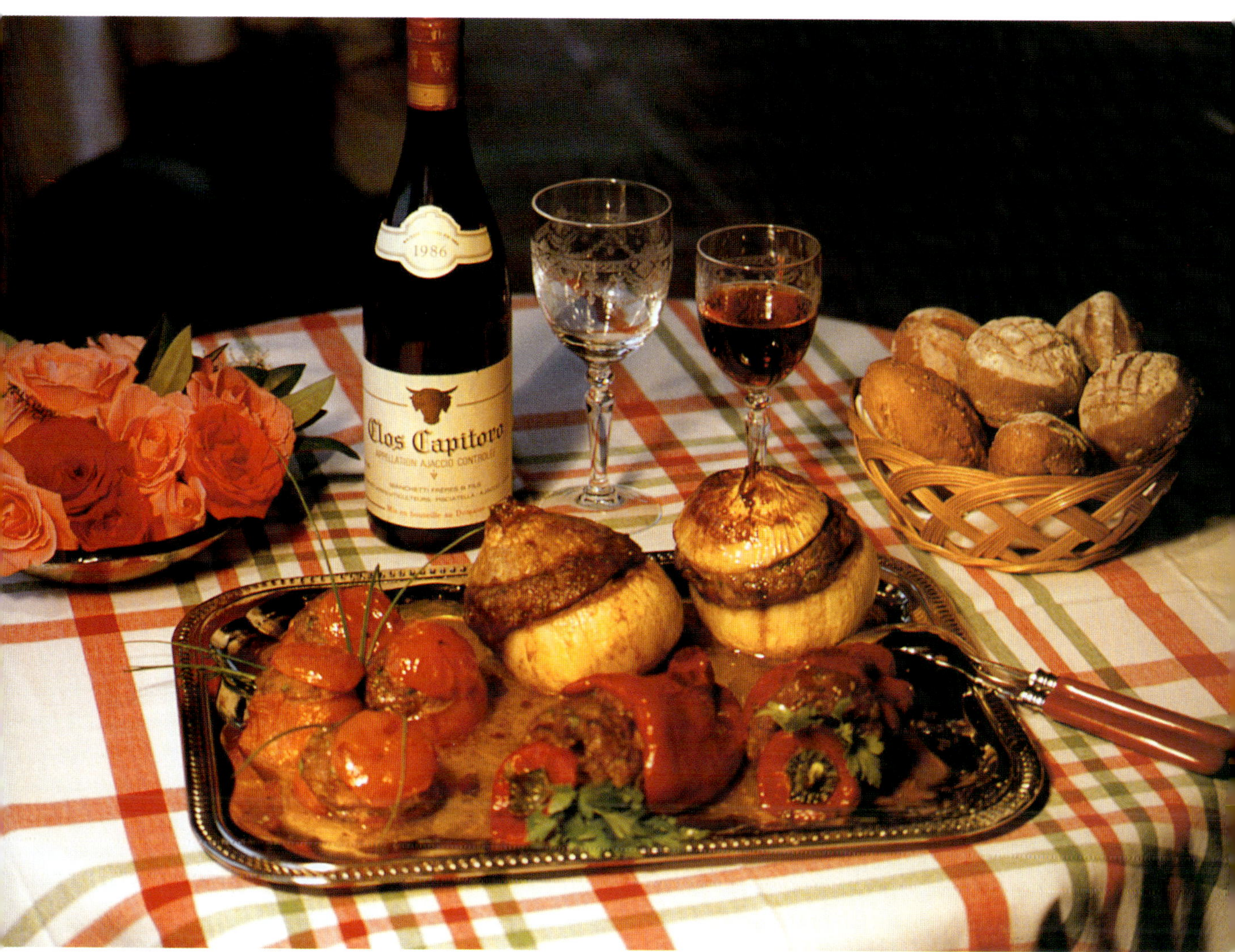
1986
Clos Capitoro
APPELLATION AJACCIO CONTROLEE

PÂTES ET LÉGUMES

PRÉPARATION : 10 mn
CUISSON : 30 mn

POUR 6 PERSONNES
1 kg d'épinards ou de blettes
1 kg de brocciu
2 œufs
30 feuilles de menthe
Sel, poivre
1 oignon
Ail, persil
Coulis de tomates (p. 6)
Fond de veau lié

NOTRE CONSEIL
Servir bien chaud avec le coulis de tomates.

QUENELLES D'ÉPINARDS OU DE BLETTES AU BROCCIU

Faire bouillir les épinards (ou blettes), les égoutter, les hacher et mélanger avec le brocciu.

Saler et poivrer, ajouter les œufs, l'ail, le persil, la menthe ciselée, l'oignon.

Préparer des boulettes de la grosseur d'une noix sur une planche farinée. Jeter ces boulettes dans une marmite d'eau salée.

Dès qu'elles remontent à la surface, les égoutter sur un papier absorbant et les placer dans un plat allant au four en ajoutant le jus de viande.

Faire mijoter et gratiner au four.

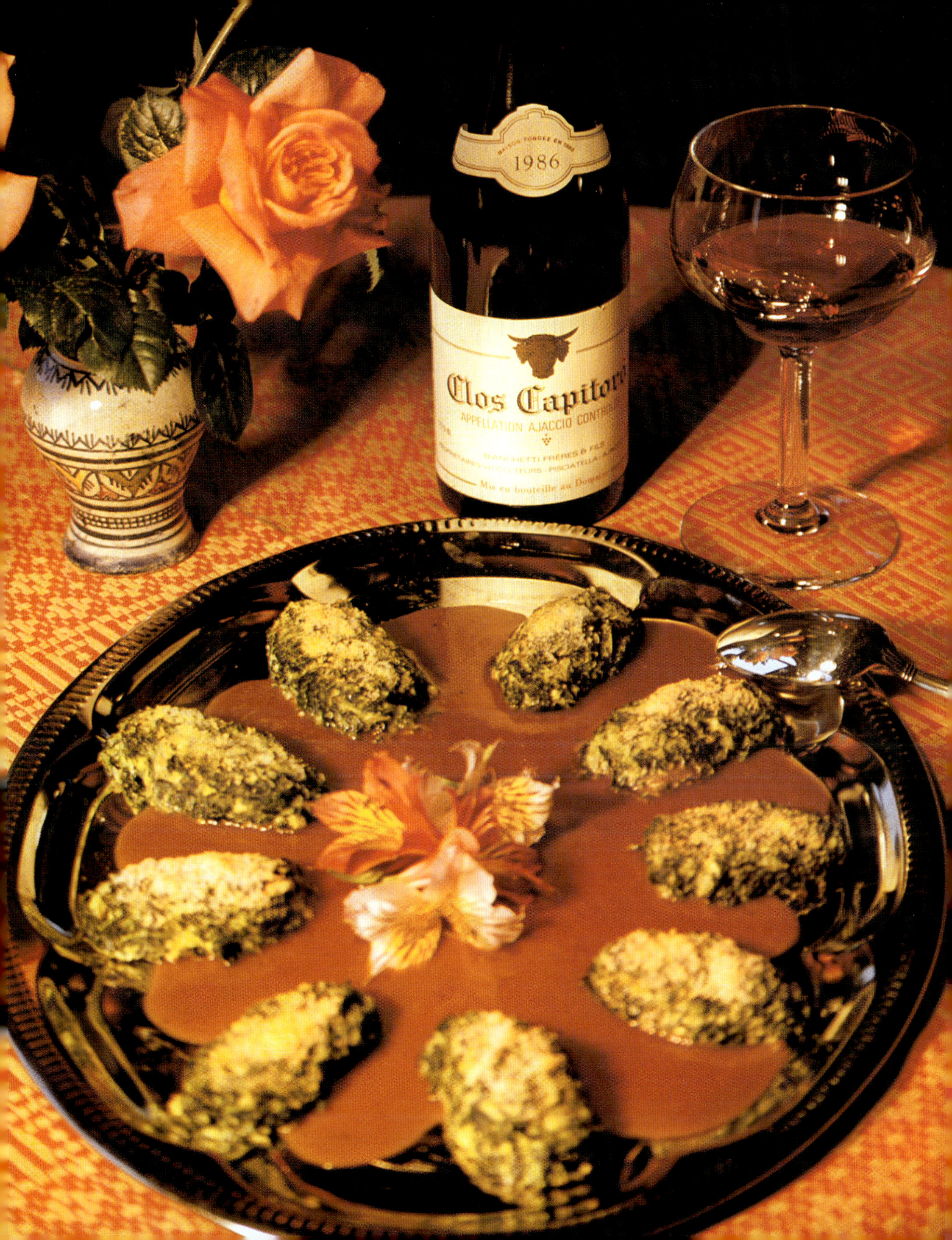
1986

LENTILLES À LA VULETTA

PRÉPARATION : 10 mn
CUISSON : 45 mn

POUR 6 PERSONNES
500 g de lentilles
1 vuletta (joue de cochon fumée)
1 oignon
3 gousses d'ail
Sel, poivre
Laurier, thym
Coulis de tomates (p. 6)

NOTRE CONSEIL
Faire cuire les lentilles 10 mn à l'eau salée. Jeter l'eau. Les rafraîchir à l'eau froide avant la cuisson définitive.

Faire cuire les lentilles à l'eau froide. Les saler légèrement et les égoutter.

Couper la vuletta en tranches et faire dorer dans un faitout en fonte.

Ajouter l'oignon et l'ail haché.

Déglacer au coulis de tomates et laisser mijoter 1/4 d'heure.

Incorporer le tout aux lentilles et bien mélanger.

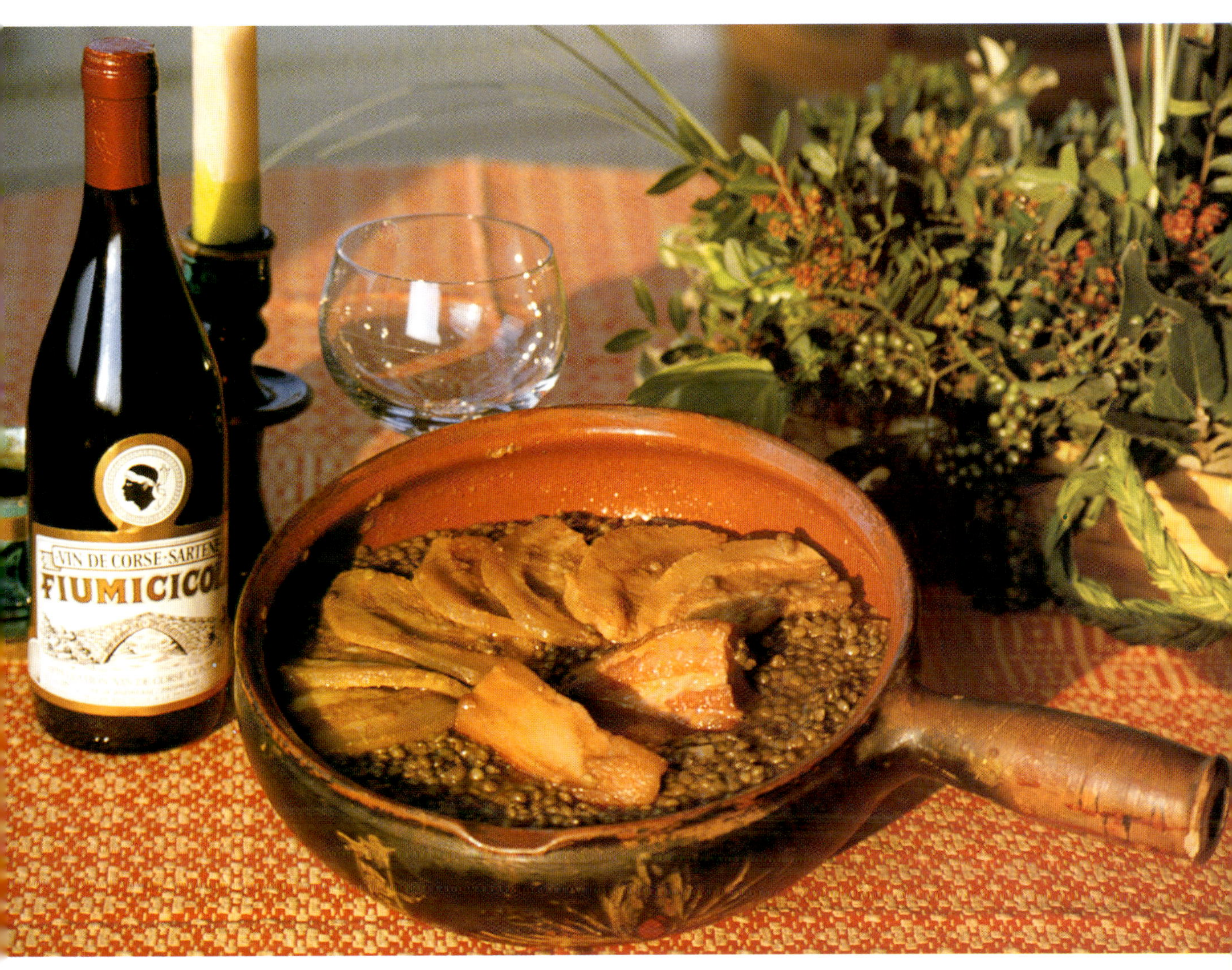
VIN DE CORSE·SARTE
FIUMICICO

PRÉPARATION : 15 mn
CUISSON : 20 mn

POUR 6 PERSONNES
6 courgettes

POUR LA FARCE
500 g de brocciu
2 œufs
Persil
Chapelure
Huile d'olive
Sel, poivre

NOTRE CONSEIL
Vous pouvez également ajouter à la farce, la chair des courgettes. Elles n'en auront que plus de saveur.

COURGETTES FARCIES AU BROCCIU

Couper les extrémités des courgettes. Les faire blanchir dans de l'eau bouillante salée, puis les égoutter. Les évider délicatement avec une cuillère.

Préparer la farce : Écraser le brocciu. Ajouter les œufs, le persil haché, saler poivrer.

Remplir les courgettes de cette farce. Parsemer de chapelure.

Disposer les courgettes dans un plat à gratin huilé, et mettre à four moyen (180°) pendant 20 mn.

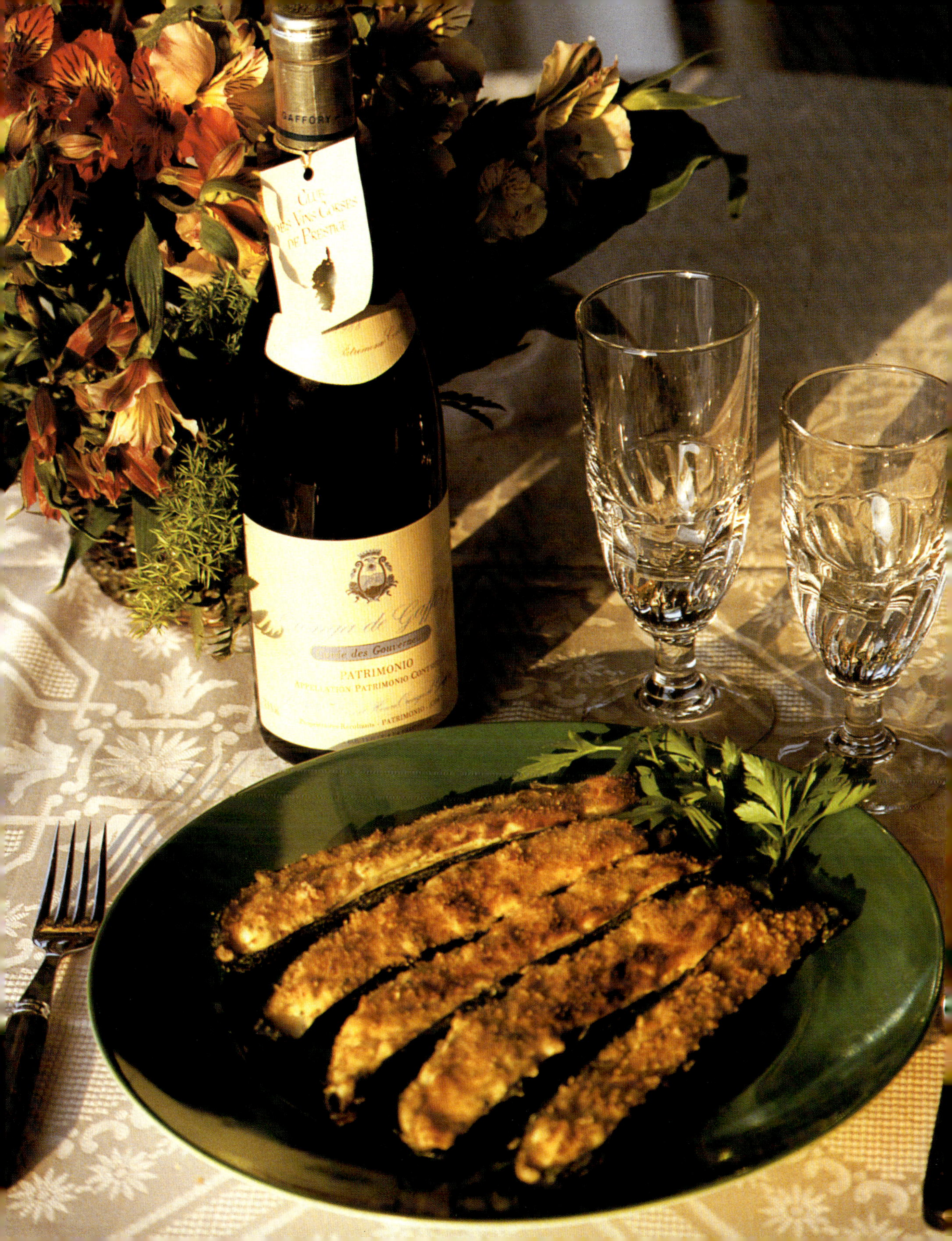
CLUB DES VINS CORSES DE PRESTIGE
PATRIMONIO

PRÉPARATION : 30 mn
CUISSON : 2 h 30

POUR 6 PERSONNES
500 g de haricots Soissons
Échine de porc
Poitrine fumée
Coulis de tomates (p. 6)
Oignons
Ail, sel, poivre, laurier

NOTRE CONSEIL
Tenir compte de la durée de la préparation.

HARICOTS SOISSONS AUX CÈPES DE MONTAGNE

Faire tremper les haricots pendant 24 h à l'eau froide, les rincer puis les recouvrir d'eau froide, et les amener à ébullition. Les égoutter et les remettre à cuire à feu doux avec de l'eau salée.

Pendant ce temps, dans la poitrine fumée, tailler des lardons et les faire revenir dans une poêle, ensuite les égoutter.

Dans l'échine, tailler des dés d'environ 2 cm puis les faire revenir dans la même huile que les lardons. Une fois bien dorés, les égoutter.

Déglacer la poêle avec 2 louches d'eau de cuisson des haricots et mettre de côté.

Dans une marmite assez grande, faire revenir les oignons finement hachés à l'huile d'olive, l'ail et la viande. Ajouter le laurier. Bien remuer, puis mettre le coulis de tomates. Saler et poivrer.

Puis verser les haricots déjà à mi-cuisson dans cette préparation et couvrir avec l'eau de cuisson. Ajouter les champignons (cueillis et séchés sur place) mis à tremper la veille et préalablement blanchis.

Laisser mijoter une demi-heure.

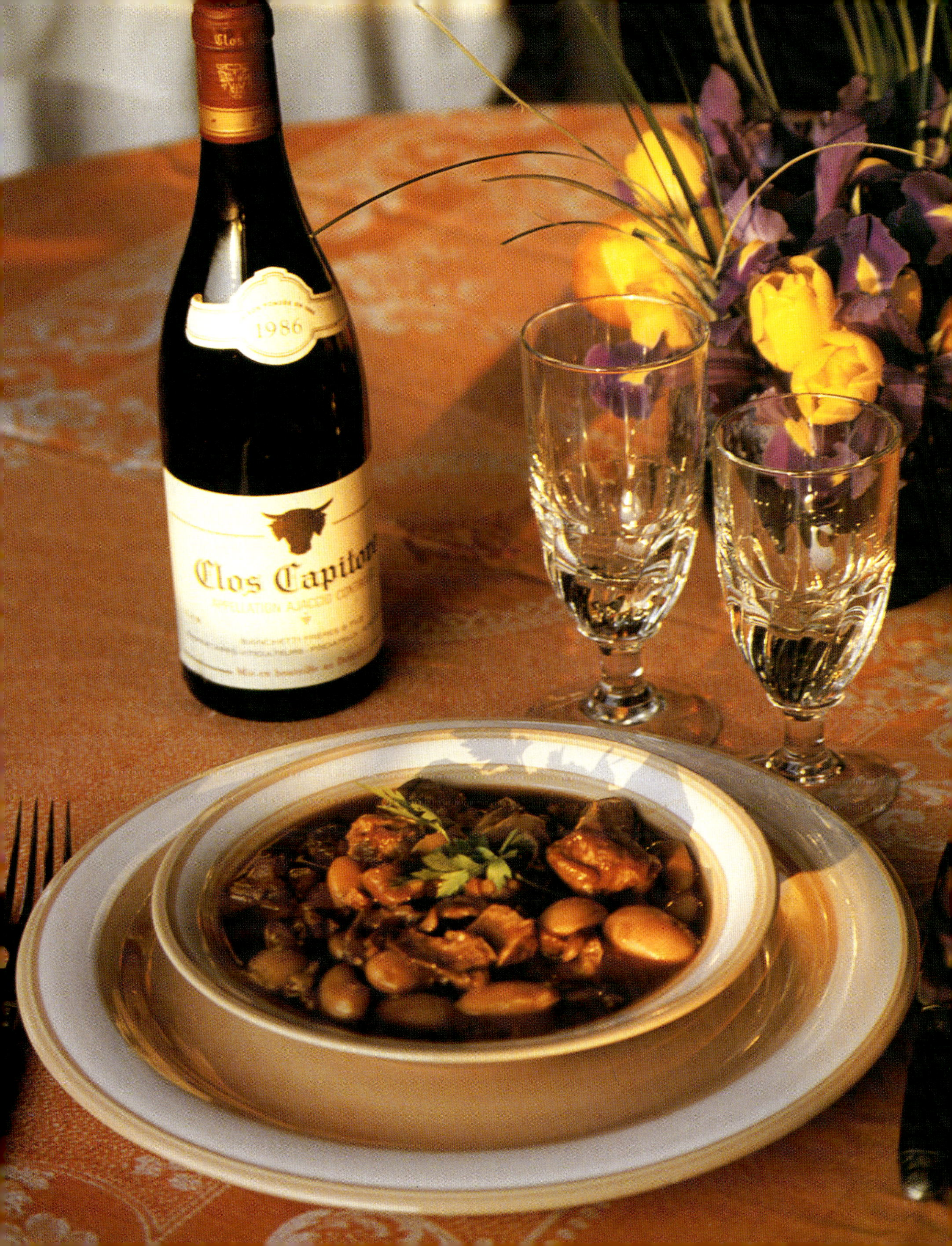
Clos
1986
Clos Capito

PÂTES ET LÉGUMES

PRÉPARATION : 10 mn
CUISSON : 20 mn

POUR 6 PERSONNES
1 kg 500 de farine de châtaignes
1 l 1/2 d'eau
Sel

NOTRE CONSEIL
Servir avec du brocciu frais, du figatellu grillé, et des œufs au plat.

POLENTA À LA FARINE DE CHÂTAIGNES

Tamiser la farine de châtaignes.

Mettre de l'eau à bouillir et la saler.

Au premier bouillon, verser la farine, et la délayer avec un bâton de châtaignier très sec, pour éviter la formation de grumeaux.

La faire cuire à feu doux jusqu'à l'obtention d'une bouillie épaisse.

La polenta est prête lorsqu'elle forme une boule et qu'elle se détache des côtés de la casserole.

En renverser le contenu sur un linge blanc, saupoudré de farine.

Diviser la boule de polenta en quatre, puis en tranches à l'aide d'un fil.

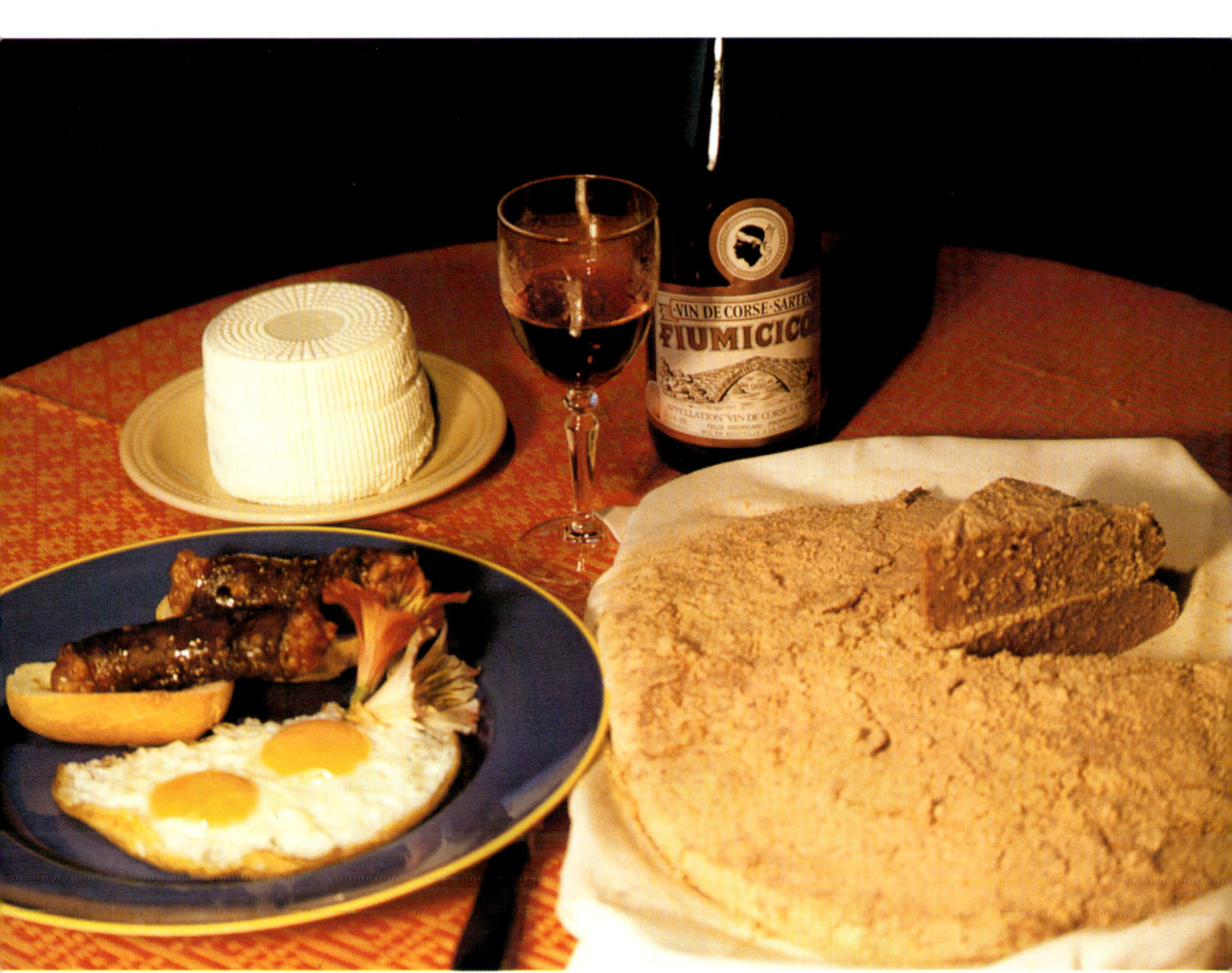
VIN DE CORSE
FIUMICIC

PÂTES ET LÉGUMES

PRÉPARATION : 15 mn
CUISSON : 1 h

POUR 6 PERSONNES
800 g de veau
2 oignons
3 gousses d'ail
Persil, serpolet, laurier, girofle
Coulis de tomates (p. 6)
Sel, poivre
Macaronis

NOTRE CONSEIL
Faire blanchir les macaronis 3 mn avant de les jeter dans la marmite.

RAGOÛT DE MACARONIS

Couper la viande en gros dés, la faire revenir dans un peu d'huile avec un oignon émincé, ajouter l'ail, persil, serpolet hachés, le coulis de tomates, une feuille de laurier, un clou de girofle. Assaisonner.

Mouiller d'eau chaude pour obtenir une sauce longue.

Faire cuire à feu moyen.

Lorsque la viande est presque cuite, ajouter les macaronis qui doivent en cuisant absorber toute la sauce.

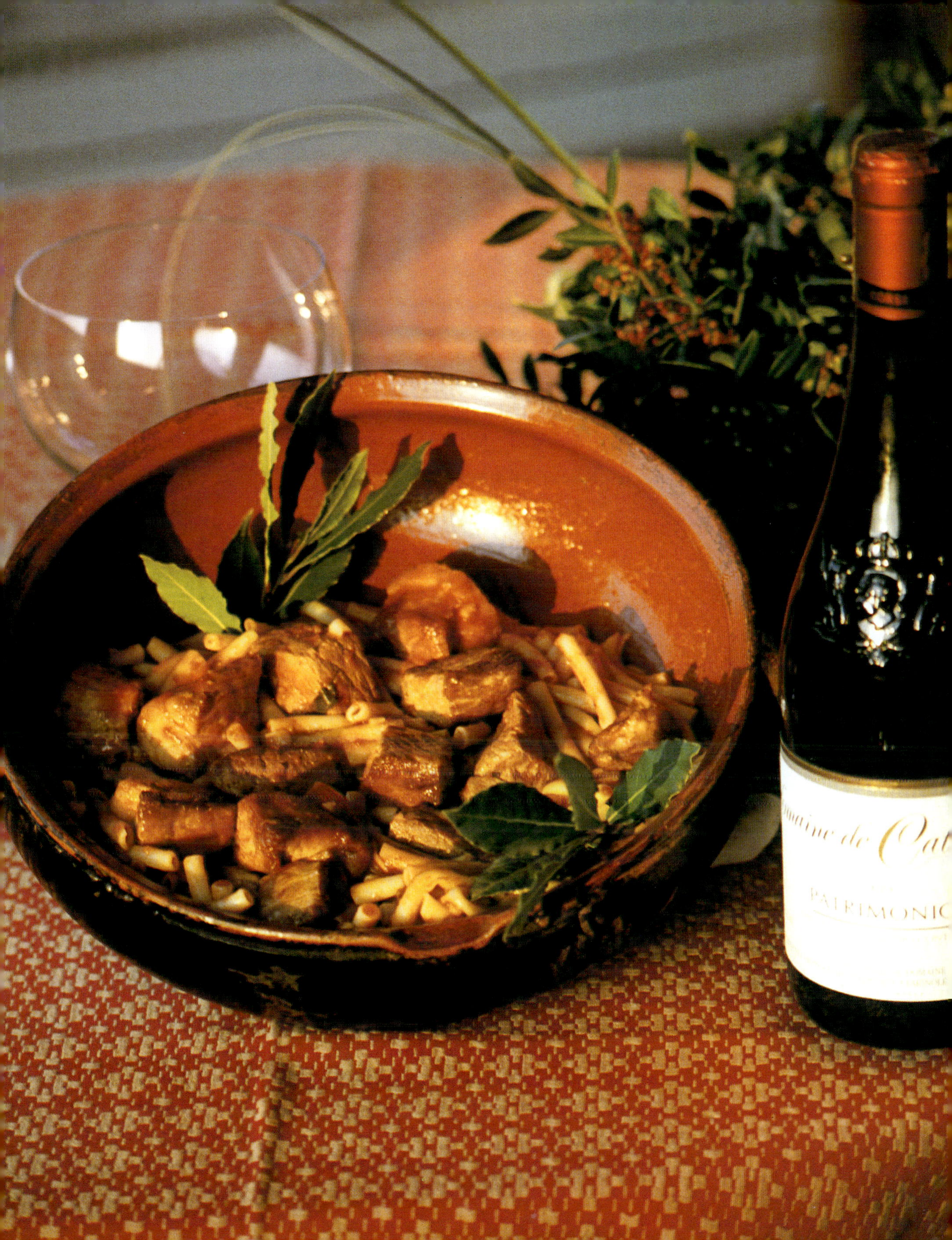

PÂTES ET LÉGUMES

PRÉPARATION : 30 mn
CUISSON : 15 mn

POUR 6 PERSONNES
Pâte à cannellonis
Coulis de tomates (p. 6)

POUR LA FARCE
1 kg de brocciu
600 g de blettes
5 œufs
Sel, poivre

NOTRE CONSEIL
Saupoudrer le plat de gruyère râpé pour faire gratiner au four.

CANNELLONIS AU BROCCIU

Préparer la farce : Écraser le brocciu à la fourchette et ajouter les œufs et les feuilles de blettes blanchies et hachées. Assaisonner.

Après avoir trempé la pâte achetée dans le commerce, placer la farce au milieu de cette pâte puis rouler.

Ranger les cannellonis dans un plat à gratin préalablement huilé ou beurré selon les goûts.

Napper d'une sauce tomate ou d'un jus de viande puis faire gratiner à four chaud pendant 1/4 h environ.

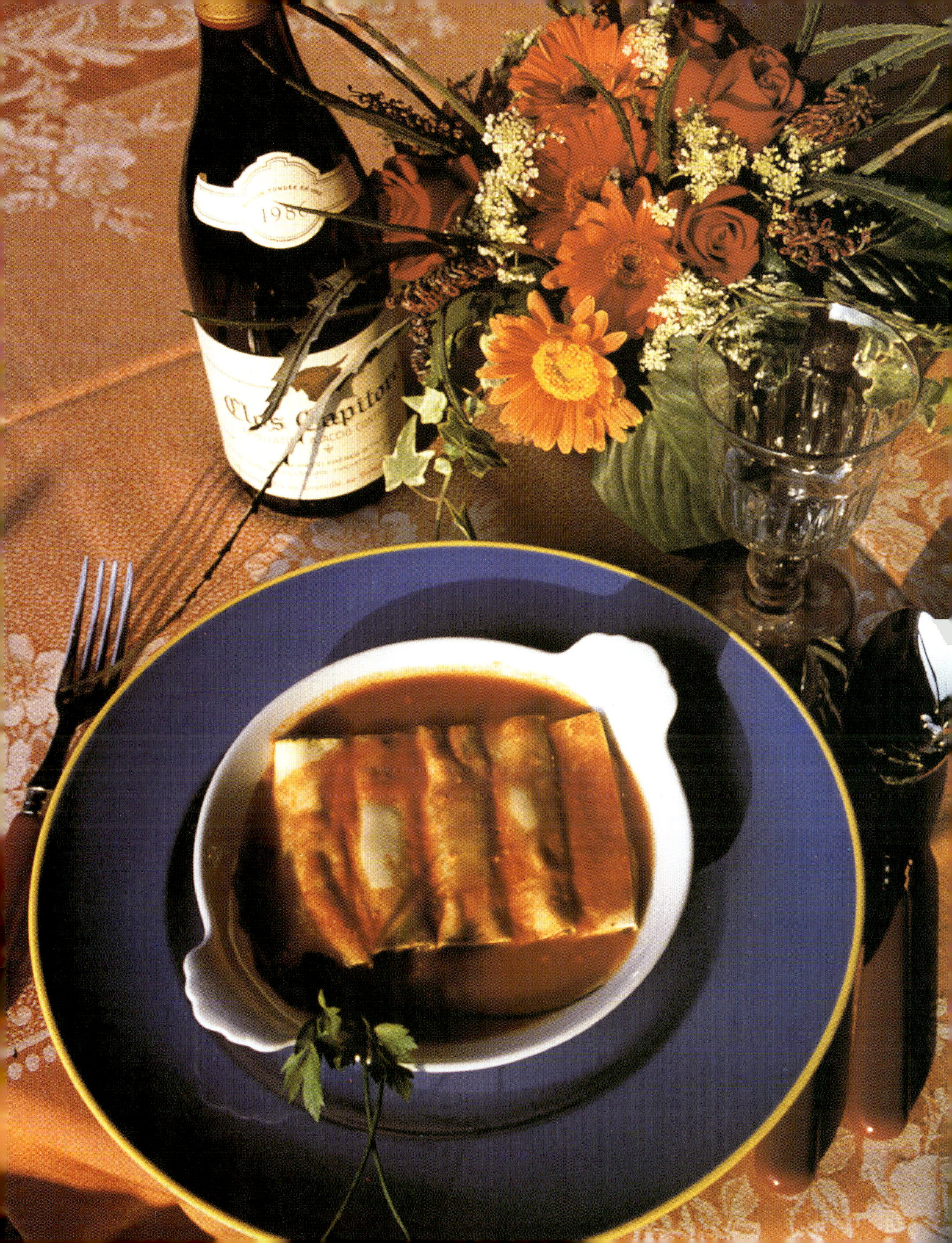

PRÉPARATION : 10 mn
CUISSON : 30 mn

POUR 8 PERSONNES
1 kg de brocciu
150 g de sucre
6 œufs
1 zeste d'orange
1 pincée de vanille en poudre

NOTRE CONSEIL
Servir tiède.

FIADONE

Mettre le brocciu dans une terrine. Ajouter les œufs, le sucre, le zeste d'orange et la vanille.

Mélanger longuement, puis verser la pâte dans un moule à bords hauts, huilé.

Enfourner à chaleur moyenne pendant 1/2 h.

Le fiadone doit être doré à la cuisson.

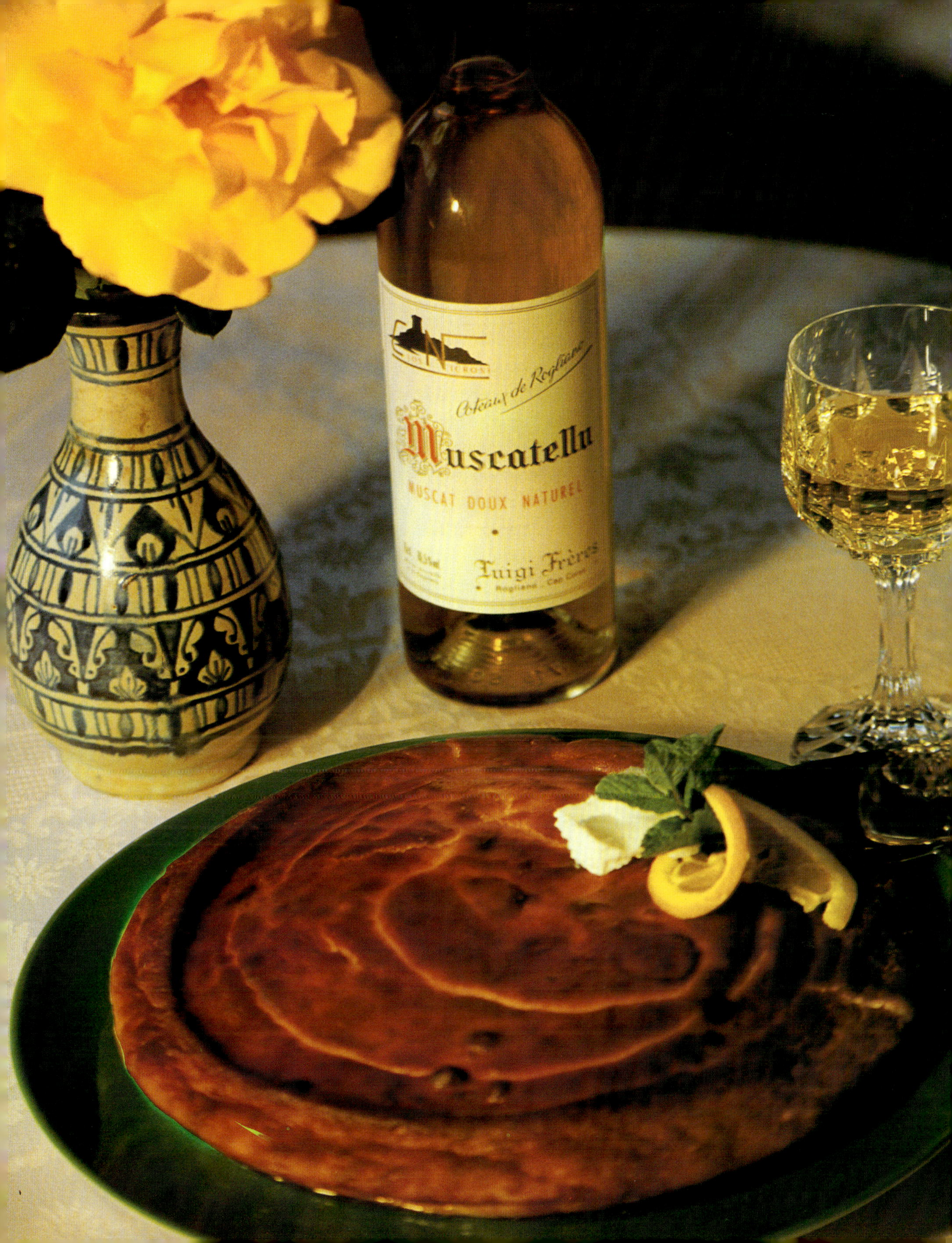
Coteaux de Rogliano
Muscatellu
MUSCAT DOUX NATUREL
Luigi Frères

PRÉPARATION : 25 mn
CUISSON : 15 mn

POUR 8 PERSONNES

Crème anglaise :
1 l de lait
10 jaunes d'œuf
250 g de sucre
1 pincée de vanille

NOTRE CONSEIL
Saupoudrer d'amandes ou de chocolat râpé.

ŒUFS À LA NEIGE

Faire bouillir le lait ; pendant ce temps casser les œufs en séparant les blancs des jaunes.

Disposer dans une terrine les jaunes, le sucre, la vanille. Battre jusqu'à coloration blanchâtre.

Verser le lait bouillant sur la préparation et bien remuer.

Remettre à feu doux.

À l'aide d'une spatule en bois, remuer sans cesse jusqu'à épaississement.

Retirer du feu et laisser refoidir.

Monter les blancs en neige bien fermes, les faire cuire dans de l'eau sucrée.

Dans un plat creux, mettre la crème anglaise et déposer les blancs dessus.

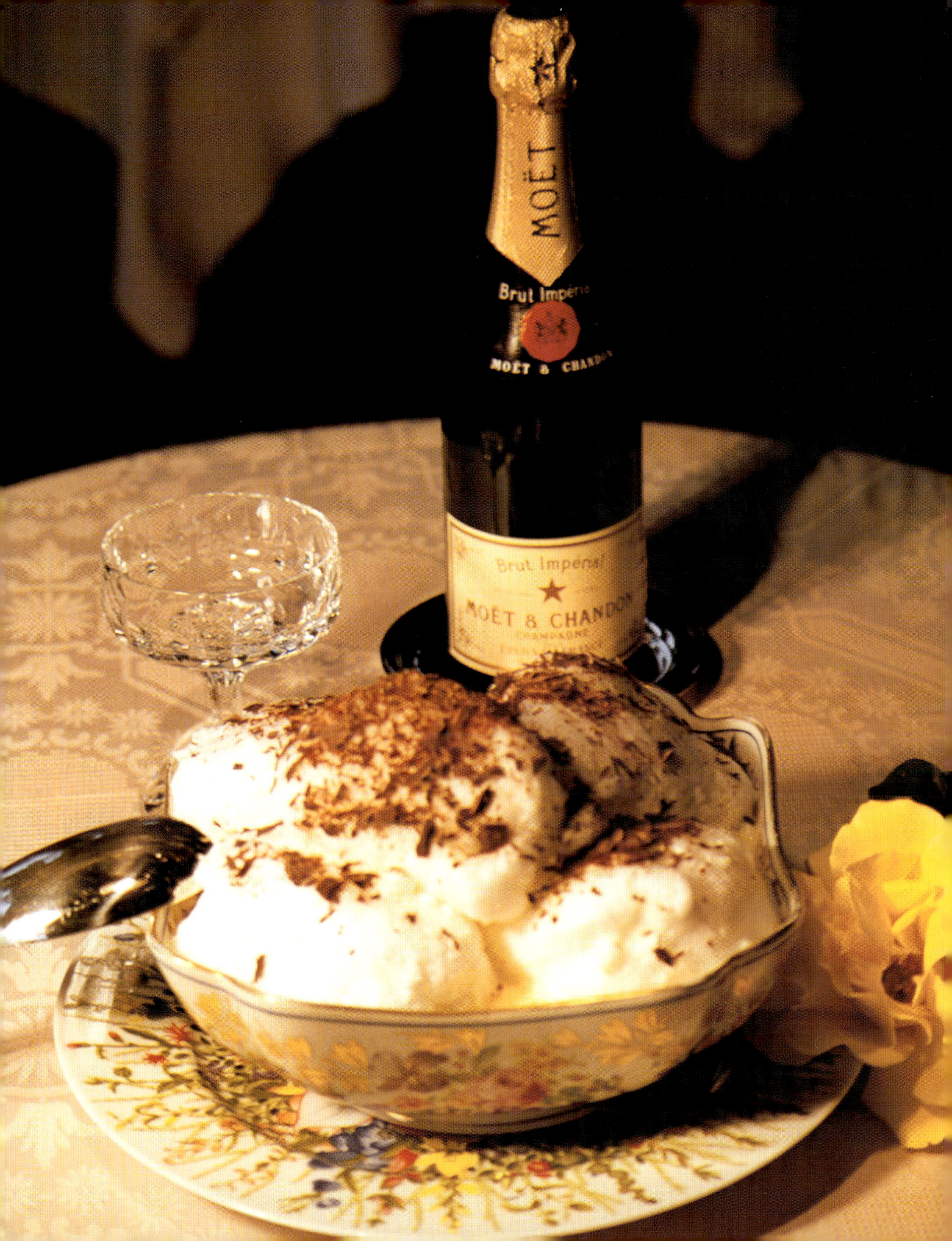
MOËT
MOËT & CHANDON
Brut Impérial
MOËT & CHANDON
CHAMPAGNE

PRÉPARATION : 25 mn
+ 2 h de repos pour la pâte
CUISSON : 10 mn

POUR 6 PERSONNES
500 g de farine
20 g de levure
2 c. à soupe d'huile
2 œufs
Beurre, crème fraîche
Sel
Zeste d'orange
Brocciu frais
Sucre en poudre
Huile pour friture

NOTRE CONSEIL
Ces beignets peuvent se servir à l'apéritif mais constituent aussi un excellent dessert.

BEIGNETS AU BROCCIU

Préparer un levain :

Délayer la levure dans un 1/2 verre d'eau tiède salée. Prélever 100 g de farine et mélanger à la levure délayée. Rouler en boule et laisser reposer 1 h environ dans un endroit tiède jusqu'à ce qu'elle soit doublée de volume.

Préparer des œufs, du beurre, de la crème fraîche, du sucre en poudre, du zeste d'orange.

Quand le levain est bien levé, mélanger le tout et pétrir en ajoutant la farine nécessaire et l'eau tiède avec un peu de sel.

Laisser reposer une heure.

Préparer une bassine avec de l'huile de cuisson. Faire chauffer (environ 100°). Couper le brocciu en petits cubes que l'on pose sur la pâte prête à cuire. Plonger dans la friture les cubes de briocciu enrobé de pâte.

Retirer une fois que les beignets sont dorés et égoutter sur une passoire.

Servir chaud, saupoudré de sucre.

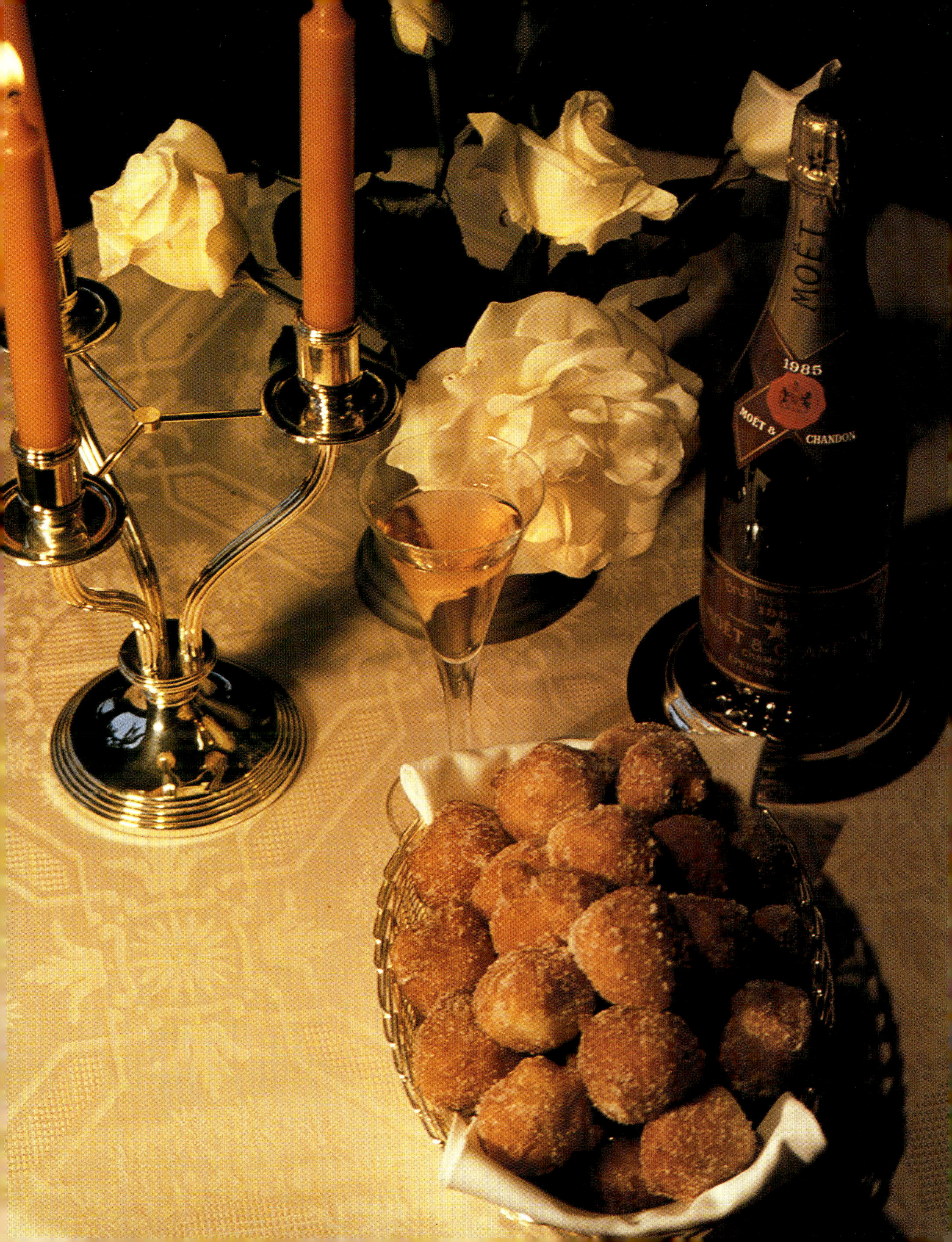
MOËT
1985
MOËT &
CHANDON

DESSERTS

PRÉPARATION : 20 mn
CUISSON : 30 mn

POUR 8 PERSONNES
500 g de farine
1 œuf
250 g de sucre
1 pincée de sel
1 petit verre d'eau de vie
1 verre d'eau
1 zeste d'orange râpé
Levure de boulanger

Pour la décoration :
5 œufs durs

NOTRE CONSEIL
Il est possible de faire des couronnes beaucoup plus petites, en prélevant moins de pâte. Un seul œuf dur suffit alors à la décoration.

CACAVELLU AUX ŒUFS

Délayer la levure de boulanger dans un peu d'eau tiède.

Dans une jatte, disposer la farine en puits.

Ajouter au centre, la levure, le sel, l'œuf, le zeste d'orange, le sucre, et l'eau de vie.

Incorporer progressivement ces éléments à la farine et pétrir la pâte avec un peu d'eau. Couvrir d'un linge, et laisser lever environ 2 h dans un endroit tiède.

La pâte doit doubler de volume.

En faire une boule.

Enfoncer l'index au milieu et faire tourner la boule autour du doigt. Vous obtiendrez une grande couronne sur laquelle vous enfoncerez 5 œufs durs en les retenant par des croisillons de pâte.

Cuire à four chaud.

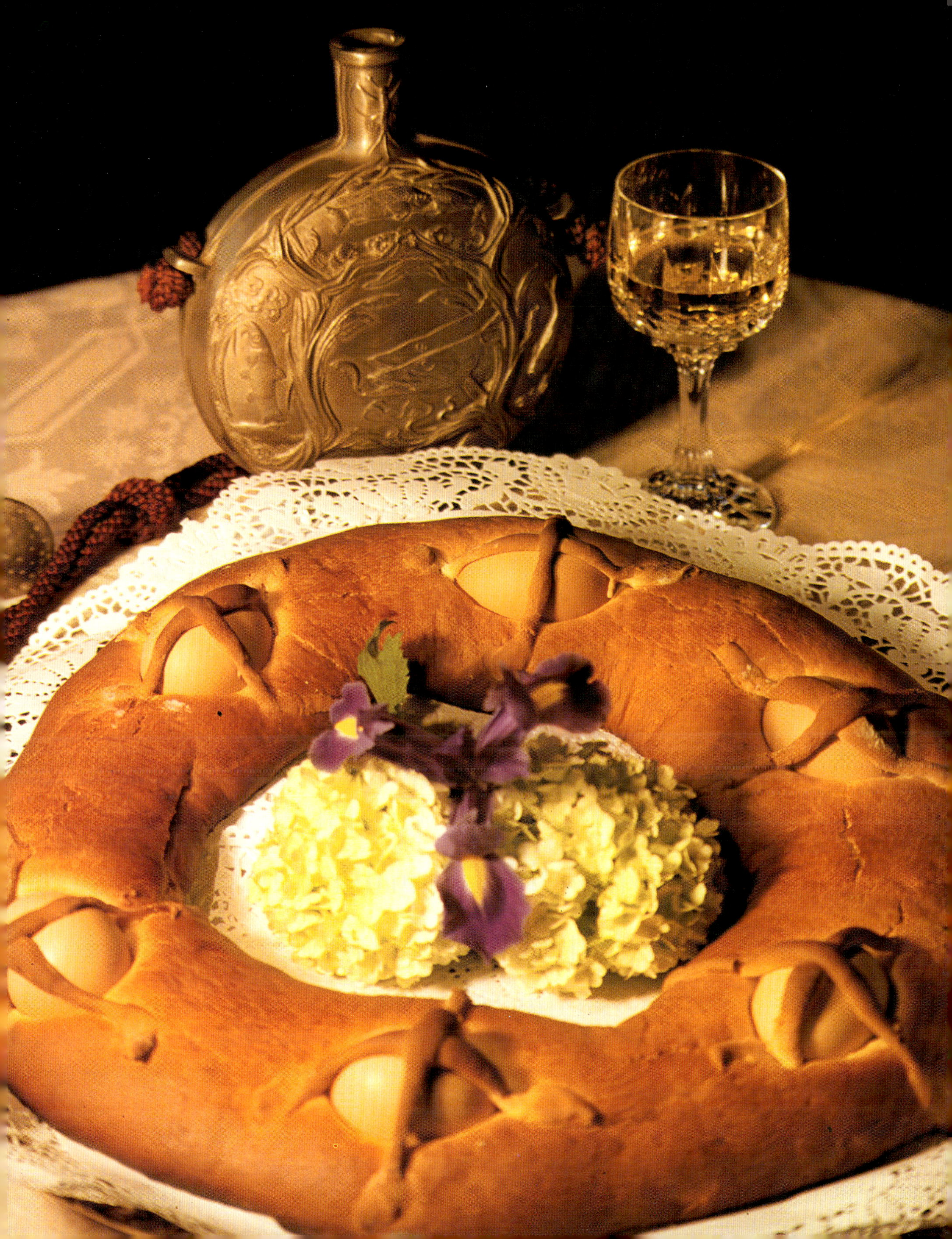

PRÉPARATION : 2 h
CUISSON : 2 h

POUR 6 PERSONNES
125 g de beurre
6 œufs
12 cuillerées de sucre ou 400 g de sucre
1 paquet de levure chimique
1 paquet de sucre vanillé
500 g de farine

NOTRE CONSEIL
Ces frappes se mangent froides.

FRAPPES

Faire une fontaine avec la farine et mettre au milieu le beurre ramolli, les œufs, le sucre, un peu de sel, du zeste de citron et d'orange, la levure, le sucre vanillé.

Mélanger le tout jusqu'à ce que vous obteniez une pâte ferme qui ne colle pas. Fariner une planche et étendre la pâte au rouleau.

Avec une roulette découper dans cette pâte de larges rectangles de 5 cm ou triangles ou rubans que l'on noue.

Faire frire dans de l'huile très chaude. Les égoutter et les saupoudrer de sucre.

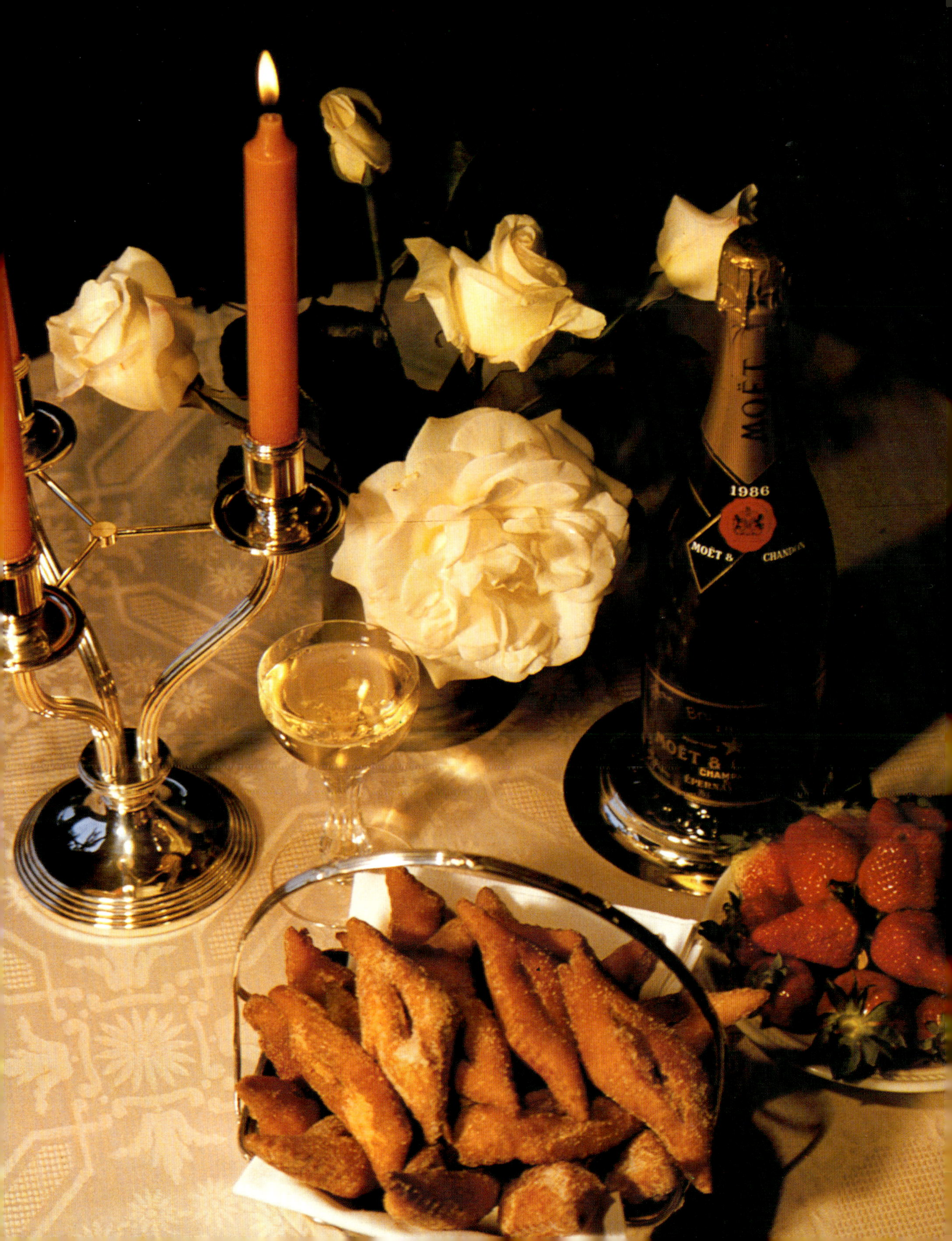
MOËT
1986
MOËT
CHANDON

PRÉPARATION : 10 mn
CUISSON : 20 mn

POUR 8 PERSONNES
600 g de farine de châtaigne
400 g de brocciu frais
1 cuillerée à soupe d'huile
Eau
Sel

NOTRE CONSEIL
Servir tiède de préférence avec un muscat du Cap.

TOURTE À LA FARINE DE CHÂTAIGNES ET AU BROCCIU

Mélanger la farine de châtaignes avec le sel et ajouter assez d'eau froide pour obtenir une pâte un peu plus épaisse qu'une pâte à crêpes.

Arroser d'un peu d'huile, puis beurrer un moule à tarte et verser la pâte dedans.

La parsemer de morceaux de brocciu, et mettre à four chaud.

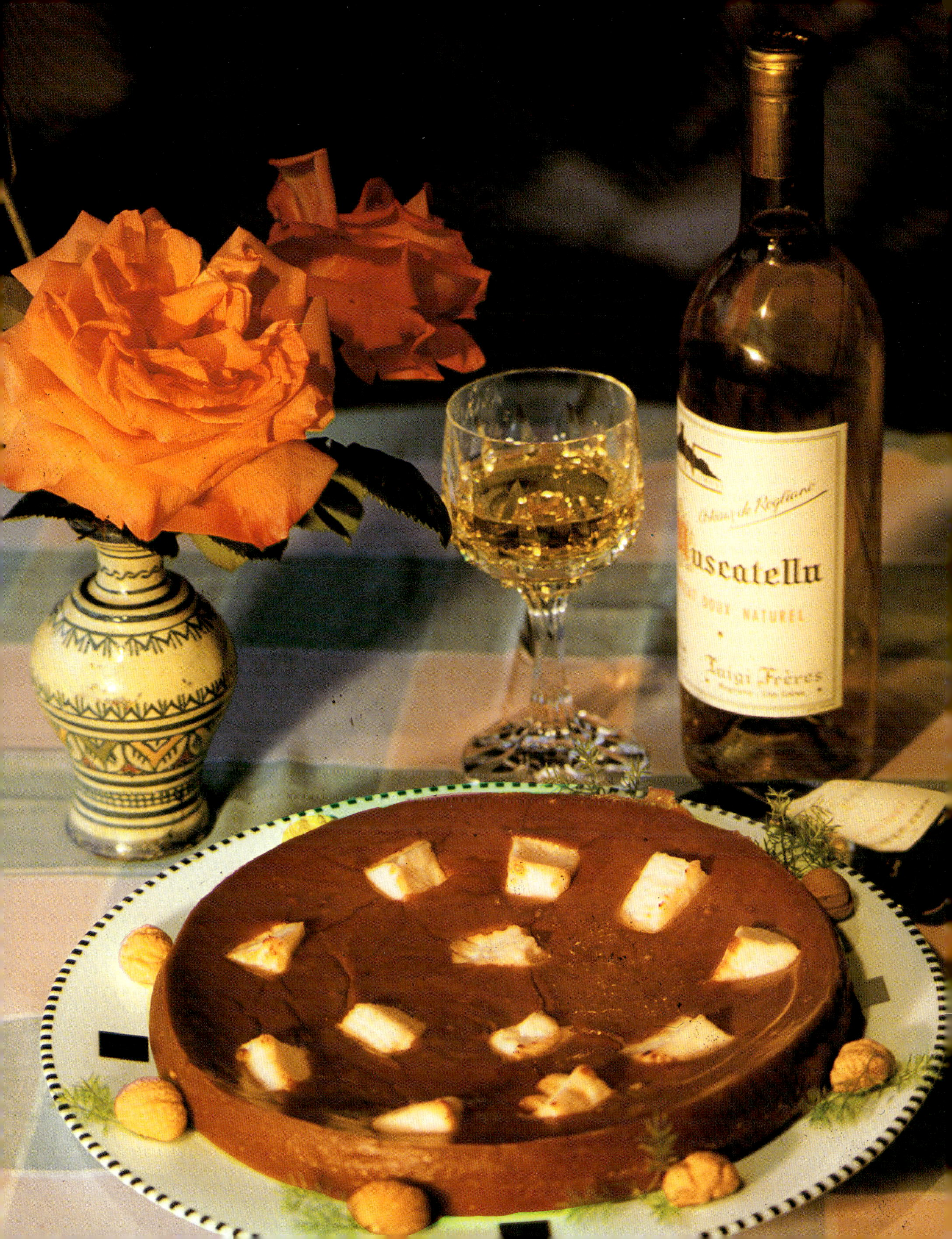
DOUX NATUREL
Luigi Frères

PRÉPARATION : 10 mn
CUISSON : 10 mn

POUR 6 PERSONNES
Farine de châtaignes
1 l d'eau
Sel
Zeste d'orange
1 c. à soupe d'anis en grains
Brocciu

NOTRE CONSEIL
Passez la farine de châtaignes au tamis pour éviter les grumeaux.

BEIGNETS À LA FARINE DE CHÂTAIGNES ET AU BROCCIU

Préparer la pâte en incorporant dans l'eau à laquelle vous avez ajouté : sel, zeste d'orange, anis, la farine jusqu'à obtention d'une pâte assez fluide.

Ajouter à cette pâte du brocciu frais coupé en gros dés.

Mettre une cuillerée à soupe de beignet comportant 1 ou 2 dés de brocciu dans l'huile bouillante.

Servir aussitôt.

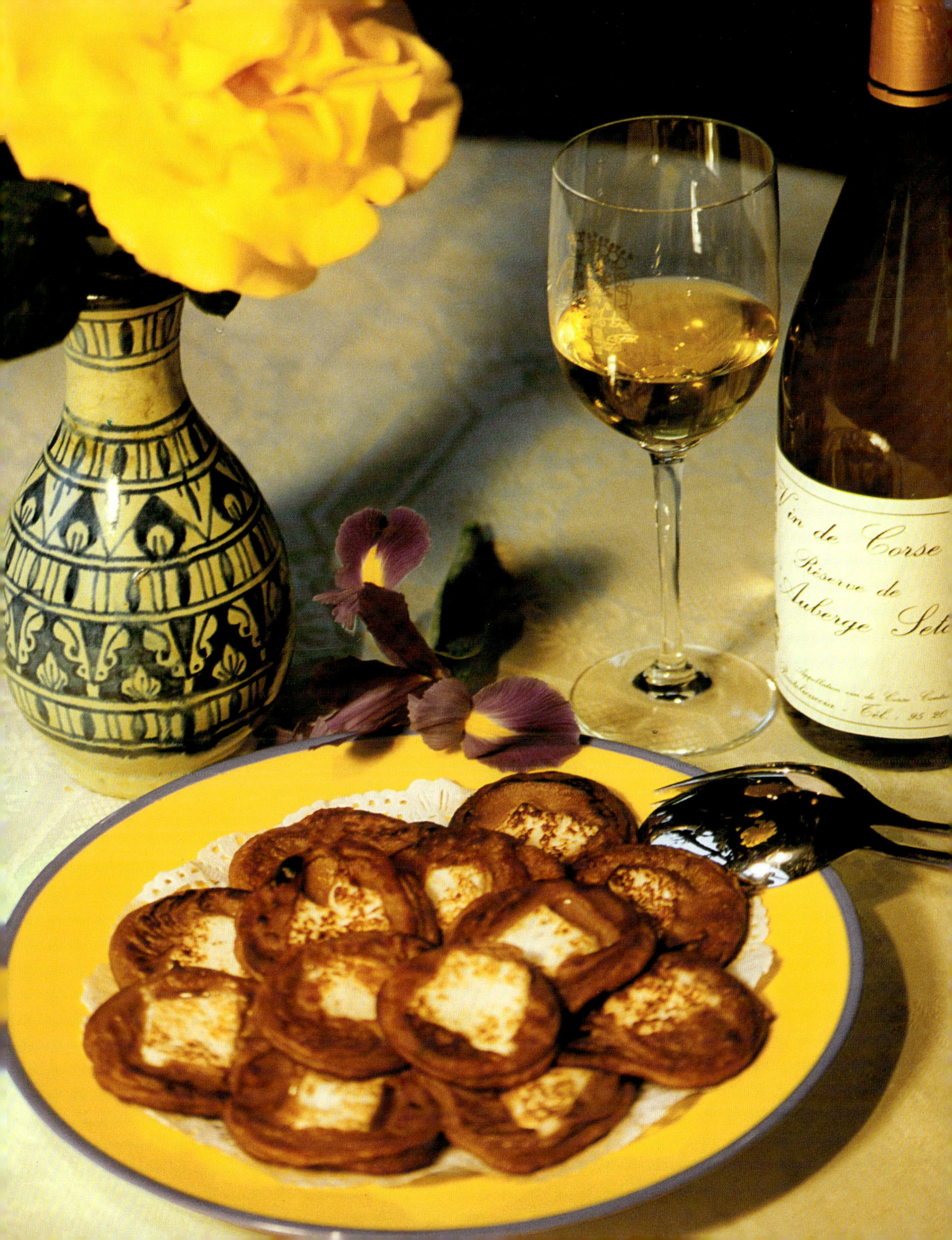
Vin de Corse
Réserve de
Auberge

INDEX

REMERCIEMENTS

L'éditeur remercie :
Pour la réalisation des plats : Toussainte SETA - Paul SETA et Daniel MONMOUSSEAU ainsi que Philippe BAUDIER - Daniel CHICHOKI - Denis RIVIÈRE - Pierre SCAGLIA
Pour la préface : Annebelle CHIOCCA
Pour la rédaction des textes : Annie CACHET - Suzanne PLACARD
Pour les couverts et la vaisselle : La Boutique ARTS ET NATIONS à Ajaccio
Pour les compositions florales : Le BOUQUET DES ÎLES à Bastelicaccia
Pour leur contribution : A.L. CULIOLI - G.X. CULIOLI

Conception et réalisation : Eugénie PERROT
Photos réalisées spécialement pour cet ouvrage par : Pierre-Antoine FOURNIL